𝕮𝖊𝖓𝖙𝖊𝖓𝖆𝖗𝖕 𝕰𝖉𝖎𝖙𝖎𝖔𝖓

THE COMPLETE WORKS OF
RALPH WALDO EMERSON

WITH

A BIOGRAPHICAL

INTRODUCTION AND NOTES

BY EDWARD WALDO EMERSON AND

A GENERAL INDEX

VOLUME

I

1854

RALPH WALDO EMERSON

From a daguerreotype taken in 1854

NATURE

ADDRESSES AND LECTURES

BY

RALPH WALDO EMERSON

BOSTON AND NEW YORK
HOUGHTON, MIFFLIN AND COMPANY
The Riverside Press, Cambridge
1904

PREFACE

IT has seemed fitting in the one hundredth
year since the birth of Emerson to prepare
a new edition of his writings in prose and verse.
Nearly twenty years have gone by since the last
edition was · published. Mr. Emerson in his
later years, when he found himself unequal to
the task of revising the manuscript of his lectures
and arranging the matter in permanent form,
with hesitation approached on the subject the
one man in whose taste and judgment he most
confided, Mr. James Elliot Cabot. His friend
consented, and came constantly to Concord to
work on the papers, with most gratifying results.
By him *Letters and Social Aims* was prepared for
the press. Mr. Emerson in his will appointed
him his literary executor.

Two years after Mr. Emerson's death, eleven
volumes, carefully edited by Mr. Cabot, were
published in the " Riverside Edition"; and a
twelfth was added in 1893. The preparation of
the three posthumous volumes required much
care and labor, and this work was excellently
done.

Messrs. Houghton, Mifflin and Company last summer urged the fitness of preparing a Centenary Edition with full annotation, and the matter was submitted by me to Mr. Cabot. He concurred in their view, but felt unable to undertake the task and advised me to do so. With the sanction of his wish, and because of more ready access to the manuscript and other sources of information than another could have, I assumed the duty, hoping for the benefit of the advice of my father's friend. This hope was cut off by Mr. Cabot's death in January. But his admirable arrangement of the manuscript, years ago, in which task the help of his wife, now also gone, is gratefully remembered, had made the work lighter.

The first eight volumes contain the collected Essays as Mr. Emerson left them, except revision in punctuation and correction of obvious mistakes. The ninth volume comprises the pieces chosen by him from the " Poems " and " May-Day " to form the " Selected Poems," with some restored that he omitted, and the addition of some poems and fragments never published in his lifetime, most of which appeared in the Riverside Edition. All verbal emendations in the poems have the sanction of his pencillings on the margin of his printed poems. The tenth, eleventh, and twelfth volumes consist of lectures unprinted during Mr. Emerson's lifetime and of "Occasional Addresses" and other prose writings which have appeared separately or in periodicals.

In the edition which was published soon after Mr. Emerson's death it did not seem best either to his family or to Mr. Cabot to present to the public any passages from Mr. Emerson's journals or the earlier writings. The continued interest in his life and work, and the lapse of years and the death of his contemporaries, have made it seem perhaps well now to print some selections. Mr. Cabot sanctioned the consideration of this project. As the journals cover nearly half a century (although the greater part of their contents appears in the printed books), the editing would require time and care. It is hoped that a few volumes may be prepared from these.

I undertook the annotation of the works at the desire of the publishers, sharing their feeling that to the student of Emerson side-lights on the man, his surroundings, his work, and method might be welcome, gathered from the journals, the correspondence, reminiscences, and works written about him. In supplying the notes I have had to rely on my own judgment. The pressure due to the late undertaking of the work has prevented my revising and condensing them. Remembering that notes seem to many readers an interruption and even an impertinence, they have been placed at the end of each volume. Repetitions occur, because a reader who wishes information cannot search all the volumes. The occurrence of the same thought or expression in the prose and poems has been pointed out.

I thankfully acknowledge the help of friends in finding the more unusual quotations. I also gratefully recognize the help received from the works of various writers about my father.

EDWARD WALDO EMERSON.

CONCORD, April 8th, 1903.

CONTENTS

The portrait prefixed to this volume is from a daguerreotype taken in 1854, in the possession of the Emerson family.

BIOGRAPHICAL SKETCH

BIOGRAPHICAL SKETCH

I F *there be power in good. intention, in fidelity
and in toil, the North wind shall be purer, the
stars in heaven shall glow with a kindlier beam,
that I have lived. I am primarily engaged to myself to be a public servant of all the gods, to demonstrate to all men that there is intelligence and
good will at the heart of things, and ever higher
and yet higher leadings. These are my engagements ; how can your law further or hinder me in
what I shall do to men? . . . Wherever there are
men, are the objects of my study and love. Sooner
or later all men will be my friends and will testify
.in all methods the energy of their regards.*

Such is the hero's attitude in facing life, Emerson said, in one of his early lectures. After
his death, forty years later, his friend Dr.
Holmes in writing of him said, "Consciously or
unconsciously men describe themselves in the
characters they draw. One must have the mor-
dant in his own personality or he will not take
the color of his subject," and the Doctor goes
on to show how well the test applies to his prose,
and especially to his verse. And as for the
North wind and the stars, Emerson held their

bracing and uplifting influence dependent on
the preparation of the soul : —

Light-loving, asking, life in me
Feeds those eternal lamps I see.

His spiritual autobiography might be given
almost in its completeness in impersonal extracts,
duly ordered, from his prose and verse. There,
as he said of Shakspeare, "in place of meagre
fact we have really the information which is
material: that which describes character and fortune, that which, if we were about to meet the
man and deal with him, would most import us
to know. We have his recorded convictions on
those questions which knock for answer at every
heart — on life and death, on love, on wealth and
poverty, on the prizes of life and the ways
whereby we come at them ; on the characters of
men and the influences, occult and open, which
affect their fortunes ; and on those mysterious
and demoniacal powers which defy our science
and which yet interweave their malice and their
gift in our brightest hours." In his journal for
1841 Mr. Emerson wrote, "Seemed to me that
I had the keeping of a secret too great to be
confided to one man : that a divine man dwelt
near me in a hollow tree." And again, "All
that is said of the wise man by Stoic or Oriental

or Modern essayist, describes to each reader his
own idea, describes his unattained but attainable
self; . . . he hears the commendation, not of himself, but, more sweet, of that character he seeks,
in every word that is said concerning character,
yea further, in every fact and circumstance — in
the running river and the rustling corn." This
purified man, — he named him Osman, — an
organ of the Universal Spirit, yet with his own
temperament and subject to his experiences,
often appears in the Journals : —

1841. " When I wish, it is permitted me to
say, These hands, this body, this history of
Waldo Emerson are profane and wearisome, but
I, I descend not to mix myself with that or with
any man. Above his life, above all creatures, I
flow down forever a sea of benefit into races of
individuals. Nor can the stream ever roll backward or the sin or death of a man taint the immutable energy which distributes itself into men,
as the sun into rays, or the sea into drops."

In the notes to this edition of Emerson's
Works, the correspondence between the passages
and his own traits and experiences will be often
shown. But a sketch of his personal history
must here be briefly given.

He was born in Boston, May 25, 1803, the

son of William Emerson, pastor of the Second
Church, and Ruth Haskins, his wife. His father, son of the patriotic young minister of Concord at the outbreak of the Revolution, was a
preacher, liberal for his day, social and a man of
letters; his mother, a lady of serene sweetness
and courage.

She was left a widow in 1811 with her family
of five little boys, and helped by kind friends,
brought them up in straitened circumstances,
wisely and well. The Emerson ancestry, almost
all ministers, after Thomas, who came to Ipswich
in 1638, were men who, living frugally and
prayerfully in the clearings of wild New England, had striven to keep before the minds of
their people

" The invisible things of God, before things seen and known."

They were humble and earnest scholars. Mr.
Emerson told that, in his childhood, "Dr.
Frothingham one day found me in his parlor,
and coming close and looking at the form of
my head, said, ' If you are good, it is no thanks
to you.'" These Emerson boys, "born to be
educated," as their Aunt Mary Emerson,[1] the

---

[1] An account of her is given by her nephew in *Lectures
and Biographical Sketches.*

strange sibyl and inspirer of their youth, said
of them, helped the matter on by their eager
reading, especially of poetry, their ventures in
writing, and declamation to one another of fine
passages in which they delighted. There were
almost no children's books then, and they soon
were versed in the best authors. Mr. Emerson,
in the essay "Domestic Life" in the volume
Society and Solitude, gives a touching and true
picture of the life of these brothers in their
childhood, and speaking of their air castles says,
"Woe to them if their wishes were crowned.
The angels that dwell with them and are weav-
ing laurels of life for their youthful brows are
Toil and Want, Truth and Mutual Faith."

Rev. Ezra Ripley, the successor of their
grandfather in the church of Concord, and married to his widow, welcomed the boys to the
Old Manse in the holidays. So, long before he
settled there, Mr. Emerson had loving memories
of Concord woods and meadows.

Emerson entered Harvard College at the
age of fourteen; he graduated with his class in
1821. Like a great part of the students of his
day, he helped himself through his course by
various services, either to the college or by teaching. Though his instincts drove him much to

solitude, he found enjoyment too in the social life of the small classes of his day, and was a member of the Pythologian, a convivio-literary club for which he furnished the songs. Alluding to himself in his Journal, he writes of "the youth who has no faculty for mathematics and weeps over the impossible analytical geometry, to console his defeats with Chaucer and Montaigne, with Plutarch and Plato at night." These were to him the living professors, and became his friends for life. He loved Latin and Greek — not for their syntax—and every paragraph of his English shows the value of these now neglected studies: the Elizabethan authors too, and the ancient philosophers, though the modern metaphysicians did not interest him. He was only in the upper half of his class, yet he won prizes for declamation and dissertations.[1] "Even in college I was already content to be 'screwed' in the recitation room if on my return I could accurately paint the fact in my journal."

From boyhood to old age he kept a journal, not of events, but wherein to note the thoughts that were given him, his trials at versifying, a

[1] Two of his prize dissertations are printed in Dr. Edward Everett Hale's *Ralph Waldo Emerson*. Boston: Brown & Co., 1899.

quotation that charmed, or an anecdote that pleased him. In an early lecture, and often through life, he gave to scholars these two maxims, 1. "*Sit alone:* in your arrangements for residence see you have a chamber to yourself, though you sell your coat and wear a blanket. 2. *Keep a journal:* pay so much honor to the visits of Truth to your mind as to record them."

In the Journal for 1837 he wrote: "This book is my savings-bank. I grow richer because I have somewhere to deposit my earnings, and fractions are worth more to me because corresponding fractions are waiting here that shall be made integers by their addition."

Neglecting the college text-books and incurring admonition for so doing, he joyfully pastured in the library, not reading serially or thoroughly, but with the sure instinct for what was for him in a book, — "reading for lustres," as he called it. Looking backward, he said, "I wiil trust my instincts . . . I was the true philosopher in college, and Mr. Farrar and Mr. Hedge and Dr. Ware the false. Yet what seemed then to me less probable?"

Four of the Emerson boys went through college, and each had by teaching to help the others; the younger ones, when their turn to work came, in some measure freeing the elder brothers to pursue their education for the ministry. Ralph, at the age of nineteen, assisted William, the eldest and the prop of the family, in his "finishing school" for the first young ladies of Boston. Later, he taught the school alone, a sore trial for a bashful boy. The relief when he got away from these daunting fair ones to his rural home found expression in "Goodbye, Proud World." He taught later in Brookline, Cambridge and Chelmsford, and began his studies at the Divinity School.

The health of the young teacher suffered from too ascetic a life, and unmistakable danger-signals began to appear, fortunately heeded in time. Disappointment and delay resulted, borne, however, with sense and courage. A certain serene acceptance of physical and temperamental limitations came even at that early age into play and saved his life, balancing the drivings of conscience or ambition which cost his two brilliant younger brothers their lives, and made William, the brave and faithful bearer of the family burdens, a sufferer through most of his life.

William studied for the ministry at Göttingen, but the same honest doubts which later came to

his brother turned him aside to the Law, and
the hereditary mantle fell on Waldo's shoulders.
Weak lungs and eyes interrupted his studies;
nevertheless, in October, 1826, he was "appro-
bated to preach" by the Middlesex Association
of Ministers. A winter at the North at this
time threatened to prove fatal, so, helped by
his generous kinsman, Rev. Samuel Ripley, he
sailed for Charleston and thence to Florida,
where he passed the winter with benefit at St.
Augustine. In the spring he worked northward,
preaching in the cities through which he passed,
and later near home, as opportunity offered,
while pursuing his studies.

In 1829 Mr. Emerson was ordained in the
Second or Old North Church in Boston as
associate pastor with Rev. Henry Ware, and
soon after, because of his senior's delicate health,
was called on to assume the full duty. In this
year he also was chosen chaplain of the Senate.
The young minister entered earnestly upon his
duties, although, quoting the words of one of
the Fathers of the Church, he called it *Onus
angelicis humeris formidandum.* Theological dogmas, even such as the Unitarians of Channing's
day accepted, did not appeal to Emerson, nor
did the supernatural in religion, in its ordinary

acceptation, interest him. The living God, the solicitations of the Spirit, the daily miracle of the universe, the secure compensations, the dignity of man, were what he taught, and, though the older members of the congregation may have been disquieted that he did not dwell upon revealed religion or the offices of the Christ, his words reached the young people, stirred thought, and wakened aspiration.

Because of his shyness the pastoral visits to his parishioners were less easy for him than helping them by his thought. At this time he lived with his young wife, Ellen Tucker, and his mother, in Chardon Street. For nearly four years he ministered to his people in Boston, then his expanding spirit found itself cramped by custom and tradition even in the most liberal church of his day. Though endeavoring to conform to blameless usage, he presently felt it his duty to tell his congregation that he could not regard the rite of the Lord's Supper as a sacrament established by Christ for observance through the ages, and proposed to them a merely commemorative service without the elements. This change was not adopted, and the question whether he ought to resign his charge came to him. To decide this he went for solitary thought to the

White Mountains. The temptation not to sacrifice, on a matter of form, a position of usefulness for which he had been trained, and in which he was happy and valued, was great, but he put it behind him and bravely offered his resignation. He and his people parted in all friendship, many desiring that he should remain on his own terms. The use of prayer at stated times, whether the spirit moved or not, had been distressing to Mr. Emerson, and thereafter he always declined engagements where this was required. In his farewell to his church he spoke of himself as still " engaged to the love and service of the same eternal cause. . . . To me, as one disciple, is the ministry of truth, as far as I can discern and declare it, committed."

This was the darkest time in Mr. Emerson's life. His wife, a beautiful and spiritual woman, had died. His noble brother Edward had broken down from overwork, and gone to Porto Rico, where, after three years' exile for health, he died. He himself was sick and sad. On Christmas Day, 1832, he sailed for the Mediterranean to recover as he might.

He landed in Malta and went thence to Sicily and Naples. The sea always helped him, and, though never a sight-seer and constantly urged homeward by his spirit to begin the new life, he found useful diversion in these old-world sights. As the philosophy and poetry of ancient Greeks always spoke to him, so now in Italy, seeing their sculptured deities and heroes and the contrast between these faces and those of the living throng around, he said, " These are the countenances of the first-born, the face of man in the morning of the world." The Elgin marbles, seen later in London, he always remembered with delight. Sculpture seemed nobler to him than painting, and, though greatly moved by Raphael's Transfiguration, the work of Michel Angelo — St. Peter's, his statues, and the sculpture-painting in the Sistine Chapel — was the principal gift that Rome had for him. The engravings of the Sibyls and a copy of the Fates thereafter adorned his study walls. He tarried in Florence and enjoyed acquaintance with Landor. There, he tells us, he did homage at the tomb of Galileo. But he quickly sped northward, over the Alps, made but short stay in Paris, crossed the Channel, and in the lonely moorlands of the Scottish Border sought out the man, then hardly recognized in England, whose writings had stirred him at home, and who drew him thither like a magnet. There began the friendship of Emerson and Carlyle, a blessing to both, and lasting through life.

"That man," wrote Carlyle to a friend, "came to see me. I don't know what brought him, and we kept him one night, and then he left us. I saw him go up the hill. I did n't go with him to see him descend. I preferred to watch him mount and vanish like an angel!"

On September 1, 1833, Emerson, in his journal at Liverpool, thanks God "that He has brought me to the shore and the ship that steers westward. He has shown me the men I wished to see, Landor, Coleridge, Carlyle, Wordsworth: He has thereby comforted and confirmed me in my convictions. . . . I am very glad my travelling is done." His health was restored, and he was eager to begin life anew. For the thought which he expressed in "The Over-Soul" was then burning within him, — "When we have broken our god of tradition and ceased from our god of rhetoric, then may God fire the soul." In his journal at sea he wrote, "That which I cannot yet declare has been my angel from childhood until now. It has separated me from men. It has watered my pillow. . . . It has inspired me with hope. It cannot be defeated by my defeats. . . . It is the 'open secret' of the Universe. . . .

I believe in *this* life. I believe it continues. As long as I am here, I plainly read my duties as writ with pencil of fire. They speak not of death; they are woven of immortal thread."

Thus he landed at Boston within the year in good health and hope, and joined his mother and youngest brother Charles in Newton. Frequent invitations to preach still came, and were accepted, and he even was sounded as to succeeding Dr. Dewey in the church at New Bedford; but, as he stipulated for freedom from ceremonial, this came to nothing. In his visits to New Bedford the Friends, with their doctrine of Obedience, interested him.

In the autumn of 1834 he moved to Concord, living with his kinsman, Dr. Ripley, at the Manse, but soon bought house and land on the Boston Road, on the edge of the village towards Walden woods. Thither, in the following autumn, he brought his wife, Miss Lidian Jackson, of Plymouth, and this was their home during the rest of their lives.

The new life to which he had been called opened pleasantly and increased in happiness and opportunity, except for the sadness of bereavements, for, in the first few years, his brilliant brothers Edward and Charles died, and soon afterward Waldo, his first-born son, and later his mother. Emerson had left traditional religion, the city, the Old World, behind, and now went to Nature as his teacher, his inspiration. His first book, *Nature*, which he was meditating while in Europe, was finished here, and published in 1836. When, as a boy, he went with William to the Maine woods, he wrote to his Aunt Mary that he found enjoyment there, but not inspiration. "You should have gone alone," the sibyl answered. And now he went to the woods near his door to find her word true. As God *liveth*, he said, —

> The word unto the prophet spoken
> Was writ on tablets still unbroken,
> Still floats upon the morning wind,
> Still whispers to the willing mind.

From this time on, to the last days of his life, except when on his lecturing trips, he went almost daily to the woods to listen for the thoughts, not originated by him, he held, though colored by the temperament of the individual through which these inspirations of the Universal Mind passed.

> Oh what are heroes, prophets, men
> But pipes through which the breath of Pan doth blow
> A momentary music?

The singing of the pine-tree, or the Æolian harp, passive to be played on by the wild wind, his favorite music,[1] symbolized his belief.

One song of the pine-tree to him was of

> The genesis of things,
> Of tendency through endless ages,
> Of star-dust and star-pilgrimages,
> The rushing metamorphosis.

And in 1836, in *Nature*, he told how —

> Striving to be man, the worm
> Mounts through countless spires of form.

The early recognition by Emerson of Evolution as the plan of the Universe in his first book, and everywhere in his prose and verse, has often attracted notice, first, I think, of Mr. Moncure D. Conway in his *Emerson at Home and Abroad*.

A question so interesting should be considered here — necessarily briefly. A study of Mr. Emerson's history and reading suggests these steps as those by which his beliefs were reached.

1. His open mind and hopeful temperament.

2. His poetic nature looked on beneficent law as universal, working alike on matter or

[1] See his two poems "The Harp," and "Maiden Speech of the Æolian Harp."

spirit; hence analogies could be read either way from one to the other.

3. The facts of Astronomy and the Nebular-hypothesis early delighted him.

4. The poetic teachings of the ancient philosophers, especially " The Flowing of the Universe" by Heracleitus and the " Identity " by Xenophanes and others, prepared his mind.

5. He had undoubtedly early read of Leibnitz's *scale of being* from minerals through plants to animals, from monad to man, and from Coleridge knew something of the speculations of Schelling and Oken.

He also, in 1830, read with interest Lee's Life of Cuvier, and probably in Buffon.

6. He recorded in his Journal and in his lecture before the Natural History Society, just after his return from Europe in 1833, the strange feelings of relationship that had been stirred in him by the sight of the animal forms graded from lowest to highest in the *Jardin des Plantes* Museum in Paris " and the upheaving principle of life everywhere incipient, in the very rock aping organized forms. . . . I am impressed with the singular conviction that not a form so grotesque, so savage, or so beautiful but is an expression of something in man, the

observer. We feel that there is an occult relation between the very worm, the crawling scorpion and man. I am moved to strange sympathies. I say, I will listen to this invitation. I will be a Naturalist."

In December, 1833, in his lecture "The Relation of Man to the Globe," he spoke of the recent discovery of a fact the "most sublime," that man is no upstart in Creation, but has been prophesied in Nature for a thousand thousand ages before he appeared; that from times incalculably remote there has been a progressive preparation for him, an effort (as physiologists say) to produce him.

7. In 1835 Lyell's book on Geology came out and was read by Emerson, in which the ideas of Lamarck, first announced in 1800, were mentioned. Mr. Emerson probably came on them there. These doctrines of Variation in animals through environment and "effort," and the transmission of these peculiarities, were at first ridiculed or neglected, but are now recognized as equally necessary in Evolution with Darwin's Natural Selection. Darwin's *Origin of Species* was not published until 1859.

In 1836, in a lecture given in Boston on "The Humanity of Science," Mr. Emerson alluded to Lamarck as " finding a monad of organic life common to every animal, and becoming a worm, a mastiff or a man, according to circumstances. He says to the caterpillar, How dost thou, brother? Please God you shall yet be a philosopher."

Lastly. In his Essay " Poetry and Imagination," made up from lectures, some of which were given early, Mr. Emerson credits John Hunter with " the electric word *arrested* and *progressive* development, indicating the way upward from the invisible protoplasm to the highest organism which gave the poetic key to Natural Science."

Mr. Conway after long search found interesting evolutionary ideas only in a note to Palmers' edition of Hunter's works, but not this phrase.

Mr. Emerson, in some notes on the sketch of John Hunter in the *Biographie Générale* (Paris, 1858), speaks of these words as found by Richard Owen in Hunter's *Manuscripts*,[1] and in 1866 wrote in his Journal : —

" The idea which haunted John Hunter, that

---

[1] The writer in the *Biographie Générale*, dwelling on a likeness between the ideas of Hunter and Harvey, says : " Cette filiation se retrouve également dans un autre ordre

life was independent of organization protecting and re-creating the parts and varying its means of action, he never succeeded in expressing but in his museum." Possibly Owen himself said this to Emerson, as the word *progressive* does not appear in the *Biographie Générale* notice.

From books, and from men, alike in the laboratory, the counting-room, on the farm, he eagerly collected his material — "dull, despised facts" which he found were "pearls and rubies to his discourse." "They do not know what to do with their facts. I know;" for behind each was a law of spirit as well as of matter, in however humble guise. The great significance of Evolution was its warrant with him. After leaving his church he found that "the man of to-day scarcely recognizes the man of yesterday," yet the high aim in both was the same — "as the shellfish crawls out of its beautiful but

d'idées dans cette phrase remarquable que M. Owen a trouvée dans les manuscrits de Hunter, et qui contient en germe, quoique avec une expression très-peu nette, les théories actuelles *sur l'arrêt de développement ;*" and then gives a quotation of some length, the substance of which may be thus translated : "If we take a series of animals from the most imperfect to the most perfect, we there shall probably find an imperfect animal corresponding to each stage of the development of the most perfect."

stony cave because it no longer admits of its growth." Now he spoke on week days to hearers, who did not come from custom, on the same high themes, but in freer language and with richer illustration, and found ready acceptance from the young in years or spirit. Those who shared the general social, intellectual, and spiritual awakening that came from various causes to New England at that time, were called Transcendentalists. " I told Mr. M——," said Mr. Emerson, " that he need not consult the Germans, but if he wished at any time to know what the Transcendentalists believed, he might simply omit what in his own mind he added [to his simple perception] from the tradition, and the rest would be Transcendentalism."

In 1837 Mr. Emerson made his notable address, " The American Scholar," to the Phi Beta Kappa Society at Cambridge. It was well received and advanced his repute as a thinker and writer. But the next year, when, invited by the graduating class at the Divinity School, he made up his mind to tell them bravely that they could well spare tradition, and the soul might regard any mediation between itself and the living God as impertinent, he had the old conditions to deal with, — the presence, alert for heresy, of men pledged and committed to the tradition. These pained or outraged guardians of the flock remonstrated, or fiercely disclaimed complicity in this occurrence.

> The stern old war-gods shook their heads,
> The seraphs frowned from myrtle beds ;
> Seemed to the holy festival
> The rash word boded ill to all.

Mr. Emerson declined to argue his case. The thought given to his earnest prayer he had delivered, and he withdrew, leaving it to do its work. "As like a sunbeam he glided into the conclave, so like a sunbeam he glided out." Returning to his woodlands to contemplate the daily miracle of Nature, he said with St. Augustine, Wrangle who will, I will work. His poem "Uriel," if carefully read, will be seen to be an exact but sublimed account of this experience. Uriel, archangel of the sun, was chosen as one who from a central position sees all things in their ordered courses, where those in eccentric positions see perturbations. Yet Emerson did not lack defenders who then could see that he was no Atheist, — denied personality to God "because it was too little, not too much." As for the Pantheism of his "Universal Mind," their

Bibles told of " Him in whom we live and move and have our being." Mr. Emerson was more troubled by the notoriety involved than by the attacks. Yet his Journal at this time shows that he thought his heresies might cut off his source of earning by lectures, and felt that he must become a more skilful gardener and rely on his planting. He mentions the discovery that " if you put one potato in the ground you found ten, the true miracle of the loaves and fishes."

For thirty years thereafter the official doors of Harvard College were shut to him. But the tempest was, as he said, " in a wash bowl," and the country colleges still bade him to speak to them, a service in which he always expressed delight, — the showing them that " the Scholar had drawn the white lot in life," and that his responsibility was proportionate. At this time he prepared his two volumes of Essays.

Although he had few close friendships and said that he had not animal spirits enough even for near friends, he was always surrounded by friends known and unknown. He was fortunate in having two noble women close by him, Miss Hoar, the betrothed of his brother Charles, and Mrs. Samuel Ripley, the wife of his uncle, a woman of eager interest in all that was good. Her brother, Mr. Bradford, a gentle scholar, was a near friend, and Mr. Emerson took great delight in the manly sincerity and knowledge of Nature of Henry Thoreau, who for some years was a member of his household. He sometimes met the shy and interesting Hawthorne, his neighbor, and soon Mr. Alcott came also to Concord. Of him he said, "The ideal world I might have treated as cloud-land, had I not known Alcott, who is a native of that country and makes it as solid as Massachusetts for me."

Mr. Emerson's wide hospitality, to the souls as well as bodies of men, brought to his door many visitors, inspiring or exacting, inspired or possessed. His habit of imputing virtue, or of "taking people by their best handles," brought out their best, but some were hopeless "monotones," of one of whom he said: "He will not *listen* in company which is much, but, what is worse, *when he is alone.*" He writes : —

"When the narrow-minded and unworthy shall knock at my gate, I will say come, now will I sacrifice to the gods below; then will I entertain my guests heartily and handsomely. Besides, is it for thee to choose what shadows shall pass over thy magical mirror?"

Of one he made this humorous parable: "As for walking with Heraclitus," said Theanor, " I know nothing less interesting. I had as lief talk with my own conscience." He often had Swedenborg's statement in mind: "Angels have no idea of time." One of his nearest friends, still living, has lately published anonymously some of Emerson's letters to him showing his ideals of friendship.[1]

The Lyceum was Emerson's open pulpit. His main occupation through life was reading lectures to who would hear, at first in courses in Boston, but later all over the country, for the Lyceum sprang up in New England in these years in every town, and spread westward to the new settlements even beyond the Mississippi. His winters were spent in these rough, but to him interesting journeys, for he loved to watch the growth of the Republic, in which he had faith. His summers were spent in study and writing. The thoughts gathering in his journals presently found their affinities, one with another, and suggested the theme for the next course of lectures. Tested by this trial-trip, the joints looked after (but not too closely, for it was important that the *spark should pass* in the mind

[1] Emerson's *Letters to a Friend.* Houghton, Mifflin & Co.

of the hearer), the roughnesses smoothed, and with every superfluous passage or word cut away, the best in the lectures appeared later as the Essays, of which seven volumes of different names appeared between 1841 and 1876. The courses in Boston, which at first were given in the Masonic Temple, were always well attended by earnest and thoughtful people. The young, whether in years or in spirit, were always and to the end his audience of the spoken or written word. The freedom of the Lyceum platform pleased Emerson. He found that people would hear on Wednesday with approval and unsuspectingly doctrines from which on Sunday they felt officially obliged to dissent.

Mr. Lowell, in his essays, has spoken of these early lectures and what they were worth to him and others suffering from the generous discontent of youth with things as they were. Emerson used to say, " My strength and my doom is to be solitary "; but to a retired scholar a wholesome offset to this seclusion was the travelling and lecturing in cities and in raw frontier towns, bringing him into touch with the people, and this he knew and valued. He was everywhere a learner, expecting light from the youngest and least educated companion.

From the first he never "came down to his audience." He had faith in the intelligence and ideals of Americans, and his lectures were well received, and called for again. The astonished curiosity about American audiences for such thoughts as his, expressed by both Carlyle and Sterling in their letters to him, is amusing. Herman Grimm says that Emerson preferred not to speak to those who read or had read, but to those that had ears to hear, and that he resembled Shakspeare in that he can be read without preparation.

In 1847 Emerson was invited to read lectures in England, and he went thither and remained abroad a year, seeing old friends and new. *English Traits* was the result. At that time he made also a short visit to France in her troublous times.

In writing to John Sterling in 1840, in acknowledgment of his volume of poems, Mr. Emerson had expressed his faith, founded on his ardent wish, "that one day — I ask not where or when — I shall attain to the speech of this splendid dialect; . . . and these wishes, I suppose, are ever only the buds of power, but up to this hour I have never had a true success in such attempts."

From boyhood he had written verses, at first correct in metre and stilted in expression, on eighteenth-century models; but in the ten years preceding his visit to England his verse had shown the influence of his growth; indeed the thoughts in all the essays had been cast in poetic mould, many of them showing the influence of the Bardic poems, the thought roughly cast at white heat. Many of his poems first appeared in the *Dial*. The *Poems* were published in 1846. *May-Day*, a second collection, more mellowed and finished, followed in 1867. Both are now included in one volume, in which the history of some of the poems will be given in the notes. Emerson was primarily a poet, whether in prose or rhyme, though he struggled long to attain rhythmical expression. He said, " I like my poems best because it is not I who write them." He consoled himself for not having a musical ear in having " musical eyes." He said, " Good poetry must be affirmative. *Thus saith the Lord* should begin the song."

The reforms of the day were honored and helped by Emerson, but he would not " mistake others' chivalries for his own." He said : " My reforms include theirs " ; and again, " I have quite other slaves to free than those negroes, to

wit, imprisoned spirits, imprisoned thoughts."
But in times of doubt and danger he failed not
to bring his lance to help as a brave volunteer.
Early and always he spoke out for human
freedom. In his ode at the celebration of the
Fourth of July in 1856 were the lines as he
would write them again to-day —

> United States ! the ages plead, —
>   Present and Past, in under-song,
> Go put your creed into your deed,
>   Nor speak with double tongue.
>
> For sea and land don't understand,
>   Nor skies without a frown
> See rights for which the one hand fights
>   By the other cloven down.

As he was a good citizen of his village and a
patriotic American, so he was a happy and trusting soul in the Universe, seeing everywhere, in
Protean forms, the inseparable Trinity of Truth,
Goodness and Beauty.

Mr. Emerson tells us that as a boy he
pleased himself as he lay on his bed with the
beauty of the Lord's equilibrium in the Universe, instead of shuddering at the terrors of
his judgment, — that all was so intelligible and
sweet, instead of inscrutable and dire.

Secure and happy in his assurance of the law of compensation, though in his manhood he fell on evil times, when even in Boston free thought, free speech, free action were unpopular to the verge of danger, Unitarian and Transcendental heresies scourged or ridiculed and the cause of human freedom, in the hands of a despised few, seemed almost hopeless, he lived to see these causes everywhere winning, and their champions honored. Mr. John Albee in his *Remembrances of Emerson*[1] said: "I am impressed with the fact that he never made any mistakes throughout his career. He faced one way and continued to face that way. He never had to recant, to make a new start, to modify, or apologize." He said in his early manhood, "If the single man plant himself indomitably on his instincts, and there abide, the huge world will come round to him."

The year after the end of the Civil War, in the triumph of freedom, Mr. Emerson was again invited to give the Phi Beta Kappa address at Harvard, and was shortly after chosen a member of the Board of Overseers. In 1870 and 1871 he delivered a course of lectures on Philosophy there, but the undertaking was too much for his

[1] *Remembrances of Emerson*, by John Albee.

strength, which had begun to fail. A friend carried him with a pleasure party to California for rest and recreation. Professor James B. Thayer, a member of the party, wrote the story of that trip.[1] But Mr. Emerson's forces had failed more than was then realized, and the next year the exposure and fatigue incident to the accidental burning of his house prostrated him seriously. Loyal friends took upon themselves the gracious task of restoring his house completely, and meanwhile sent him to the Old World to recruit his forces. A winter with his daughter in Italy and on the Nile helped, but could not restore him. On his return he found himself unable to prepare a promised book of essays (*Letters and Social Aims*). This task was cheerfully accomplished by his trusted and valued friend, the late Mr. James Elliot Cabot, who afterward, at the desire of the family, wrote the admirable *Memoir of Emerson*, and in 1883 prepared the posthumous edition of the *Works*.

Mr. Emerson, unable to do active literary work, lived a quiet and happy life among his friends and his books, still going often to hear the song of the pines by Walden, until the last days of April,

[1] *A Western Journey with Emerson*, by James B. Thayer.

1882, when he died of pneumonia after a short illness.

His life, brave, serene and happy, was in exact accord with his words : —

> The sun set, but set not his hope ;
> Stars rose, his faith was earlier up.

E. W. E.

NATURE

A SUBTLE chain of countless rings
The next unto the farthest brings ;
The eye reads omens where it goes,
And speaks all languages the rose ;
And, striving to be man, the worm
Mounts through all the spires of form.[1]

INTRODUCTION

OUR age is retrospective. It builds the sep-
ulchres of the fathers. It writes biographies, histories, and criticism. The foregoing
generations beheld God and nature face to face;
we, through their eyes. Why should not we also
enjoy an original relation to the universe? Why
should not we have a poetry and philosophy of
insight and not of tradition, and a religion by
revelation to us, and not the history of theirs?
Embosomed for a season in nature, whose floods
of life stream around and through us, and invite
us, by the powers they supply, to action proportioned to nature, why should we grope among
the dry bones of the past, or put the living
generation into masquerade out of its faded
wardrobe? The sun shines to-day also. There
is more wool and flax in the fields. There are
new lands, new men, new thoughts. Let us demand our own works and laws and worship.

Undoubtedly we have no questions to ask
which are unanswerable. We must trust the
perfection of the creation so far as to believe
that whatever curiosity the order of things has

awakened in our minds, the order of things can
satisfy. Every man's condition is a solution in
hieroglyphic to those inquiries he would put.[1]
He acts it as life, before he apprehends it as
truth. In like manner, nature is already, in its
forms and tendencies, describing its own design.
Let us interrogate the great apparition that shines
so peacefully around us. Let us inquire, to what
end is nature?

All science has one aim, namely, to find a
theory of nature. We have theories of races and
of functions, but scarcely yet a remote approach
to an idea of creation.[2] We are now so far from
the road to truth, that religious teachers dis-
pute and hate each other, and speculative men
are esteemed unsound and frivolous. But to a
sound judgment, the most abstract truth is the
most practical. Whenever a true theory appears,
it will be its own evidence. Its test is, that
it will explain all phenomena. Now many are
thought not only unexplained but inexplicable;
as language, sleep, madness, dreams, beasts, sex.

Philosophically considered, the universe is
composed of Nature and the Soul. Strictly
speaking, therefore, all that is separate from us,
all which Philosophy distinguishes as the NOT
ME, that is, both nature and art, all other men

and my own body, must be ranked under this
name, NATURE. In enumerating the values of
nature and casting up their sum, I shall use the
word in both senses;—in its common and in its
philosophical import. In inquiries so general as
our present one, the inaccuracy is not material ;
no confusion of thought will occur. *Nature*, in
the common sense, refers to essences unchanged
by man ; space, the air, the river, the leaf. *Art*
is applied to the mixture of his will with the
same things, as in a house, a canal, a statue, a
picture. But his operations taken together are
so insignificant, a little chipping, baking, patch-
ing, and washing, that in an impression so grand
as that of the world on the human mind, they
do not vary the result.

NATURE

I

TO go into solitude, a man needs to retire as much from his chamber as from society. I am not solitary whilst I read and write, though nobody is with me. But if a man would be alone, let him look at the stars. The rays that come from those heavenly worlds will separate between him and what he touches. One might think the atmosphere was made transparent with this design, to give man, in the heavenly bodies, the perpetual presence of the sublime. Seen in the streets of cities, how great they are! If the stars should appear one night in a thousand years, how would men believe and adore; and preserve for many generations the remembrance of the city of God which had been shown! But every night come out these envoys of beauty, and light the universe with their admonishing smile.[1]

The stars awaken a certain reverence, because though always present, they are inaccessible; but all natural objects make a kindred impression, when the mind is open to their influence. Nature never wears a mean appearance. Neither does the wisest man extort her secret, and lose his curiosity by finding out all her perfection. Nature never became a toy to a wise spirit. The flowers, the animals, the mountains, reflected the wisdom of his best hour, as much as they had delighted the simplicity of his childhood.

When we speak of nature in this manner, we have a distinct but most poetical sense in the mind. We mean the integrity of impression made by manifold natural objects. It is this which distinguishes the stick of timber of the wood-cutter from the tree of the poet. The charming landscape which I saw this morning is indubitably made up of some twenty or thirty farms. Miller owns this field, Locke that, and Manning the woodland beyond. But none of them owns the landscape. There is a property in the horizon which no man has but he whose eye can integrate all the parts, that is, the poet. This is the best part of these men's farms, yet to this their warranty-deeds give no title.

To speak truly, few adult persons can see nature. Most persons do not see the sun. At least they have a very superficial seeing. The sun illuminates only the eye of the man, but shines into the eye and the heart of the child.

The lover of nature is he whose inward and
outward senses are still truly adjusted to each
other; who has retained the spirit of infancy
even into the era of manhood.[1] His intercourse
with heaven and earth becomes part of his daily
food.[2] In the presence of nature a wild delight
runs through the man, in spite of real sorrows.
Nature says, — he is my creature, and maugre
all his impertinent griefs, he shall be glad with
me. Not the sun or the summer alone, but
every hour and season yields its tribute of delight; for every hour and change corresponds to
and authorizes a different state of the mind, from
breathless noon to grimmest midnight. Nature
is a setting that fits equally well a comic or a
mourning piece.[3] In good health, the air is a
cordial of incredible virtue. Crossing a bare
common, in snow puddles, at twilight, under a
clouded sky, without having in my thoughts
any occurrence of special good fortune, I have
enjoyed a perfect exhilaration. I am glad to the
brink of fear. In the woods, too, a man casts
off his years, as the snake his slough, and at what
period soever of life is always a child. In the
woods is perpetual youth. Within these plantations of God, a decorum and sanctity reign, a
perennial festival is dressed, and the guest sees

not how he should tire of them in a thousand
years. In the woods, we return to reason and
faith. There I feel that nothing can befall me
in life, — no disgrace, no calamity (leaving me
my eyes), which nature cannot repair. Standing
on the bare ground, — my head bathed by the
blithe air and uplifted into infinite space, — all
mean egotism vanishes. I become a transparent
eyeball; I am nothing; I see all; the currents
of the Universal Being circulate through me; I
am part or parcel of God.[1] The name of the
nearest friend sounds then foreign and accidental: to be brothers, to be acquaintances, master or servant, is then a trifle and a disturbance.
I am the lover of uncontained and immortal
beauty. In the wilderness, I find something
more dear and connate than in streets or villages. In the tranquil landscape, and especially
in the distant line of the horizon, man beholds
somewhat as beautiful as his own nature.

The greatest delight which the fields and
woods minister is the suggestion of an occult
relation between man and the vegetable. I am
not alone and unacknowledged. They nod to
me, and I to them. The waving of the boughs
in the storm is new to me and old. It takes
me by surprise, and yet is not unknown. Its

effect is like that of a higher thought or a better emotion coming over me, when I deemed I was thinking justly or doing right.

Yet it is certain that the power to produce this delight does not reside in nature, but in man, or in a harmony of both. It is necessary to use these pleasures with great temperance. For nature is not always tricked in holiday attire, but the same scene which yesterday breathed perfume and glittered as for the frolic of the nymphs is overspread with melancholy to-day. Nature always wears the colors of the spirit. To a man laboring under calamity, the heat of his own fire hath sadness in it. Then there is a kind of contempt of the landscape felt by him who has just lost by death a dear friend. The sky is less grand as it shuts down over less worth in the population.[1]

II

COMMODITY

WHOEVER considers the final cause of the world will discern a multitude of uses that enter as parts into that result. They all admit of being thrown into one of the following classes : Commodity; Beauty; Language; and Discipline.

Under the general name of commodity, I rank all those advantages which our senses owe to nature. This, of course, is a benefit which is temporary and mediate, not ultimate, like its service to the soul. Yet although low, it is perfect in its kind, and is the only use of nature which all men apprehend. The misery of man appears like childish petulance, when we explore the steady and prodigal provision that has been made for his support and delight on this green ball which floats him through the heavens. What angels invented these splendid ornaments, these rich conveniences, this ocean of air above, this ocean of water beneath, this firmament of earth between? this zodiac of lights, this tent of dropping clouds, this striped coat of climates, this fourfold year?[1] Beasts, fire, water, stones, and corn serve him. The field is at once his floor, his work-yard, his play-ground, his garden, and his bed.

> " More servants wait on man
> Than he'll take notice of."[2]

Nature, in its ministry to man, is not only the material, but is also the process and the result. All the parts incessantly work into each other's hands for the profit of man. The wind sows the seed; the sun evaporates the sea; the wind blows the vapor to the field; the ice, on the other side of the planet, condenses rain on this; the rain feeds the plant; the plant feeds the animal; and thus the endless circulations of the divine charity nourish man.

The useful arts are reproductions or new combinations by the wit of man, of the same natural benefactors. He no longer waits for favoring gales, but by means of steam, he realizes the fable of Æolus's bag, and carries the two and thirty winds in the boiler of his boat. To diminish friction, he paves the road with iron bars, and, mounting a coach with a ship-load of men, animals, and merchandise behind him, he darts through the country, from town to town, like an eagle or a swallow through the air. By the aggregate of these aids, how is the face of the world changed, from the era of Noah to that of Napoleon! The private poor man hath cities, ships, canals, bridges, built for him. He goes to the post-office, and the human race run on his errands; to the book-shop, and the human race read and write of all that happens, for him; to the court-house, and nations repair his wrongs. He sets his house upon the road, and the human race go forth every morning, and shovel out the snow, and cut a path for him.

But there is no need of specifying particulars in this class of uses. The catalogue is endless, and the examples so obvious, that I shall,leave them to the reader's reflection, with the general remark, that this mercenary benefit is one which has respect to a farther good. A man is fed, not that he may be fed, but that he may work.[1]

III

BEAUTY

A NOBLER want of man is served by nature, namely, the love of Beauty.

The ancient Greeks called the world κόσμος, beauty. Such is the constitution of all things, or such the plastic power of the human eye, that the primary forms, as the sky, the mountain, the tree, the animal, give us a delight *in and for themselves;* a pleasure arising from outline, color, motion, and grouping. This seems partly owing to the eye itself. The eye is the best of artists. By the mutual action of its structure and of the laws of light, perspective is produced, which integrates every mass of objects, of what character soever, into a well colored and shaded globe, so that where the particular objects are mean and unaffecting, the landscape which they compose is round and symmetrical. And as the eye is the best composer, so light is the first of painters. There is no object so foul that intense light will not make beautiful. And the stimulus it affords to the sense, and a sort of infinitude which it hath, like space and time, make all matter gay.

Even the corpse has its own beauty.' But besides this general grace diffused over nature,
almost all the individual forms are agreeable to
the eye, as is proved by our endless imitations
of some of them, as the acorn, the grape, the
pine-cone, the wheat-ear, the egg, the wings and
forms of most birds, the lion's claw, the serpent, the butterfly, sea‑shells, flames, clouds,
buds, leaves, and‧ the forms of many trees, as the
palm.

For better consideration, we may distribute
the aspects of Beauty in a threefold manner.

1. First, the simple perception of natural
forms is a delight. The influence of the forms
and actions in nature is so needful to man, that,
in its lowest functions, it seems to lie on the
confines of commodity and beauty. To the
body and mind which have been cramped by
noxious work or company, nature is medicinal
and restores their tone. The tradesman, the
attorney comes out of the din and craft of the
street and sees the sky and the woods, and is a
man again. In their eternal calm, he finds himself. The health of the eye seems to demand a
horizon. We are never tired, so long as we can
see far enough.

But in other hours, Nature satisfies by its

loveliness, and without any mixture of corpóreal
benefit. I see the spectacle of morning from the
hilltop over against my house, from daybreak
to sunrise, with emotions which an angel might
share. The long slender bars of cloud float like
fishes in the sea of crimson light. From the
earth, as a shore, I look out into that silent sea.
I seem to partake its rapid transformations; the
active enchantment reaches my dust, and I dilate and conspire with the morning wind.[1] How
does Nature deify us with a few and cheap elements! Give me health and a day, and I will
make the pomp of emperors ridiculous. The
dawn is my Assyria; the sunset and moonrise
my Paphos, and unimaginable realms of faerie;
broad noon shall be my England of the senses
and the understanding; the night shall be my
Germany of mystic philosophy and dreams.

Not less excellent, except for our less susceptibility in the afternoon, was the charm,
last evening, of a January sunset. The western
clouds divided and subdivided themselves into
pink flakes modulated with tints of unspeakable
softness, and the air had so much life and sweetness that it was a pain to come within doors.
What was it that nature would say? Was there
no meaning in the live repose of the valley be-

hind the mill, and which Homer or Shakspeare could not re-form for me in words? The leaf-less trees become spires of flame in the sunset, with the blue east for their background, and the stars of the dead calices of flowers, and every withered stem and stubble rimed with frost, contribute something to the mute music.

The inhabitants of cities suppose that the country landscape is pleasant only half the year. I please myself with the graces of the winter scenery, and believe that we are as much touched by it as by the genial influences of summer. To the attentive eye, each moment of the year has its own beauty, and in the same field, it beholds, every hour, a picture which was never seen before, and which shall never be seen again. The heavens change every moment, and reflect their glory or gloom on the plains beneath. The state of the crop in the surrounding farms alters the expression of the earth from week to week. The succession of native plants in the pastures and roadsides, which makes the silent clock by which time tells the summer hours, will make even the divisions of the day sensible to a keen observer.[1] The tribes of birds and insects, like the plants punctual to their time, follow each other, and the year has room for all. By water-

courses, the variety is greater. In July, the blue
pontederia or pickerel-weed blooms in large
beds in the shallow parts of our pleasant river,
and swarms with yellow butterflies in continual
motion. Art cannot rival this pomp of purple
and gold. Indeed the river is a perpetual gala,
and boasts each month a new ornament.

But this beauty of Nature which is seen and
felt as beauty, is the least part. The shows of day,
the dewy morning, the rainbow, mountains, orchards in blossom, stars, moonlight, shadows in
still water, and the like, if too eagerly hunted,
become shows merely, and mock us with their
unreality. Go out of the house to see the moon,
and 't is mere tinsel; it will not please as when its
light shines upon your necessary journey. The
beauty that shimmers in the yellow afternoons
of October, who ever could clutch it? Go forth
to find it, and it is gone; 't is only a mirage as
you look from the windows of diligence.

2. The presence of a higher, namely, of the
spiritual element is essential to its perfection.
The high and divine beauty which can be loved
without effeminacy, is that which is found in
combination with the human will. Beauty is
the mark God sets upon virtue. Every natural
action is graceful. Every heroic act is also de-

cent, and causes the place and the bystanders
to shine. We are taught by great actions that
the universe is the property of every individual
in it. Every rational creature has all nature for
his dowry and estate. It is his, if he will. He
may divest himself of it; he may creep into
a corner, and abdicate his kingdom, as most
men do, but he is entitled to the world by his
constitution. In proportion to the energy of
his thought and will, he takes up the world
into himself. " All those things for which men
plough, build, or sail, obey virtue ; " said Sal-
lust. " The winds and waves," said Gibbon,
" are always on the side of the ablest naviga-
tors." [1] So are the sun and moon and all the
stars of heaven. When a noble act is done, —
perchance in a scene of great natural beauty;
when Leonidas and his three hundred martyrs consume one day in dying, and the sun
and moon come each and look at them once in
the steep defile of Thermopylæ; when Arnold
Winkelried, in the high Alps, under the shadow
of the avalanche, gathers in his side a sheaf of
Austrian spears to break the line for his com-
rades ; are not these heroes entitled to add the
beauty of the scene to the beauty of the deed ?
When the bark of Columbus nears the shore

of America ; — before it the beach lined with
savages, fleeing out of all their huts of cane ;
the sea behind ; and the purple mountains of
the Indian Archipelago around, can we separate
the man from the living picture ? Does not the
New World clothe his form with her palm-
groves and savannahs as fit drapery ? Ever does
natural beauty steal in like air, and envelope
great actions. When Sir Harry Vane was dragged
up the Tower-hill, sitting on a sled, to suffer
death as the champion of the English laws, one
of the multitude cried out to him, " You never
sate on so glorious a seat ! " Charles II., to
intimidate the citizens of London, caused the
patriot Lord Russell to be drawn in an open
coach through the principal streets of the city
on his way to the scaffold. " But," his biographer
says, " the multitude imagined they saw liberty
and virtue sitting by his side." In private places,
among sordid objects, an act of truth or heroism
seems at once to draw to itself the sky as its
temple, the sun as its candle. Nature stretches
out her arms to embrace man, only let his
thoughts be of equal greatness. Willingly does
she follow his steps with the rose and the violet,
and bend her lines of grandeur and grace to the
decoration of her darling child. Only let his

thoughts be of equal scope, and the frame will suit the picture. A virtuous man is in unison with her works, and makes the central figure of the visible sphere. Homer, Pindar, Socrates, Phocion, associate themselves fitly in our memory with the geography and climate of Greece. The visible heavens and earth sympathize with Jesus. And in common life whosoever has seen a person of powerful character and happy genius, will have remarked how easily he took all things along with him, — the persons, the opinions, and the day, and nature became ancillary to a man.

3. There is still another aspect under which the beauty of the world may be viewed, namely, as it becomes an object of the intellect. Beside the relation of things to virtue, they have a relation to thought. The intellect searches out the absolute order of things as they stand in the mind of God, and without the colors of affection. The intellectual and the active powers seem to succeed each other, and the exclusive activity of the one generates the exclusive activity of the other. There is something unfriendly in each to the other, but they are like the alternate periods of feeding and working in animals; each prepares and will be followed by the other. Therefore does beauty, which, in

relation to actions, as we have seen, comes unsought, and comes because it is unsought, remain for the apprehension and pursuit of the
intellect; and then again, in its turn, of the
active power. Nothing divine dies. All good
is eternally reproductive. The beauty of nature
re-forms itself in the mind, and not for barren
contemplation, but for new creation.

All men are in some degree impressed by the
face of the world ; some men even to delight.
This love of beauty is Taste. Others have the
same love in such excess, that, not content with
admiring, they seek to embody it in new forms.
The creation of beauty is Art.

The production of a work of art throws a
light upon the mystery of humanity. A work
of art is an abstract or epitome of the world. It
is the result or expression of nature, in minia-
ture. For although the works of nature are innumerable and all different, the result or the
expression of them all is similar and single. Nature is a sea of forms radically alike and even
unique. A leaf, a sunbeam, a landscape, the
ocean, make an analogous impression on the
mind. What is common to them all, — that per-
fectness and harmony, is beauty.[1] The standard
of beauty is the entire circuit of natural forms,

— the totality of nature ; which the Italians expressed by defining beauty " il più nell' uno."
Nothing is quite beautiful alone ; nothing but
is beautiful in the whole. A single object is only
so far beautiful as it suggests this universal
grace.[1] The poet, the painter, the sculptor, the
musician, the architect, seek each to concentrate
this radiance of the world on one point, and each
in his several work to satisfy the love of beauty
which stimulates him to produce. Thus is Art a
nature passed through the alembic of man. Thus
in art does Nature work through the will of a
man filled with the beauty of her first works.

The world thus exists to the soul to satisfy
the desire of beauty. This element I call an
ultimate end. No reason can be asked or given
why the soul seeks beauty.[2] Beauty, in its
largest and profoundest sense, is one expression
for the universe. God is the all-fair. Truth,
and goodness, and beauty, are but different
faces of the same All. But beauty in nature is
not ultimate. It is the herald of inward and
eternal beauty, and is not alone a solid and sat-
isfactory good. It must stand as a part, and not
as yet the last or highest expression of the final
cause of Nature.[3]

IV

LANGUAGE

LANGUAGE is a third use which Nature subserves to man. Nature is the vehicle of thought, and in a simple, double, and three-fold degree.

1. Words are signs of natural facts.

2. Particular natural facts are symbols of particular spiritual facts.

3. Nature is the symbol of spirit.

1. Words are signs of natural facts. The use of natural history is to give us aid in supernatural history ; the use of the outer creation, to give us language for the beings and changes of the inward creation. Every word which is used to express a moral or intellectual fact, if traced to its root, is found to be borrowed from some material appearance. *Right* means *straight;* *wrong* means *twisted.* *Spirit* primarily means *wind; transgression,* the crossing of a *line; supercilious,* the *raising of the eyebrow.* We say the *heart* to express emotion, the *head* to denote thought ; and *thought* and *emotion* are words borrowed from sensible things, and now appro-

priated to spiritual nature. Most of the process by which this transformation is made, is hidden from us in the remote time when language was framed ; but the same tendency may be daily observed in children. Children and savages use only nouns or names of things, which they convert into verbs, and apply to analogous mental acts.

2. But this origin of all words that convey a spiritual import, — so conspicuous a fact in the history of language, — is our least debt to nature. It is not words only that are emblematic ; it is things which are emblematic. Every natural fact is a symbol of some spiritual fact. Every appearance in nature corresponds to some state of the mind, and that state of the mind can only be described by presenting that natural appearance as its picture. An enraged man is a lion, a cunning man is a fox, a firm man is a rock, a learned man is a torch. A lamb is innocence ; a snake is subtle spite ; flowers express to us the delicate affections. Light and darkness are our familiar expression for knowledge and ignorance ; and heat for love. Visible distance behind and before us, is respectively our image of memory and hope.

Who looks upon a river in a meditative hour

and is not reminded of the flux of all things ?
Throw a stone into the stream, and the circles
that propagate themselves are the beautiful type
of all influence.[1] Man is conscious of a universal soul within or behind his individual life,
wherein, as in a firmament, the natures of Justice, Truth, Love, Freedom, arise and shine.
This universal soul he calls Reason : it is not
mine, or thine, or his, but we are its ; we are
its property and men. And the blue sky in
which the private earth is buried, the sky with
its eternal calm, and full of everlasting orbs, is
the type of Reason. That which intellectually
considered we call Reason, considered in relation
to nature, we call Spirit. Spirit is the Creator.
Spirit hath life in itself. And man in all ages
and countries embodies it in his language as the
FATHER.

It is easily seen that there is nothing lucky
or capricious in these analogies, but that they
are constant, and pervade nature. These are
not the dreams of a few poets, here and there,
but man is an analogist, and studies relations in
all objects. He is placed in the centre of beings,
and a ray of relation passes from every other
being to him. And neither can man be understood without these objects, nor these objects

without man. All the facts in natural history
taken by themselves, have no value, but are
barren, like a single sex. But marry it to human
history, and it is full of life. Whole floras, all
Linnæus' and Buffon's volumes, are dry catalogues of facts ; but the most trivial of these
facts, the habit of a plant, the organs, or work,
or noise of an insect, applied to the illustration
of a fact in intellectual philosophy, or in any
way associated to human nature, affects us in
the most lively and agreeable manner. The
seed of a plant, — to what affecting analogies
in the nature of man is that little fruit made
use of, in all discourse, up to the voice of Paul,
who calls the human corpse a seed, — " It is
sown a natural body; it is raised a spiritual
body." The motion of the earth round its axis
and round the sun, makes the day and the year.
These are certain amounts of brute light and
heat. But is there no intent of an analogy between man's life and the seasons? And do the
seasons gain no grandeur or pathos from that
analogy ? The instincts of the ant are very
unimportant considered as the ant's ; but the
moment a ray of relation is seen to extend from
it to man, and the little drudge is seen to be a
monitor, a little body with a mighty heart, then

all its habits, even that said to be recently observed, that it never sleeps, become sublime.

Because of this radical correspondence between
visible things and human thoughts, savages,
who have only what is necessary, converse in
figures. As we go back in history, language
becomes more picturesque, until its infancy,
when it is all poetry ; or all spiritual facts are
represented by natural symbols. The same symbols are found to make the original elements of
all languages. It has moreover been observed,
that the idioms of all languages approach each
other in passages of the greatest eloquence and
power. And as this is the first language, so is
it the last. This immediate dependence of language upon nature, this conversion of an outward phenomenon into a type of somewhat in
human life, never loses its power to affect us.
It is this which gives that piquancy to the conversation of a strong-natured farmer or back-
woodsman, which all men relish.

A man's power to connect his thought with
its proper symbol, and so to utter it, depends
on the simplicity of his character, that is, upon
his love of truth and his desire to communicate
it without loss. The corruption of man is followed by the corruption of language. When

simplicity of character and the sovereignty of
ideas is broken up by the prevalence of secondary desires, — the desire of riches, of pleasure,
of power, and of praise, — and duplicity and
falsehood take place of simplicity and truth, the
power over nature as an interpreter of the will
is in a degree lost; new imagery ceases to be
created, and old words are perverted to stand for
things which are not; 'a paper currency is employed, when there is no bullion in the vaults.
In due time the fraud is manifest, and words
lose all power to stimulate the understanding
or the affections. Hundreds of writers may be
found in every long-civilized nation who for a
short time believe and make others believe that
they see and utter truths, who do not of themselves clothe one thought in its natural garment,
but who feed unconsciously on the language created by the primary writers of the country, those,
namely, who hold primarily on nature.[1]

But wise men pierce this rotten diction and
fasten words again to visible things ; so that picturesque language is at once a commanding certificate that he who employs it is a man in alliance
with truth and God. The moment our discourse
rises above the ground line of familiar facts and
is inflamed with passion or exalted by thought,

it clothes itself in images. A man conversing in earnest, if he watch his intellectual processes, will find that a material image more or less luminous arises in his mind, contemporaneous with every thought, which furnishes the vestment of the thought. Hence, good writing and brilliant discourse are perpetual allegories. This imagery is spontaneous. It is the blending of experience with the present action of the mind. It is proper creation. It is the working of the Original Cause through the instruments he has already made.

These facts may suggest the advantage which the country-life possesses, for a powerful mind, over the artificial and curtailed life of cities. We know more from nature than we can at will communicate. Its light flows into the mind evermore, and we forget its presence. The poet, the orator, bred in the woods, whose senses have been nourished by their fair and appeasing changes, year after year, without design and without heed, — shall not lose their lesson altogether, in the roar of cities or the broil of politics. Long hereafter, amidst agitation and terror in national councils, — in the hour of revolution, — these solemn images shall reappear in their morning lustre, as fit symbols and words of the thoughts which the passing events shall awaken. At the call of a

noble sentiment, again the woods wave, the pines
murmur, the river rolls and shines, and the cattle
low upon the mountains, as he saw and heard
them in his infancy. And with these forms, the
spells of persuasion, the keys of power are put
into his hands.

3. We are thus assisted by natural objects in
the expression of particular meanings. But how
great a language to convey such pepper-corn informations! Did it need such noble races of creatures, this profusion of forms, this host of orbs
in heaven, to furnish man with the dictionary
and grammar of his municipal speech? Whilst
we use this grand cipher to expedite the affairs
of our pot and kettle, we feel that we have not
yet put it to its use, neither are able. We are
like travellers using the cinders of a volcano to
roast their eggs. Whilst we see that it always
stands ready to clothe what we would say, we
cannot avoid the question whether the characters
are not significant of themselves. Have mountains, and waves, and skies, no significance but
what we consciously give them when we employ
them as emblems of our thoughts?[1] The world
is emblematic. Parts of speech are metaphors,
because the whole of nature is a metaphor of
the human mind. The laws of moral nature an-

swer to those of matter as face to face in a glass. " The visible world and the relation of its parts, is the dial plate of the invisible." The axioms of physics translate the laws of ethics. Thus, " the whole is greater than its part; " " reaction is equal to action ; " " the smallest weight may be made to lift the greatest, the difference of weight being compensated by time; " and many the like propositions, which have an ethical as well as physical sense. These propositions have a much more extensive and universal sense when applied to human life, than when confined to technical use.

In like manner, the memorable words of history and the proverbs of nations consist usually of a natural fact, selected as a picture or parable of a moral truth. Thus ; A rolling stone gathers no moss ; A bird in the hand is worth two in the bush ; A cripple in the right way will beat a racer in the wrong ; Make hay while the sun shines ; 'T is hard to carry a full cup even ; Vinegar is the son of wine ; The last ounce broke the camel's back ; Long-lived trees make roots first ; — and the like. In their primary sense these are trivial facts, but we repeat them for the value of their analogical import. What is true of proverbs, is true of all fables, parables, and allegories.

This relation between the mind and matter is

not fancied by some poet, but stands in the will
of God, and so is free to be known by all men.
It appears to men, or it does not appear. When
in fortunate hours we ponder this miracle, the
wise man doubts if at all other times he is not
blind and deaf;

> " Can such things be,
> And overcome us like a summer's cloud,
> Without our special wonder ? " [1]

for the universe becomes transparent, and the
light of higher laws than its own shines through
it. It is the standing problem which has exercised the wonder and the study of every fine
genius since the world began; from the era
of the Egyptians and the Brahmins to that of
Pythagoras, of Plato, of Bacon, of Leibnitz,
of Swedenborg. There sits the Sphinx at the
road-side, and from age to age, as each prophet
comes by, he tries his fortune at reading her riddle. There seems to be a necessity in spirit to
manifest itself in material forms; and day and
night, river and storm, beast and bird, acid and
alkali, preëxist in necessary Ideas in the mind
of God, and are what they are by virtue of preceding affections in the world of spirit. A Fact
is the end or last issue of spirit. The visible
creation is the terminus or the circumference of

the invisible world. " Material objects," said a
French philosopher, " are necessarily kinds of
scoriæ of the substantial thoughts of the Creator,
which must always preserve an exact relation to
their first origin; in other words, visible nature
must have a spiritual and moral side."

This doctrine is abstruse, and though the images of " garment," " scoriæ," " mirror," etc.,
may stimulate the fancy, we must summon the
aid of subtler and more vital expositors to make
it plain. " Every scripture is to be interpreted
by the same spirit which gave it forth," — is the
fundamental law of criticism. A life in harmony
with Nature, the love of truth and of virtue, will
purge the eyes to understand her text. By degrees we may come to know the primitive sense
of the permanent objects of nature, so that the
world shall be to us an open book, and every
form significant of its hidden life and final cause.

A new interest surprises us, whilst, under the
view now suggested, we contemplate the fearful
extent and multitude of objects; since " every
object rightly seen, unlocks a new faculty of the
soul." That which was unconscious truth, becomes, when interpreted and defined in an object, a part of the domain of knowledge, — a
new weapon in the magazine of power.

V

DISCIPLINE

IN view of the significance of nature, we arrive at once at a new fact, that nature is a discipline. This use of the world includes the preceding uses, as parts of itself.

Space, time, society, labor, climate, food, locomotion, the animals, the mechanical forces, give us sincerest lessons, day by day, whose meaning is unlimited. They educate both the Understanding and the Reason. Every property of matter is a school for the understanding, — its solidity or resistance, its inertia, its extension, its figure, its divisibility. The understanding adds, divides, combines, measures, and finds nutriment and room for its activity in this worthy scene. Meantime, Reason transfers all these lessons into its own world of thought, by perceiving the analogy that marries Matter and Mind.

1. Nature is a discipline of the understanding in intellectual truths. Our dealing with sensible objects is a constant exercise in the necessary lessons of difference, of likeness, of order, of being and seeming, of progressive arrangement;

of ascent from particular to general; of combination to one end of manifold forces. Proportioned to the importance of the organ to be
formed, is the extreme care with which its tuition
is provided, — a care pretermitted in no single
case. What tedious training, day after day, year
after year, never ending, to form the common
sense; what continual reproduction of annoy-
ances, inconveniences, dilemmas; what rejoicing
over us of little men; what disputing of prices,
what reckonings of interest, — and all to form
the Hand of the mind; — to instruct us that
" good thoughts are no better than good dreams,
unless they be executed ! "

The same good office is performed by Property and its filial systems of debt and credit.
Debt, grinding debt, whose iron face the widow,
the orphan, and the sons of genius fear and
hate ; — debt, which consumes so much time,
which so cripples and disheartens a great spirit
with cares that seem so base, is a preceptor
whose lessons cannot be foregone, and is needed
most by those who suffer from it most. Moreover, property, which has been well compared
to snow, — " if it fall level to-day, it will be
blown into drifts to-morrow," — is the surface
action of internal machinery, like the index on

the face of a clock. Whilst now it is the gymnastics of the understanding, it is hiving, in the foresight of the spirit, experience in profounder laws.

The whole character and fortune of the individual are affected by the least inequalities in the culture of the understanding ; for example, in the perception of differences. Therefore is Space, and therefore Time, that man may know that things are not huddled and lumped, but sundered and individual. A bell and a plough have each their use, and neither can do the office of the other. Water is good to drink, coal to burn, wool to wear ; but wool cannot be drunk, nor water spun, nor coal eaten. The wise man shows his wisdom in separation, in gradation, and his scale of creatures and of merits is as wide as nature. The foolish have no range in their scale, but suppose every man is as every other man. What is not good they call the worst, and what is not hateful, they call the best.

In like manner, what good heed Nature forms in us ! She pardons no mistakes. Her yea is yea, and her nay, nay.

The first steps in Agriculture, Astronomy, Zoölogy (those first steps which the farmer, the hunter, and the sailor take), teach that Nature's dice are always loaded;¹ that in her heaps and rubbish are concealed sure and useful re- sults.

How calmly and genially the mind appre- hends one after another the laws of physics! What noble emotions dilate the mortal as he enters into the councils of the creation, and feels by knowledge the privilege to BE! His insight refines him. The beauty of nature shines in his own breast. Man is greater that he can see this, and the universe less, because Time and Space relations vanish as laws are known.

Here again we are impressed and even daunted by the immense Universe to be explored. "What we know is a point to what we do not know." Open any recent journal of science, and weigh the problems suggested concerning Light, Heat, Electricity, Magnetism, Physiology, Geology, and judge whether the interest of natural science is likely to be soon exhausted.

Passing by many particulars of the discipline of nature, we must not omit to specify two.

The exercise of the Will, or the lesson of power, is taught in every event. From the child's successive possession of his several senses up to the hour when he saith, "Thy will be done!" he is learning the secret that he can reduce under

his will not only particular events but great
classes, nay, the whole series of events, and so
conform all facts to his character. Nature is
thoroughly mediate. It is made to serve. It
receives the dominion of man as meekly as the
ass on which the Saviour rode. It offers all its
kingdoms to man as the raw material which he
may mould into what is useful. Man is never
weary of working it up. He forges the subtile
and delicate air into wise and melodious words,
and gives them wing as angels of persuasion
and command. One after another his victorious
thought comes up with and reduces all things,
until the world becomes at last only a realized
will, — the double of the man.

2. Sensible objects conform to the premoni-
tions of Reason and reflect the conscience. All
things are moral ; and in their boundless changes
have an unceasing reference to spiritual nature.
Therefore is nature glorious with form, color,
and motion ; that every globe in the remotest
heaven, every chemical change from the rudest
crystal up to the laws of life, every change of
vegetation from the first principle of growth in
the eye of a leaf, to the tropical forest and ante-
diluvian coal-mine, every animal function from
the sponge up to Hercules, shall hint or thun-

der to man the laws of right and wrong, and
echo the Ten Commandments.' Therefore is
Nature ever the ally of Religion : lends all her
pomp and riches to the religious sentiment.
Prophet and priest, David, Isaiah, Jesus, have
drawn deeply from this source. This ethical
character so penetrates the bone and marrow of
nature, as to seem the end for which it was made.
Whatever private purpose is answered by any
member or part, this is its public and universal function, and is never omitted. Nothing
in nature is exhausted in its first use. When
a thing has served an end to the uttermost, it
is wholly new for an ulterior service. In God,
every end is converted into a new means. Thus
the use of commodity, regarded by itself, is
mean and squalid. But it is to the mind an
education in the doctrine of Use, namely, that
a thing is good only so far as it serves ; that a
conspiring of parts and efforts to the production
of an end is essential to any being. The first
and gross manifestation of this truth is our inevitable and hated training in values and wants, in
corn and meat.

It has already been illustrated, that every natural process is a version of a moral sentence.
The moral law lies at the centre of nature and

radiates to the circumference. It is the pith
and marrow of every substance, every relation,
and every process. All things with which we
deal, preach to us. What is a farm but a mute
gospel? The chaff and the wheat, weeds and
plants, blight, rain, insects, sun, — it is a sacred
emblem from the first furrow of spring to the
last stack which the snow of winter overtakes
in the fields. But the sailor, the shepherd, the
miner, the merchant, in their several resorts,
have each an experience precisely parallel, and
leading to the same conclusion : because all organizations are radically alike. Nor can it be
doubted that this moral sentiment which thus
scents the air, grows in the grain, and impreg-
nates the waters of the world, is caught by man
and sinks into his soul.[1] The moral influence
of nature upon every individual is that amount
of truth which it illustrates to him. Who can
estimate this? Who can guess how much firmness the sea-beaten rock has taught the fisher-
man? how much tranquillity has been reflected
to man from the azure sky, over whose unspotted
deeps the winds forevermore drive flocks of
stormy clouds, and leave no wrinkle or stain?[2]
how much industry and providence and affection we have caught from the pantomime of

brutes ? What a searching preacher of self-command is the varying phenomenon of Health !

Herein is especially apprehended the unity of Nature, — the unity in variety, — which meets us everywhere. All the endless variety of things make an identical impression. Xenophanes complained in his old age, that, look where he would, all things hastened back to Unity. He was weary of seeing the same entity in the tedious variety of forms.[1] The fable of Proteus has a cordial truth. A leaf, a drop, a crystal, a moment of time, is related to the whole, and partakes of the perfection of the whole. Each particle is a microcosm, and faithfully renders the likeness of the world.

Not only resemblances exist in things whose analogy is obvious, as when we detect the type of the human hand in the flipper of the fossil saurus,[2] but also in objects wherein there is great superficial unlikeness. Thus architecture is called "frozen music," by De Staël and Goethe. Vitruvius thought an architect should be a musician. " A Gothic church," said Coleridge, " is a petrified religion." Michael Angelo maintained, that, to an architect, a knowledge of anatomy is essential. In Haydn's oratorios, the notes present to the imagination not only motions, as of

the snake, the stag, and the elephant, but colors
also ; as the green grass. The law of harmonic
sounds reappears in the harmonic colors. The
granite is differenced in its laws only by the
more or less of heat from the river that wears
it away. The river, as it flows, resembles the
air that flows over it ; the air resembles the light
which traverses it with more subtile currents;
the light resembles the heat which rides with it
through Space. Each creature is only a modi-
fication of the other ; the likeness in them is
more than the difference, and their radical law
is one and the same. A rule of one art, or a
law of one organization, holds true throughout nature. So intimate is this Unity, that, it is
easily seen, it lies under the undermost garment
of Nature, and betrays its source in Universal
Spirit. For it pervades Thought also. Every
universal truth which we express in words, implies or supposes every other truth. *Omne verum
vero consonat.* It is like a great circle on a sphere,
comprising all possible circles ; which, however,
may be drawn and comprise it in like manner.
Every such truth is the absolute Ens seen from
one side. But it has innumerable sides.

The central Unity is still more conspicuous
in actions. Words are finite organs of the infi-

nite mind. They cannot cover the dimensions
of what is in truth. They break, chop, and impoverish it. An action is the perfection and publication of thought. A right action seems to fill
the eye, and to be related to all nature. " The
wise man, in doing one thing, does all ; or, in
the one thing he does rightly, he sees the likeness of all which is done rightly."

Words and actions are not the attributes of
brute nature. They introduce us to the human
form, of which all other organizations appear to
be degradations.[1] When this appears among
so many that surround it, the spirit prefers it to
all others. It says, "From such as this have
I drawn joy and knowledge ; in such as this
have I found and beheld myself; I will speak
to it ; it can speak again ; it can yield me thought
already formed and alive." In fact, the eye, —
the mind, — is always accompanied by these
forms, male and female ; and these are incom-
parably the richest informations of the power
and order that lie at the heart of things. Un-
fortunately every one of them bears the marks
as of some injury ; is marred and superficially
defective. Nevertheless, far different from the
deaf and dumb nature around them, these all
rest like fountain-pipes on the unfathomed sea

of thought and virtue whereto they alone, of all organizations, are the entrances.[1]

It were a pleasant inquiry to follow into detail their ministry to our education, but where would it stop? We are associated in adolescent and adult life with some friends, who, like skies and waters, are coextensive with our idea; who, answering each to a certain affection of the soul, satisfy our desire on that side ; whom we lack power to put at such focal distance from us, that we can mend or even analyze them. We cannot choose but love them. When much intercourse with a friend has supplied us with a standard of excellence, and has increased our respect for the resources of God who thus sends a real person to outgo our ideal ; when he has, moreover, become an object of thought, and, whilst his character retains all its unconscious effect, is converted in the mind into solid and sweet wisdom, — it is a sign to us that his office is closing, and he is commonly withdrawn from our sight in a short time.[2]

VI

IDEALISM [1]

THUS is the unspeakable but intelligible
and practicable meaning of the world con-
veyed to man, the immortal pupil, in every object of sense.   To this one end of Discipline,
all parts of nature conspire.

A noble doubt perpetually suggests itself, —
whether this end be not the Final Cause of the
Universe ; and whether nature outwardly exists.
It is a sufficient account of that Appearance we
call the World, that God will teach a human
mind, and so makes it the receiver of a certain
number of congruent sensations, which we call
sun and moon, man and woman, house and trade.
In my utter impotence to test the authenticity
of the report of my senses, to know whether
the impressions they make on me correspond
with outlying objects, what difference does it
make, whether Orion is up there in heaven, or
some god paints the image in the firmament of
the soul ?   The relations of parts and the end
of the whole remaining the same, what is the
difference, whether land and sea interact, and
worlds revolve and intermingle without number

or end, — deep yawning under deep, and galaxy balancing galaxy, throughout absolute space, — or whether, without relations of time and space, the same appearances are inscribed in the constant faith of man? Whether nature enjoy a substantial existence without, or is only in the apocalypse of the mind, it is alike useful and alike venerable to me. Be it what it may, it is ideal to me so long as I cannot try the accuracy of my senses.

The frivolous make themselves merry with the Ideal theory, as if its consequences were burlesque ; as if it affected the stability of nature. It surely does not. God never jests with us, and will not compromise the end of nature by permitting any inconsequence in its procession. Any distrust of the permanence of laws would paralyze the faculties of man. Their permanence is sacredly respected, and his faith therein is perfect. The wheels and springs of man are all set to the hypothesis of the permanence of nature. We are not built like a ship to be tossed, but like a house to stand. It is a natural consequence of this structure, that so long as the active powers predominate over the reflective, we resist with indignation any hint that nature is more short-lived or mutable than

spirit.   The broker, the wheelwright, the car-
penter, the tollman, are much displeased at the
intimation.

But whilst we acquiesce entirely in the permanence of natural laws, the question of the
absolute existence of nature still remains open.
It is the uniform effect of culture on the human
mind, not to shake our faith in the stability of
particular phenomena, as of heat, water, azote ;
but to lead us to regard nature as phenomenon,
not a substance ; to attribute necessary existence
to spirit ; to esteem nature as an accident and
an effect.

To the senses and the unrenewed understanding, belongs a sort of instinctive belief in
the absolute existence of nature.   In their view
man and nature are indissolubly joined. Things
are ultimates, and they never look beyond their
sphere. The presence of Reason mars this faith.
The first effort of thought tends to relax this
despotism of the senses which binds us to nature as if we were a part of it, and shows us
nature aloof, and, as it were, afloat. Until this
higher agency intervened, the animal eye sees,
with wonderful accuracy, sharp outlines and
colored surfaces. When the eye of Reason
opens, to outline and surface are at once added

grace and expression. These proceed from imagination and affection, and abate somewhat of
the angular distinctness of objects. If the Reason
be stimulated to more earnest vision, outlines
and surfaces become transparent, and are no
longer seen; causes and spirits are seen through
them. The best moments of life are these delicious awakenings of the higher powers, and the
reverential withdrawing of nature before its God.

Let us proceed to indicate the effects of culture.

1. Our first institution in the Ideal philosophy is a hint from Nature herself.

Nature is made to conspire with spirit to
emancipate us. Certain mechanical changes, a
small alteration in our local position, apprizes
us of a dualism. We are strangely affected by
seeing the shore from a moving ship, from a
balloon, or through the tints of an unusual sky.
The least change in our point of view gives the
whole world a pictorial air. A man who seldom
rides, needs only to get into a coach and traverse
his own town, to turn the street into a puppet-
show. The men, the women, — talking, running, bartering, fighting, — the earnest mechanic,
the lounger, the beggar, the boys, the dogs, are
unrealized at once, or, at least, wholly detached

from all relation to the observer, and seen as apparent, not substantial beings. What new thoughts are suggested by seeing a face of country quite familiar, in the rapid movement of the railroad car! Nay, the most wonted objects, (make a very slight change in the point of vision,) please us most. In a camera obscura, the butcher's cart, and the figure of one of our own family amuse us. So a portrait of a well-known face gratifies us. Turn the eyes upside down, by looking at the landscape through your legs, and how agreeable is the picture, though you have seen it any time these twenty years!

In these cases, by mechanical means, is suggested the difference between the observer and the spectacle — between man and nature. Hence arises a pleasure mixed with awe; I may say, a low degree of the sublime is felt, from the fact, probably, that man is hereby apprized that whilst the world is a spectacle, something in himself is stable.

2. In a higher manner the poet communicates the same pleasure. By a few strokes he delineates, as on air, the sun, the mountain, the camp, the city, the hero, the maiden, not different from what we know them, but only lifted from the ground and afloat before the eye. He unfixes

the land and the sea, makes them revolve around
the axis of his primary thought, and disposes
them anew. Possessed himself by a heroic passion, he uses matter as symbols of it. The
sensual man conforms thoughts to things; the
poet conforms things to his thoughts. The one
esteems nature as rooted and fast; the other, as
fluid, and impresses his being thereon. To him,
the refractory world is ductile and flexible; he
invests dust and stones with humanity, and
makes them the words of the Reason.[1] The
Imagination may be defined to be the use which
the Reason makes of the material world. Shakspeare possesses the power of subordinating nature for the purposes of expression, beyond all
poets. His imperial muse tosses the creation like
a bauble from hand to hand, and uses it to embody any caprice of thought that is uppermost
in his mind. The remotest spaces of nature are
visited, and the farthest sundered things are
brought together, by a subtile spiritual connection. We are made aware that magnitude of
material things is relative, and all objects shrink
and expand to serve the passion of the poet.
Thus in his sonnets, the lays of birds, the scents
and dyes of flowers he finds to be the *shadow*
of his beloved; time, which keeps her from him,

is his *chest;* the suspicion she has awakened, is her *ornament;*

> The ornament of beauty is Suspect,
> A crow which flies in heaven's sweetest air.[1]

His passion is not the fruit of chance; it swells, as he speaks, to a city, or a state.

> No, it was builded far from accident;
> It suffers not in smiling pomp, nor falls
> Under the brow of thralling discontent;
> It fears not policy, that heretic,
> That works on leases of short numbered hours,
> But all alone stands hugely politic.[2]

In the strength of his constancy, the Pyramids seem to him recent and transitory. The freshness of youth and love dazzles him with its resemblance to morning;

> Take those lips away
> Which so sweetly were forsworn;
> And those eyes, — the break of day,
> Lights that do mislead the morn.[3]

The wild beauty of this hyperbole, I may say in passing, it would not be easy to match in literature.

This transfiguration which all material objects undergo through the passion of the poet, — this power which he exerts to dwarf the great, to magnify the small, — might be illustrated by a

thousand examples from his Plays. I have before me the Tempest, and will cite only these few
lines.

> ARIEL. The strong based promontory
> Have I made shake, and by the spurs plucked up
> The pine and cedar.

Prospero calls for music to soothe the frantic
Alonzo, and his companions ;

> A solemn air, and the best comforter
> To an unsettled fancy, cure thy brains
> Now useless, boiled within thy skull.

Again ;

> The charm dissolves apace,
> And, as the morning steals upon the night,
> Melting the darkness, so their rising senses
> Begin to chase the ignorant fumes that mantle
> Their clearer reason.
> Their understanding
> Begins to swell : and the approaching tide
> Will shortly fill the reasonable shores
> That now lie foul and muddy.

The perception of real affinities between events
(that is to say, of *ideal* affinities, for those only
are real), enables the poet thus to make free
with the most imposing forms and phenomena
of the world, and to assert the predominance of
the soul.

3. Whilst thus the poet animates nature with his own thoughts, he differs from the philosopher only herein, that the one proposes Beauty as his main end; the other Truth. But the philosopher, not less than the poet, postpones the apparent order and relations of things to the empire of thought. "The problem of philosophy," according to Plato, "is, for all that exists conditionally, to find a ground unconditioned and absolute." It proceeds on the faith that a law determines all phenomena, which being known, the phenomena can be predicted. That law, when in the mind, is an idea. Its beauty is infinite. The true philosopher and the true poet are one, and a beauty, which is truth, and a truth, which is beauty, is the aim of both. Is not the charm of one of Plato's or Aristotle's definitions strictly like that of the Antigone of Sophocles? It is, in both cases, that a spiritual life has been imparted to nature; that the solid seeming block of matter has been pervaded and dissolved by a thought;' that this feeble human being has penetrated the vast masses of nature with an informing soul, and recognized itself in their harmony, that is, seized their law. In physics, when this is attained, the memory disburthens itself of its cumbrous catalogues of

particulars, and carries centuries of observation
in a single formula.

Thus even in physics, the material is degraded
before the spiritual. The astronomer, the geo-
meter, rely on their irrefragable analysis, and
disdain the results of observation. The sublime
remark of Euler on his law of arches, "This will
be found contrary to all experience, yet is true;"
had already transferred nature into the mind,
and left matter like an outcast corpse.'

4. Intellectual science has been observed to
beget invariably a doubt of the existence of matter. Turgot said, "He that has never doubted
the existence of matter, may be assured he has no
aptitude for metaphysical inquiries." It fastens
the attention upon immortal necessary uncreated
natures, that is, upon Ideas; and in their presence we feel that the outward circumstance is
a dream and a shade. Whilst we wait in this
Olympus of gods, we think of nature as an
appendix to the soul. We ascend into their
region, and know that these are the thoughts
of the Supreme Being. "These are they who
were set up from everlasting, from the beginning,
or ever the earth was. When he prepared the
heavens, they were there; when he established
the clouds above, when he strengthened the foun-

tains of the deep. Then they were by him, as one brought up with him. Of them took he counsel." [1]

Their influence is proportionate. As objects of science they are accessible to few men. Yet all men are capable of being raised by piety or by passion, into their region. And no man touches these divine natures, without becoming, in some degree, himself divine. Like a new soul, they renew the body. We become physically nimble and lightsome; we tread on air; life is no longer irksome, and we think it will never be so. No man fears age or misfortune or death in their serene company, for he is transported out of the district of change. Whilst we behold unveiled the nature of Justice and Truth, we learn the difference between the absolute and the conditional or relative. We apprehend the absolute. As it were, for the first time, *we exist*. We become immortal, for we learn that time and space are relations of matter; that with a perception of truth or a virtuous will they have no affinity.

5. Finally, religion and ethics, which may be fitly called the practice of ideas, or the introduction of ideas into life, have an analogous effect with all lower culture, in degrading nature and

suggesting its dependence on spirit. Ethics and
religion differ herein; that the one is the system
of human duties commencing from man; the
other, from God. Religion includes the personality of God; Ethics does not. They are one
to our present design. They both put nature
under foot. The first and last lesson of religion
is, " The things that are seen, are temporal; the
things that are unseen, are eternal." It puts an
affront upon nature. It does that for the un-
schooled, which philosophy does for Berkeley
and Viasa. The uniform language that may be
heard in the churches of the most ignorant sects
is, — " Contemn the unsubstantial shows of the
world; they are vanities, dreams, shadows, un-
realities; seek the realities of religion." The
devotee flouts nature. Some theosophists have
arrived at a certain hostility and indignation towards matter, as the Manichean and Plotinus.'
They distrusted in themselves any looking back
to these flesh - pots of Egypt. Plotinus was
ashamed of his body. In short, they might all
say of matter, what Michael Angelo said of external beauty, " It is the frail and weary weed,
in which God dresses the soul which he has
called into time."

It appears that motion, poetry, physical and

intellectual science, and religion, all tend to affect our convictions of the reality of the external
world. But I own there is something ungrate-
ful in expanding too curiously the particulars of
the general proposition, that all culture tends to
imbue us with idealism. I have no hostility to
nature, but a child's love to it. I expand and
live in the warm day like corn and melons. Let
us speak her fair. I do not wish to fling stones
at my beautiful mother, nor soil my gentle nest.
I only wish to indicate the true position of nature in regard to man, wherein to establish man
all right education tends; as the ground which
to attain is the object of human life, that is, of
man's connection with nature. Culture inverts
the vulgar views of nature, and brings the mind
to call that apparent which it uses to call real,
and that real which it uses to call visionary.
Children, it is true, believe in the external world.
The belief that it appears only, is an afterthought, but with culture this faith will as surely
arise on the mind as did the first.

The advantage of the ideal theory over the
popular faith is this, that it presents the world
in precisely that view which is most desirable to
the mind. It is, in fact, the view which Reason,
both speculative and practical, that is, philoso-

phy and virtue, take. For seen in the light of thought, the world always is phenomenal; and virtue subordinates it to the mind. Idealism sees the world in God. It beholds the whole circle of persons and things, of actions and events, of country and religion, not as painfully accumulated, atom after atom, act after act, in an aged creeping Past, but as one vast picture which God paints on the instant eternity for the contemplation of the soul. Therefore the soul holds itself off from a too trivial and microscopic study of the universal tablet. It respects the end too much to immerse itself in the means. It sees something more important in Christianity than the scandals of ecclesiastical history or the niceties of criticism; and, very incurious concerning persons or miracles, and not at all disturbed by chasms of historical evidence, it accepts from God the phenomenon, as it finds it, as the pure and awful form of religion in the world. It is not hot and passionate at the appearance of what it calls its own good or bad fortune, at the union or opposition of other persons. No man is its enemy. It accepts whatsoever befalls, as part of its lesson. It is a watcher more than a doer, and it is a doer, only that it may the better watch.

VII

SPIRIT

IT is essential to a true theory of nature
and of man, that it should contain somewhat progressive. Uses that are exhausted or
that may be, and facts that end in the statement, cannot be all that is true of this brave
lodging wherein man is harbored, and wherein
all his faculties find appropriate and endless exercise. And all the uses of nature admit of being
summed in one, which yields the activity of man
an infinite scope. Through all its kingdoms, to
the suburbs and outskirts of things, it is faithful
to the cause whence it had its origin. It always
speaks of Spirit. It suggests the absolute. It is
a perpetual effect. It is a great shadow pointing
always to the sun behind us.

The aspect of Nature is devout. Like the
figure of Jesus, she stands with bended head,
and hands folded upon the breast. The happiest man is he who learns from nature the
lesson of worship.

Of that ineffable essence which we call Spirit,
he that thinks most, will say least. We can fore-

see God in the coarse, and, as it were, distant
phenomena of matter; but when we try to de-
fine and describe himself, both language and
thought desert us, and we are as helpless as
fools and savages.[1] That essence refuses to be
recorded in propositions, but when man has
worshipped him intellectually, the noblest ministry of nature is to stand as the apparition of
God. It is the organ through which the universal spirit speaks to the individual, and strives
to lead back the individual to it.

When we consider Spirit, we see that the
views already presented do not include the
whole circumference of man. We must add
some related thoughts.

Three problems are put by nature to the
mind: What is matter? Whence is it? and
Whereto? The first of these questions only, the
ideal theory answers. Idealism saith: matter is
a phenomenon, not a substance. Idealism ac-
quaints us with the total disparity between the
evidence of our own being and the evidence of
the world's being. The one is perfect; the other,
incapable of any assurance; the mind is a part
of the nature of things; the world is a divine
dream, from which we may presently awake to
the glories and certainties of day. Idealism is a

hypothesis to account for nature by other principles than those of carpentry and chemistry. Yet, if it only deny the existence of matter, it does not satisfy the demands of the spirit. It leaves God out of me. It leaves me in the splendid labyrinth of my perceptions, to wander without end. Then the heart resists it, because it balks the affections in denying substantive being to men and women. Nature is so pervaded with human life that there is something of humanity in all and in every particular. But this theory makes nature foreign to me, and does not account for that consanguinity which we acknowledge to it.

Let it stand then, in the present state of our knowledge, merely as a useful introductory hypothesis, serving to apprize us of the eternal distinction between the soul and the world.

But when, following the invisible steps of thought, we come to inquire, Whence is matter? and Whereto? many truths arise to us out of the recesses of consciousness. We learn that the highest is present to the soul of man; that the dread universal essence, which is not wisdom, or love, or beauty, or power, but all in one, and each entirely, is that for which all things exist, and that by which they are; that spirit creates;

that behind nature, throughout nature, spirit is
present; one and not compound it does not act
upon us from without, that is, in space and time,
but spiritually, or through ourselves : therefore,
that spirit, that is, the Supreme Being, does not
build up nature around us, but puts it forth
through us, as the life of the tree puts forth new
branches and leaves through the pores of the
old. As a plant upon the earth, so a man rests
upon the bosom of God; he is nourished by
unfailing fountains, and draws at his need inexhaustible power. Who can set bounds to the
possibilities of man? Once inhale the upper air,
being admitted to behold the absolute natures
of justice and truth, and we learn that man has
access to the entire mind of the Creator, is himself the creator in the finite. This view, which
admonishes me where the sources of wisdom and
power lie, and points to virtue as to

"The golden key
Which opes the palace of eternity,"[1]

carries upon its face the highest certificate of
truth, because it animates me to create my own
world through the purification of my soul.

The world proceeds from the same spirit as
the body of man. It is a remoter and inferior
incarnation of God, a projection of God in the

unconscious. But it differs from the body in one important respect. It is not, like that, now subjected to the human will. Its serene order is inviolable by us. It is, therefore, to us, the present expositor of the divine mind. It is a fixed .point whereby we may measure our departure. As we degenerate, the contrast between us and our house is more evident. We are as much strangers in nature as we are aliens from God. We do not understand the notes of birds. The fox and the deer run away from us ; the bear and tiger rend us. We do not know the uses of more than a few plants, as corn and the apple, the potato and the vine. Is not the landscape, every glimpse of which hath a grandeur, a face of him ? Yet this may show us what discord is between man and nature, for you cannot freely admire a noble landscape if laborers are digging in the field hard by. The poet finds something ridiculous in his delight until he is out of the sight of men.

VIII

PROSPECTS

IN inquiries respecting the laws of the world
and the frame of things, the highest reason
is always the truest. That which seems faintly
possible, it is so refined, is often faint and dim
because it is deepest seated in the mind among
the eternal verities. Empirical science is apt to
cloud the sight, and by the very knowledge of
functions and processes to bereave the student
of the manly contemplation of the whole. The
savant becomes unpoetic. But the best read naturalist who lends an entire and devout attention to truth, will see that there remains much
to learn of his relation to the world, and that
it is not to be learned by any addition or sub-
traction or other comparison of known quantities, but is arrived at by untaught sallies of the
spirit, by a continual self-recovery, and by entire
humility. He will perceive that there are far
more excellent qualities in the student than pre-
ciseness and infallibility; that a guess is often
more fruitful than an indisputable affirmation,
and that a dream may let us deeper into the

secret of nature than a hundred concerted experiments.

For the problems to be solved are precisely
those which the physiologist and the naturalist omit to state.   It is not so pertinent to
man to know all the individuals of the animal
kingdom, as it is to know whence and whereto
is this tyrannizing unity in his constitution,
which evermore separates and classifies things,
endeavoring to reduce the most diverse to one
form.   When I behold a rich landscape, it is
less to my purpose to recite correctly the order
and superposition of the strata, than to know
why all thought of multitude is lost in a tranquil sense of unity.   I cannot greatly honor
minuteness in details, so long as there is no
hint to explain the relation between things and
thoughts; no ray upon the *metaphysics* of con-
chology, of botany, of the arts, to show the relation of the forms of flowers, shells, animals,
architecture, to the mind, and build science
upon ideas.   In a cabinet of natural history, we
become sensible of a certain occult recognition
and sympathy in regard to the most unwieldy
and eccentric forms of beast, fish, and insect.[1]
The American who has been confined, in his
own country, to the sight of buildings designed

after foreign models, is surprised on entering
York Minster or St. Peter's at Rome, by the
feeling that these structures are imitations also,
— faint copies of an invisible archetype. Nor
has science sufficient humanity, so long as the
naturalist overlooks that wonderful congruity
which subsists between man and the world; of
which he is lord, not because he is the most
subtile inhabitant, but because he is its head and
heart, and finds something of himself in every
great and small thing, in every mountain stra-
tum, in every new law of color, fact of astronomy,
or atmospheric influence which observation or
analysis lays open. A perception of this mystery
inspires the muse of George Herbert, the beautiful psalmist of the seventeenth century. The
following lines are part of his little poem on
Man.

> Man is all symmetry,
> Full of proportions, one limb to another,
>   And all to all the world besides.
>   Each part may call the farthest, brother;
> For head with foot hath private amity,
>   And both with moons and tides.
>
>   Nothing hath got so far
> But man hath caught and kept it as his prey;
>   His eyes dismount the highest star:

He is in little all the sphere.
Herbs gladly cure our flesh, because that they
    Find their acquaintance there.

For us, the winds do blow,
The earth doth rest, heaven move, and fountains flow;
    Nothing we see, but means our good,
    As our delight, or as our treasure ;
The whole is either our cupboard of food,
    Or cabinet of pleasure.

The stars have us to bed :
Night draws the curtain; which the sun withdraws.
    Music and light attend our head.
    All things unto our flesh are kind,
In their descent and being; to our mind,
    In their ascent and cause.

More servants wait on man
Than he 'll take notice of.   In every path,
    He treads down that which doth befriend him
    When sickness makes him pale and wan.
Oh mighty love! Man is one world, and hath
    Another to attend him.

The perception of this class of truths makes
the attraction which draws men to science, but
the end is lost sight of in attention to the
means. In view of this half-sight of science, we
accept the sentence of Plato, that "poetry
comes nearer to vital truth than history."

Every surmise and vaticination of the mind is entitled to a certain respect, and we learn to prefer imperfect theories, and sentences which contain glimpses of truth, to digested systems which have no one valuable suggestion. A wise writer will feel that the ends of study and composition are best answered by announcing undiscovered regions of thought, and so communicating, through hope, new activity to the torpid spirit.

I shall therefore conclude this essay with some traditions of man and nature, which a certain poet sang to me; and which, as they have always been in the world, and perhaps reappear to every bard, may be both history and prophecy.'

'The foundations of man are not in matter, but in spirit. But the element of spirit is eternity. To it, therefore, the longest series of events, the oldest chronologies are young and recent. In the cycle of the universal man, from whom the known individuals proceed, centuries are points, and all history is but the epoch of one degradation.

'We distrust and deny inwardly our sympathy with nature. We own and disown our relation to it, by turns. We are like Nebuchadnezzar, dethroned, bereft of reason, and eating grass like an ox. But who can set limits to the remedial force of spirit?

'A man is a god in ruins. When men are innocent, life shall be longer, and shall pass into the immortal as gently as we awake from dreams. Now, the world would be insane and rabid, if these disorganizations should last for hundreds of years. It is kept in check by death and infancy. Infancy is the perpetual Messiah, which comes into the arms of fallen men, and pleads with them to return to paradise.

'Man is the dwarf of himself. Once he was permeated and dissolved by spirit. He filled nature with his overflowing currents. Out from him sprang the sun and moon; from man the sun, from woman the moon. The laws of his mind, the periods of his actions externized themselves into day and night, into the year and the seasons. But, having made for himself this huge shell, his waters retired; he no longer fills the veins and veinlets; he is shrunk to a drop. He sees that the structure still fits him, but fits him colossally. Say, rather, once it fitted him, now it corresponds to him from far and on high. He adores timidly his own work. Now is man the follower of the sun, and woman the follower of the moon. Yet sometimes he starts in his slumber, and wonders at himself and his house, and muses strangely at the resemblance betwixt him and it. He perceives that if his law is still paramount, if still he have elemental power, if his word is sterling yet in nature, it is not conscious power, it is not inferior but superior to his will. It is instinct.' Thus my Orphic poet sang.[1]

At present, man applies to nature but half his force. He works on the world with his understanding alone. He lives in it and masters it by a penny-wisdom; and he that works most in it is but a half-man, and whilst his arms are strong and his digestion good, his mind is imbruted, and he is a selfish savage. His relation to nature, his power over it, is through the understanding, as by manure; the economic use of fire, wind, water, and the mariner's needle; steam, coal, chemical agriculture; the repairs of the human body by the dentist and the surgeon. This is such a resumption of power as if a banished king should buy his territories inch by inch, instead of vaulting at once into his throne. Meantime, in the thick darkness, there are not wanting gleams of a better light, — occasional examples of the action of man upon nature with his entire force, — with reason as

well as understanding. Such examples are, the
traditions of miracles in the earliest antiquity
of all nations; the history of Jesus Christ; the
achievements of a principle, as in religious and
political revolutions, and in the abolition of
the slave-trade; the miracles of enthusiasm,
as those reported of Swedenborg, Hohenlohe,[1]
and the Shakers; many obscure and yet con-
tested facts, now arranged under the name of
Animal Magnetism; prayer; eloquence; self-
healing; and the wisdom of children. These
are examples of Reason's momentary grasp of
the sceptre; the exertions of a power which exists not in time or space, but an instantaneous
in-streaming causing power. The difference
between the actual and the ideal force of man
is happily figured by the schoolmen, in saying,
that the knowledge of man is an evening knowledge, *vespertina cognitio*, but that of God is a
morning knowledge, *matutina cognitio.*[2]

The problem of restoring to the world original and eternal beauty is solved by the redemption of the soul. The ruin or the blank that we
see when we look at nature, is in our own eye.
The axis of vision is not coincident with the
axis of things, and so they appear not transparent but opaque. The reason why the world

lacks unity, and lies broken and in heaps, is because man is disunited with himself. He cannot
be a naturalist until he satisfies all the demands
of the spirit. Love is as much its demand as
perception. Indeed, neither can be perfect without the other. In the uttermost meaning of
the words, thought is devout, and devotion is
thought. Deep calls unto deep. But in actual
life, the marriage is not celebrated. There are
innocent men who worship God after the tradition of their fathers, but their sense of duty has
not yet extended to the use of all their faculties.
And there are patient naturalists, but they freeze
their subject under the wintry light of the understanding. Is not prayer also a study of truth,
— a sally of the soul into the unfound infinite?
No man ever prayed heartily without learning
something. But when a faithful thinker, reso-
lute to detach every object from personal relations and see it in the light of thought, shall, at
the same time, kindle science with the fire of the
holiest affections, then will God go forth anew
into the creation.

It will not need, when the mind is prepared
for study, to search for objects. The invariable
mark of wisdom is to see the miraculous in the
common. What is a day? What is a year?

What is summer? What is woman? What is
a child? What is sleep? To our blindness,
these things seem unaffecting. We make fables
to hide the baldness of the fact and conform it,
as we say, to the higher law of the mind. But
when the fact is seen under the light of an idea,
the gaudy fable fades and shrivels. We behold
the real higher law. To the wise, therefore, a
fact is true poetry, and the most beautiful of
fables. These wonders are brought to our own
door. You also are a man. Man and woman
and their social life, poverty, labor, sleep, fear,
fortune, are known to you. Learn that none
of these things is superficial, but that each phenomenon has its roots in the faculties and affections of the mind. Whilst the abstract question
occupies your intellect, nature brings it in the
concrete to be solved by your hands. It were
a wise inquiry for the closet, to compare, point
by point, especially at remarkable crises in life,
our daily history with the rise and progress of
ideas in the mind.

So shall we come to look at the world with
new eyes. It shall answer the endless inquiry
of the intellect, — What is truth? and of the
affections, — What is good? by yielding itself
passive to the educated Will. Then shall come

to pass what my poet said : ' Nature is not fixed but fluid. Spirit alters, moulds, makes it. The immobility or bruteness of nature is the absence of spirit ; to pure spirit it is fluid, it is volatile, it is obedient. Every spirit builds itself a house, and beyond its house a world, and beyond its world a heaven. Know then that the world exists for you. For you is the phenomenon perfect. What we are, that only can we see. All that Adam had, all that Cæsar could, you have and can do. Adam called his house, heaven and earth ; Cæsar called his house, Rome ; you perhaps call yours, a cobbler's trade ; a hundred acres of ploughed land ; or a scholar's garret. Yet line for line and point for point your dominion is as great as theirs, though without fine names. Build therefore your own world. As fast as you conform your life to the pure idea in your mind, that will unfold its great proportions. A correspondent revolution in things will attend the influx of the spirit. So fast will disagreeable appearances, swine, spiders, snakes, pests, mad-houses, prisons, enemies, vanish ; they are temporary and shall be no more seen. The sordor and filths of nature, the sun shall dry up and the wind exhale.[1] As when the summer comes from the south the snow-banks melt and the face of the earth becomes green before it, so shall the advancing spirit create its ornaments along its path, and carry with it the beauty it visits and the song which enchants it; it shall draw beautiful faces, warm hearts, wise discourse, and heroic acts, around its way, until evil is no more seen. The kingdom of man over nature, which cometh not with observation, — a dominion such as now is beyond his dream of God, — he shall enter without more wonder than the blind man feels who is gradually restored to perfect sight.'

THE AMERICAN SCHOLAR

AN ORATION DELIVERED BEFORE THE PHI BETA
KAPPA SOCIETY, AT CAMBRIDGE,
AUGUST 31, 1837.

THE AMERICAN SCHOLAR

I GREET you on the recommencement of
our literary year. Our anniversary is one of
hope, and, perhaps, not enough of labor. We
do not meet for games of strength or skill, for
the recitation of histories, tragedies, and odes,
like the ancient Greeks; for parliaments of love
and poesy, like the Troubadours; nor for the
advancement of science, like our contemporaries
in the British and European capitals. Thus far,
our holiday has been simply a friendly sign of
the survival of the love of letters amongst a people too busy to give to letters any more. As
such it is precious as the sign of an indestructi-
ble instinct. Perhaps the time is already come
when it ought to be, and will be, something else;
when the sluggard intellect of this continent will
look from under its iron lids and fill the post-
poned expectation of the world with something
better than the exertions of mechanical skill.
Our day of dependence, our long apprenticeship
to the learning of other lands, draws to a close.[1]

The millions that around us are rushing into life, cannot always be fed on the sere remains of foreign harvests. Events, actions arise, that must be sung, that will sing themselves. Who can doubt that poetry will revive and lead in a new age, as the star in the constellation Harp, which now flames in our zenith, astronomers announce, shall one day be the pole-star for a thousand years?

In this hope I accept the topic which not only usage but the nature of our association seem to prescribe to this day,—the AMERICAN SCHOLAR. Year by year we come up hither to read one more chapter of his biography. Let us inquire what light new days and events have thrown on his character and his hopes.

It is one of those fables which out of an unknown antiquity convey an unlooked-for wisdom, that the gods, in the beginning, divided Man into men,¹ that he might be more helpful to himself; just as the hand was divided into fingers, the better to answer its end.

The old fable covers a doctrine ever new and sublime; that there is One Man, — present to all particular men only partially, or through one faculty; and that you must take the whole society to find the whole man. Man is not a farmer,

or a professor, or an engineer, but he is all. Man
is priest, and scholar, and statesman, and pro-
ducer, and soldier. In the *divided* or social state
these functions are parcelled out to individuals,
each of whom aims to do his stint of the joint
work, whilst each other performs his. The fable
implies that the individual, to possess himself,
must sometimes return from his own labor to
embrace all the other laborers. But, unfortu-
nately, this original unit, this fountain of power,
has been so distributed to multitudes, has been
so minutely subdivided and peddled out, that it
is spilled into drops, and cannot be gathered.
The state of society is one in which the members have suffered amputation from the trunk,
and strut about so many walking monsters, — a
good finger, a neck, a stomach, an elbow, but
never a man.

Man is thus metamorphosed into a thing, into
many things. The planter, who is Man sent out
into the field to gather food, is seldom cheered
by any idea of the true dignity of his ministry.
He sees his bushel and his cart, and nothing
beyond, and sinks into the farmer, instead of
Man on the farm. The tradesman scarcely ever
gives an ideal worth to his work, but is ridden
by the routine of his craft, and the soul is sub-

ject to dollars. The priest becomes a form ; the attorney a statute-book ; the mechanic a machine ; the sailor a rope of the ship.[1]

In this distribution of functions the scholar is the delegated intellect. In the right state he is *Man Thinking*. In the degenerate state, when the victim of society, he tends to become a mere thinker, or still worse, the parrot of other men's thinking.

In this view of him, as Man Thinking, the theory of his office is contained. Him Nature solicits with all her placid, all her monitory pictures ; him the past instructs ; him the future invites. Is not indeed every man a student, and do not all things exist for the student's behoof? And, finally, is not the true scholar the only true master? But the old oracle said, "All things have two handles : beware of the wrong one." In life, too often, the scholar errs with mankind and forfeits his privilege. Let us see him in his school, and consider him in reference to the main influences he receives.

I. The first in time and the first in importance of the influences upon the mind is that of nature. Every day, the sun ; and, after sunset, Night and her stars. Ever the winds blow ; ever

the grass grows. Every day, men and women,
conversing — beholding and beholden. The
scholar is he of all men whom this spectacle
most engages. He must settle its value in his
mind. What is nature to him? There is never
a beginning, there is never an end, to the inexplicable continuity of this web of God, but always
circular power returning into itself.[1] Therein it
resembles his own spirit, whose beginning, whose
ending, he never can find, — so entire, so boundless. Far too as her splendors shine, system on
system shooting like rays, upward, downward,
without centre, without circumference, — in the
mass and in the particle, Nature hastens to render account of herself to the mind. Classification begins. To the young mind every thing is
individual, stands by itself. By and by, it finds
how to join two things and see in them one nature; then three, then three thousand; and so,
tyrannized over by its own unifying instinct, it
goes on tying things together, diminishing ano-
malies, discovering roots running under ground
whereby contrary and remote things cohere and
flower out from one stem. It presently learns
that since the dawn of history there has been a
constant accumulation and classifying of facts.
But what is classification but the perceiving that

these objects are not chaotic, and are not foreign, but have a law which is also a law of the human mind? The astronomer discovers that geometry, a pure abstraction of the human mind, is the measure of planetary motion. The chemist finds proportions and intelligible method throughout matter; and science is nothing but the finding of analogy, identity, in the most remote parts.[1] The ambitious soul sits down before each refractory fact; one after another reduces all strange constitutions, all new powers, to their class and their law, and goes on forever to animate the last fibre of organization, the outskirts of nature, by insight.

Thus to him, to this schoolboy under the bending dome of day, is suggested that he and it proceed from one root; one is leaf and one is flower; relation, sympathy, stirring in every vein. And what is that root? Is not that the soul of his soul? A thought too bold; a dream too wild. Yet when this spiritual light shall have revealed the law of more earthly natures, — when he has learned to worship the soul, and to see that the natural philosophy that now is, is only the first gropings of its gigantic hand, he shall look forward to an ever expanding knowledge as to a becoming creator.[2] He shall see

that nature is the opposite of the soul, answering to it part for part.   One is seal and one is
print.   Its beauty is the beauty of his own mind.
Its laws are the laws of his own mind.   Nature
then becomes to him the measure of his attain-
ments.   So much of nature as he is ignorant of,
so much of his own mind does he not yet possess.   And, in fine, the ancient precept, "Know
thyself," and the modern precept, "Study nature," become at last one maxim.

II. The next great influence into the spirit
of the scholar is the mind of the Past,—in
whatever form, whether of literature, of art, of
institutions, that mind is inscribed.   Books are
the best type of the influence of the past, and
perhaps we shall get at the truth, — learn the
amount of this influence more conveniently, —
by considering their value alone.

The theory of books is noble.   The scholar
of the first age received into him the world
around ; brooded thereon ; gave it the new arrangement of his own mind, and uttered it again.
It came into him life; it went out from him
truth.   It came to him short-lived actions; it
went out from him immortal thoughts.   It came
to him business; it went from him poetry.   It
was dead fact; now, it is quick thought.   It can

stand, and it can go.   It now endures, it now flies, it now inspires.   Precisely in proportion to the depth of mind from which it issued, so high does it soar, so long does it sing.'

Or, I might say, it depends on how far the process had gone, of transmuting life into truth. In proportion to the completeness of the distillation, so will the purity and imperishableness of the product be.   But none is quite perfect. As no air-pump can by any means make a perfect vacuum, so neither can any artist entirely exclude the conventional, the local, the perishable from his book, or write a book of pure thought, that shall be as efficient, in all respects, to a remote posterity, as to contemporaries, or rather to the second age.   Each age, it is found, must write its own books ; or rather, each generation for the next succeeding.   The books of an older period will not fit this.

Yet hence arises a grave mischief.   The sacredness which attaches to the act of creation, the act of thought, is transferred to the record. The poet chanting was felt to be a divine man : henceforth the chant is divine also.   The writer was a just and wise spirit : henceforward it is settled the book is perfect; as love of the hero corrupts into worship of his statue.   Instantly the book becomes noxious: the guide is a tyrant. The sluggish and perverted mind of the multitude, slow to open to the incursions of Reason, having once so opened, having once received this book, stands upon it, and makes an outcry if it is disparaged. Colleges are built on it. Books are written on it by thinkers, not by Man Thinking; by men of talent, that is, who start wrong, who set out from accepted dogmas, not from their own sight of principles. Meek young men grow up in libraries, believing it their duty to accept the views which Cicero, which Locke, which Bacon, have given; forgetful that Cicero, Locke, and Bacon were only young men in libraries when they wrote these books.[1]

Hence, instead of Man Thinking, we have the bookworm. Hence the book-learned class, who value books, as such; not as related to nature and the human constitution, but as making a sort of Third Estate with the world and the soul. Hence the restorers of readings, the emendators, the bibliomaniacs of all degrees.

Books are the best of things, well used; abused, among the worst. What is the right use? What is the one end which all means go to effect? They are for nothing but to inspire. I had better never see a book than to be warped by its attraction clean out of my own orbit, and made a satellite instead of a system. The one thing in the world, of value, is the active soul. This every man is entitled to; this every man contains within him, although in almost all men obstructed and as yet unborn. The soul active sees absolute truth and utters truth, or creates. In this action it is genius; not the privilege of here and there a favorite, but the sound estate of every man. In its essence it is progressive. The book, the college, the school of art, the institution of any kind, stop with some past utterance of genius. This is good, say they, — let us hold by this. They pin me down. They look backward and not forward. But genius looks forward: the eyes of man are set in his forehead, not in his hindhead: man hopes: genius creates. Whatever talents may be, if the man create not, the pure efflux of the Deity is not his; — cinders and smoke there may be, but not yet flame. There are creative manners, there are creative actions, and creative words; manners, actions, words, that is, indicative of no custom or authority, but springing spontaneous from the mind's own sense of good and fair.

On the other part, instead of being its own

seer, let it receive from another mind its truth, though it were in torrents of light, without periods of solitude, inquest, and self-recovery, and a fatal disservice is done.¹ Genius is always sufficiently the enemy of genius by over-influence. The literature of every nation bears me witness. The English dramatic poets have Shakspearized now for two hundred years.

Undoubtedly there is a right way of reading, so it be sternly subordinated. Man Thinking must not be subdued by his instruments. Books are for the scholar's idle times. When he can read God directly, the hour is too precious to be wasted in other men's transcripts of their readings. But when the intervals of darkness come, as come they must, — when the sun is hid and the stars withdraw their shining, — we repair to the lamps which were kindled by their ray, to guide our steps to the East again, where the dawn is. We hear, that we may speak. The Arabian proverb says, "A fig tree, looking on a fig tree, becometh fruitful."

It is remarkable, the character of the pleasure we derive from the best books. They impress us with the conviction that one nature wrote and the same reads. We read the verses of one of the great English poets, of Chaucer, of Marvell, of Dryden, with the most modern joy, — with a pleasure, I mean, which is in great part caused by the abstraction of all *time* from their verses. There is some awe mixed with the joy of our surprise, when this poet, who lived in some past world, two or three hundred years ago, says that which lies close to my own soul, that which I also had well-nigh thought and said. But for the evidence thence afforded to the philosophical doctrine of the identity of all minds, we should suppose some preëstablished harmony, some foresight of souls that were to be, and some preparation of stores for their future wants, like the fact observed in insects, who lay up food before death for the young grub they shall never see.

I would not be hurried by any love of system, by any exaggeration of instincts, to underrate the Book. We all know, that as the human body can be nourished on any food, though it were boiled grass and the broth of shoes, so the human mind can be fed by any knowledge. And great and heroic men have existed who had almost no other information than by the printed page. I only would say that it needs a strong head to bear that diet. One must be an inventor to read well. As the proverb says, " He that would bring home the wealth of the Indies, must carry out the wealth of the Indies." There is then creative reading as well as creative writing. When the mind is braced by labor and invention, the page of whatever book we read becomes luminous with manifold allusion. Every sentence is doubly significant, and the sense of our author is as broad as the world. We then see, what is always true, that as the seer's hour of vision is short and rare among heavy days and months, so is its record, perchance, the least part of his volume. The discerning will read, in his Plato or Shakspeare, only that least part, — only the authentic utterances of the oracle; — all the rest he rejects, were it never so many times Plato's and Shakspeare's.[1]

Of course there is a portion of reading quite indispensable to a wise man. History and exact science he must learn by laborious reading. Colleges, in like manner, have their indispensable office, — to teach elements. But they can only highly serve us when they aim not to drill, but to create ; when they gather from far every ray of various genius to their hospitable halls, and by the concentrated fires, set the hearts of their youth on flame. Thought and knowledge are natures in which apparatus and pretension avail nothing. Gowns and pecuniary foundations, though of towns of gold, can never countervail the least sentence or syllable of wit. Forget this, and our American colleges will recede in their public importance, whilst they grow richer every year.

III. There goes in the world a notion that the scholar should be a recluse, a valetudinarian, — as unfit for any handiwork or public labor as a penknife for an axe. The so-called " practical men " sneer at speculative men, as if, because they speculate or *see*, they could do nothing. I have heard it said that the clergy, — who are always, more universally than any other class, the scholars of their day, — are addressed as women ; that the rough, spontaneous conversation of men they do not hear, but only a mincing and diluted speech. They are often virtually disfranchised ; and indeed there are advocates for their celibacy. As far as this is true of the studious classes, it is not just and wise. Action is with the scholar subordinate, but it is essential. Without it he is not yet man. Without it thought can never ripen into truth. Whilst the world hangs before the eye as a cloud of beauty, we cannot even see its beauty. Inaction is cowardice, but there can be no scholar without the heroic mind. The preamble of thought, the transition

through which it passes from the unconscious
to the conscious, is action.   Only so much do
I know, as I have lived.   Instantly we know
whose words are loaded with life, and whose
not.[1]

The world, — this shadow of the soul, or *other
me*, — lies wide around.[2] Its attractions are the
keys which unlock my thoughts and make me
acquainted with myself.   I run eagerly into this
resounding tumult.   I grasp the hands of those
next me, and take my place in the ring to suffer
and to work, taught by an instinct that so shall
the dumb abyss be vocal with speech.   I pierce
its order ; I dissipate its fear ; I dispose of it
within the circuit of my expanding life.   So
much only of life as I know by experience, so
much of the wilderness have I vanquished and
planted, or so far have I extended my being,
my dominion.   I do not see how any man can
afford, for the sake of his nerves and his nap,
to spare any action in which he can partake.
It is pearls and rubies to his discourse.   Drudgery, calamity, exasperation, want, are instructors
in eloquence and wisdom.   The true scholar
grudges every opportunity of action past by,
as a loss of power.   It is the raw, material out
of which the intellect moulds her splendid pro-

ducts.   A strange process too, this by which
experience is converted into thought, as a mul-
berry leaf is converted into satin.   The manufacture goes forward at all hours.

The actions and events of our childhood and
youth are now matters of calmest observation.
They lie like fair pictures in the air.   Not so
with our recent actions, — with the business
which we now have in hand.   On this we are
quite unable to speculate.   Our affections as yet
circulate through it.   We no more feel or know
it than we feel the feet, or the hand, or the brain
of our body.   The new deed is yet a part of
life, — remains for a time immersed in our unconscious life.   In some contemplative hour it
detaches itself from the life like a ripe fruit,
to become a thought of the mind.   Instantly
it is raised, transfigured ; the corruptible has put
on incorruption.   Henceforth it is an object of
beauty, however base its origin and neighborhood.   Observe too the impossibility of antedating this act.   In its grub state, it cannot fly,
it cannot shine, it is a dull grub.   But suddenly,
without observation, the selfsame thing unfurls
beautiful wings, and is an angel of wisdom.   So
is there no fact, no event, in our private history, which shall not, sooner or later, lose its

adhesive, inert form, and astonish us by soar-
ing from our body into the empyrean. Cradle
and infancy, school and playground, the fear of
boys, and dogs, and ferules, the love of little
maids and berries, and many another fact that
once filled the whole sky, are gone already ;
friend and relative, profession and party, town
and country, nation and world, must also soar
and sing.

Of course, he who has put forth his total
strength in fit actions has the richest return of
wisdom. I will not shut myself out of this globe
of action, and transplant an oak into a flower-
pot, there to hunger and pine ; nor trust the
revenue of some single faculty, and exhaust one
vein of thought, much like those Savoyards,
who, getting their livelihood by carving shep-
herds, shepherdesses, and smoking Dutchmen,
for all Europe, went out one day to the mountain to find stock, and discovered that they had
whittled up the last of their pine trees. Authors
we have, in numbers, who have written out their
vein, and who, moved by a commendable prudence, sail for Greece or Palestine, follow the
trapper into the prairie, or ramble round Algiers,
to replenish their merchantable stock.

If it were only for a vocabulary, the scholar

would be covetous of action. Life is our dictionary. Years are well spent in country labors; in
town; in the insight into trades and manufactures; in frank intercourse with many men and
women; in science; in art; to the one end of
mastering in all their facts a language by which
to illustrate and embody our perceptions. I learn
immediately from any speaker how much he has
already lived, through the poverty or the splendor of his speech. Life lies behind us as the
quarry from whence we get tiles and copestones
for the masonry of to-day. This is the way to
learn grammar. Colleges and books only copy
the language which the field and the work-yard
made.[1]

But the final value of action, like that of
books, and better than books, is that it is a resource. That great principle of Undulation in
nature, that shows itself in the inspiring and
expiring of the breath; in desire and satiety; in
the ebb and flow of the sea; in day and night; in
heat and cold; and, as yet more deeply ingrained
in every atom and every fluid, is known to us
under the name of Polarity, — these "fits of
easy transmission and reflection," as Newton
called them, are the law of nature because they
are the law of spirit.

The mind now thinks, now acts, and each fit
reproduces the other. When the artist has exhausted his materials, when the fancy no longer
paints, when thoughts are no longer apprehended and books are a weariness, — he has
always the resource *to live*. Character is higher
than intellect. Thinking is the function. Living is the functionary. The stream retreats to
its source. A great soul will be strong to live,
as well as strong to think. Does he lack organ
or medium to impart his truths? He can still
fall back on this elemental force of living them.
This is a total act. Thinking is a partial act.
Let the grandeur of justice shine in his affairs.
Let the beauty of affection cheer his lowly roof.
Those "far from fame," who dwell and act with
him, will feel the force of his constitution in the
doings and passages of the day better than it
can be measured by any public and designed
display. Time shall teach him that the scholar
loses no hour which the man lives. Herein he
unfolds the sacred germ of his instinct, screened
from influence. What is lost in seemliness is
gained in strength. Not out of those on whom
systems of education have exhausted their culture, comes the helpful giant to destroy the old
or to build the new, but out of unhandselled

savage nature ; out of terrible Druids and Ber-
serkers come at last Alfred and Shakspeare.

I hear therefore with joy whatever is beginning to be said of the dignity and necessity of
labor to every citizen.   There is virtue yet in
the hoe and the spade, for learned as well as
for unlearned hands. And labor is everywhere
welcome; always we are invited to work ; only
be this limitation observed, that a man shall
not for the sake of wider activity sacrifice any
opinion to the popular judgments and modes
of action.

I have now spoken of the education of the
scholar by nature, by books, and by action.   It
remains to say somewhat of his duties.

They are such as become Man Thinking.
They may all be comprised in self-trust.   The
office of the scholar is to cheer, to raise, and
to guide men by showing them facts amidst
appearances.   He plies the slow, unhonored,
and unpaid task of observation. Flamsteed and
Herschel, in their glazed observatories, may catalogue the stars with the praise of all men, and
the results being splendid and useful, honor is
sure. But he, in his private observatory, cata-
loguing obscure and nebulous stars of the hu-

man mind, which as yet no man has thought
of as such, — watching days and months sometimes for a few facts; correcting still his old records; — must relinquish display and immediate
fame.   In the long period of his preparation he
must betray often an ignorance and shiftlessness
in popular arts, incurring the disdain of the able
who shoulder him aside.   Long he must stam-
mer in his speech; often forego the living for
the dead. Worse yet, he must accept — how
often! — poverty and solitude.   For the ease
and pleasure of treading the old road, accepting
the fashions, the education, the religion of society, he takes the cross of making his own, and,
of course, the self-accusation, the faint heart, the
frequent uncertainty and loss of time, which are
the nettles and tangling vines in the way of the
self-relying and self-directed; and the state of
virtual hostility in which he seems to stand to
society, and especially to educated society. For
all this loss and scorn, what offset?   He is to
find consolation in exercising the highest functions of human nature.   He is one who raises
himself from private considerations and breathes'
and lives on public and illustrious thoughts.
He is the world's eye.   He is the world's heart.
He is to resist the vulgar prosperity that retro-

grades ever to barbarism, by preserving and communicating heroic sentiments, noble biographies, melodious verse, and the conclusions of history. Whatsoever oracles the human heart, in all emergencies, in all solemn hours, has uttered as its commentary on the world of actions, — these he shall receive and impart. And whatsoever new verdict Reason from her inviolable seat pronounces on the passing men and events of to-day, — this he shall hear and promulgate.

These being his functions, it becomes him to feel all confidence in himself, and to defer never to the popular cry. He and he only knows the world. The world of any moment is the merest appearance. Some great decorum, some fetish of a government, some ephemeral trade, or war, or man, is cried up by half mankind and cried down by the other half, as if all depended on this particular up or down. The odds are that the whole question is not worth the poorest thought which the scholar has lost in listening to the controversy. Let him not quit his belief •that a popgun is a popgun, though the ancient and honorable of the earth affirm it to be the crack of doom. In silence, in steadiness, in severe abstraction, let him hold by himself; add observation to observation, patient of neglect, patient of reproach, and bide his own time, — happy enough if he can satisfy himself alone that this day he has seen something truly.   Success treads on every right step.   For the instinct is sure, that prompts him to tell his brother what he thinks.   He then learns that in going down into the secrets of his own mind he has descended into the secrets of all minds.   He learns that he who has mastered any law in his private thoughts, is master to that extent of all men whose language he speaks, and of all into whose language his own can be translated.[1]   The poet, in utter solitude remembering his spontaneous thoughts and recording them, is found to have recorded that which men in crowded cities find true for them also.   The orator distrusts at first the fitness of his frank confessions, his want of knowledge of the persons he addresses, until he finds that he is the complement of his hearers ; — that they drink his words because he fulfils for them their own nature; the deeper he dives into his privatest, secretest presentiment, to his wonder he finds this is the most acceptable, most public, and universally true.   The people delight in it; the better part of every man feels, This is my music; this is myself.

In self-trust all the virtues are comprehended. Free should the scholar be, — free and brave. Free even to the definition of freedom, "without any hindrance that does not arise out of his own constitution." Brave; for fear is a thing which a scholar by his very function puts behind him. Fear always springs from ignorance. It is a shame to him if his tranquillity, amid dangerous times, arise from the presumption that like children and women his is a protected class; or if he seek a temporary peace by the diversion of his thoughts from politics or vexed questions, hiding his head like an ostrich in the flowering bushes, peeping into microscopes, and turning rhymes, as a boy whistles to keep his courage up. So is the danger a danger still; so is the fear worse. Manlike let him turn and face it. Let him look into its eye and search its nature, inspect its origin, — see the whelping of this lion, — which lies no great way back; he will then find in himself a perfect comprehension of its nature and extent; he will have made his hands meet on the other side, and can henceforth defy it and pass on superior. The world is his who can see through its pretension. What deafness, what stone-blind custom, what overgrown error you behold is there only by sufferance, — by your sufferance. See it to be a lie, and you have already dealt it its mortal blow.

Yes, we are the cowed, — we the trustless. It is a mischievous notion that we are come late into nature ; that the world was finished a long time ago. As the world was plastic and fluid in the hands of God, so it is ever to so much of his attributes as we bring to it. To ignorance and sin, it is flint. They adapt themselves to it as they may; but in proportion as a man has any thing in him divine, the firmament flows before him and takes his signet and form. Not he is great who can alter matter, but he who can alter my state of mind. They are the kings of the world who give the color of their present thought to all nature and all art, and persuade men by the cheerful serenity of their carrying the matter, that this thing which they do is the apple which the ages have desired to pluck, now at last ripe, and inviting nations to the harvest. The great man makes the great thing. Wherever Macdonald sits, there is the head of the table. Linnæus makes botany the most alluring of studies, and wins it from the farmer and the herb-woman; Davy, chemistry; and Cuvier, fossils. The day is always his who works in it with serenity and great aims. The unstable estimates of men crowd to him whose mind is filled with a truth, as the heaped waves of the Atlantic follow the moon.

For this self-trust, the reason is deeper than can be fathomed, — darker than can be enlightened. I might not carry with me the feeling of my audience in stating my own belief. But I have already shown the ground of my hope, in adverting to the doctrine that man is one.[1] I believe man has been wronged; he has wronged himself. He has almost lost the light that can lead him back to his prerogatives. Men are become of no account. Men in history, men in the world of to-day, are bugs, are spawn, and are called "the mass" and "the herd." In a century, in a millennium, one or two men; that is to say, one or two approximations to the right state of every man. All the rest behold in the hero or the poet their own green and crude being, — ripened; yes, and are content to be less, so *that* may attain to its full stature. What a testimony, full of grandeur, full of pity, is borne to the demands of his own nature, by the poor clansman, the poor partisan, who rejoices in the glory of his chief. The poor and the low find some amends to their immense moral capacity, for their acquiescence in a political and social inferiority. They are content to be brushed like flies from the path of a great person, so that justice shall be done by him to that common nature which it is the dearest desire of all to see enlarged and glorified. They sun themselves in the great man's light, and feel it to be their own element. They cast the dignity of man from their down-trod selves upon the shoulders of a hero, and will perish to add one drop of blood to make that great heart beat, those giant sinews combat and conquer. He lives for us, and we live in him.

Men, such as they are, very naturally seek money or power; and power because it is as good as money, — the "spoils," so called, "of office." And why not? for they aspire to the highest, and this, in their sleep-walking, they dream is high-est. Wake them and they shall quit the false good and leap to the true, and leave governments to clerks and desks. This revolution is to be wrought by the gradual domestication of the idea of Culture. The main enterprise of the world for splendor, for extent, is the upbuilding of a man. Here are the materials strewn along the ground. The private life of one man shall be a more illustrious monarchy, more formidable to its enemy, more sweet and serene in its influence to its friend, than any kingdom in history. For

a man, rightly viewed, comprehendeth the particular natures of all men. Each philosopher,
each bard, each actor has only done for me, as by
a delegate, what one day I can do for myself.
The books which once we valued more than the
apple of the eye, we have quite exhausted. What
is that but saying that we have come up with the
point of view which the universal mind took
through the eyes of one scribe; we have been
that man, and have passed on. First, one, then
another, we drain all cisterns, and waxing greater
by all these supplies, we crave a better and more
abundant food. The man has never lived that
can feed us ever. The human mind cannot be
enshrined in a person who shall set a barrier on
any one side to this unbounded, unboundable
empire. It is one central fire, which, flaming now
out of the lips of Etna, lightens the capes of
Sicily, and now out of the throat of Vesuvius,
illuminates the towers and vineyards of Naples.
It is one light which beams out of a thousand
stars. It is one soul which animates all men.[1]

But I have dwelt perhaps tediously upon this
abstraction of the Scholar. I ought not to delay longer to add what I have to say of nearer
reference to the time and to this country.

Historically, there is thought to be a difference in the ideas which predominate over successive epochs, and there are data for marking the genius of the Classic, of the Romantic, and now of the Reflective or Philosophical age. With the views I have intimated of the oneness or the identity of the mind through all individuals, I do not much dwell on these differences. In fact, I believe each individual passes through all three. The boy is a Greek; the youth, romantic; the adult, reflective. I deny not, however, that a revolution in the leading idea may be distinctly enough traced.

Our age is bewailed as the age of Introversion. Must that needs be evil? We, it seems, are critical; we are embarrassed with second thoughts; we cannot enjoy any thing for hankering to know whereof the pleasure consists; we are lined with eyes; we see with our feet; the time is infected with Hamlet's unhappiness, —

"Sicklied o'er with the pale cast of thought."

It is so bad then? Sight is the last thing to be pitied. Would we be blind? Do we fear lest we should outsee nature and God, and drink truth dry? I look upon the discontent of the literary class as a mere announcement of the fact that they find themselves not in the state of mind of their fathers, and regret the coming state as untried ; as a boy dreads the water before he has learned that he can swim. If there is any period one would desire to be born in, is it not the age of Revolution; when the old and the new stand side by side and admit of being compared; when the energies of all men are searched by fear and by hope ; when the historic glories of the old can be compensated by the rich possibilities of the new era ? This time, like all times, is a very good one, if we but know what to do with it.

I read with some joy of the auspicious signs of the coming days, as they glimmer already through poetry and art, through philosophy and science, through church and state.

One of these signs is the fact that the same movement which effected the elevation of what was called the lowest class in the state, assumed in literature a very marked and as benign an aspect. Instead of the sublime and beautiful, the near, the low, the common, was explored and poetized. That which had been negligently trodden under foot by those who were harnessing and provisioning themselves for long journeys into far countries, is suddenly found to be richer than all foreign parts. The literature of the poor, the feelings of the child, the philosophy of the street, the meaning of household life, are the topics of the time. It is a great stride. It is a sign — is it not? — of new vigor when the extremities are made active, when currents of warm life run into the hands and the feet. I ask not for the great, the remote, the romantic; what is doing in Italy or Arabia; what is Greek art, or Provençal minstrelsy; I embrace the common, I explore and sit at the feet of the familiar, the low. Give me insight into to-day, and you may have the antique and future worlds. What would we really know the meaning of? The meal in the firkin; the milk in the pan; the ballad in the street; the news of the boat; the glance of the eye; the form and the gait of the body; — show me the ultimate reason of these matters; show me the sublime presence of the highest spiritual cause lurking, as always it does lurk, in these suburbs and extremities of nature; let me see every trifle bristling with the polarity that ranges it instantly on an eternal law; and the shop, the plough, and the ledger referred to the like cause by which light undulates and poets sing; — and the world lies no longer a dull miscellany and lumber-room, but has form and order; there is no trifle, there is no puzzle, but one design unites and animates the farthest pinnacle and the lowest trench.

This idea has inspired the genius of Gold-smith, Burns, Cowper, and, in a newer time, of Goethe, Wordsworth, and Carlyle. This idea they have differently followed and with various success. In contrast with their writing, the style of Pope, of Johnson, of Gibbon, looks cold and pedantic. This writing is blood-warm. Man is surprised to find that things near are not less beautiful and wondrous than things remote. The near explains the far. The drop is a small ocean. A man is related to all nature. This perception of the worth of the vulgar is fruitful in dis-coveries. Goethe, in this very thing the most modern of the moderns, has shown us, as none ever did, the genius of the ancients.

There is one man of genius who has done much for this philosophy of life, whose literary value has never yet been rightly estimated; — I mean Emanuel Swedenborg.[1] The most im-aginative of men, yet writing with the precision of a mathematician, he endeavored to engraft a purely philosophical Ethics on the popular Christianity of his time. Such an attempt of course must have difficulty which no genius could surmount. But he saw and showed the connection between nature and the affections of the soul. He pierced the emblematic or spiritual character of the visible, audible, tangible world. Especially did his shade - loving muse hover over and interpret the lower parts of nature ; he showed the mysterious bond that allies moral evil to the foul material forms, and has given in epical parables a theory of insanity, of beasts, of unclean and fearful things.

Another sign of our times, also marked by an analogous political movement, is the new importance given to the single person. Every thing that tends to insulate the individual, — to surround him with barriers of natural respect, so that each man shall feel the world is his, and man shall treat with man as a sovereign state with a sovereign state, — tends to true union as well as greatness. " I learned," said the melancholy Pestalozzi, " that no man in God's wide earth is either willing or able to help any other man." ' Help must come from the bosom alone. The scholar is that man who must take up into himself all the ability of the time, all the contributions of the past, all the hopes of the future. He must be an university of knowledges. If there be one lesson more than another which

should pierce his ear, it is, The world is nothing, the man is all; in yourself is the law of all
nature, and you know not yet how a globule of
sap ascends ; in yourself slumbers the whole of
Reason ; it is for you to know all ; it is for you
to dare all.   Mr. President and Gentlemen, this
confidence in the unsearched might of man belongs, by all motives, by all prophecy, by all
preparation, to the American Scholar.   We have
listened too long to the courtly muses of Europe.
The spirit of the American freeman is already
suspected to be timid, imitative, tame.   Public
and private avarice make the air we breathe thick
and fat.   The scholar is decent, indolent, complaisant.   See already the tragic consequence.
The mind of this country, taught to aim at
low objects, eats upon itself.   There is no work
for any but the decorous and the complaisant.
Young men of the fairest promise, who begin
life upon our shores, inflated by the mountain
winds, shined upon by all the stars of God, find
the earth below not in unison with these, but are
hindered from action by the disgust which the
principles on which business is managed inspire,
and turn drudges, or die of disgust, some of them
suicides.   What is the remedy ?   They did not
yet see, and thousands of young men as hopeful

now crowding to the barriers for the career do
not yet see, that if the single man plant himself
indomitably on his instincts, and there abide, the
huge world will come round to him.[1] Patience,
— patience; with the shades of all the good and
great for company; and for solace the perspective of your own infinite life; and for work the
study and the communication of principles, the
making those instincts prevalent, the conversion
of the world. Is it not the chief disgrace in the
world, not to be an unit; — not to be reckoned
one character; — not to yield that peculiar fruit
which each man was created to bear, but to be
reckoned in the gross, in the hundred, or the
thousand, of the party, the section, to which we
belong; and our opinion predicted geographi-
cally, as the north, or the south? Not so, brothers and friends — please God, ours shall not be
so. We will walk on our own feet; we will work
with our own hands; we will speak our own
minds. The study of letters shall be no longer
a name for pity, for doubt, and for sensual indulgence. The dread of man and the love of man
shall be a wall of defence and a wreath of joy
around all. A nation of men will for the first
time exist, because each believes himself inspired
by the Divine Soul which also inspires all men.

AN ADDRESS

DELIVERED BEFORE THE SENIOR CLASS IN DIVINITY
COLLEGE, CAMBRIDGE, SUNDAY EVENING,
JULY 15, 1838.

ADDRESS

IN this refulgent summer, it has been a luxury to draw the breath of life. The grass grows, the buds burst, the meadow is spotted with fire and gold in the tint of flowers. The air is full of birds, and sweet with the breath of the pine, the balm-of-Gilead, and the new hay. Night brings no gloom to the heart with its welcome shade. Through the transparent darkness the stars pour their almost spiritual rays. Man under them seems a young child, and his huge globe a toy. The cool night bathes the world as with a river, and prepares his eyes again for the crimson dawn. The mystery of nature was never displayed more happily. The corn and the wine have been freely dealt to all creatures, and the never-broken silence with which the old bounty goes forward has not yielded yet one word of explanation. One is constrained to respect the perfection of this world in which our senses converse. How wide; how rich; what invitation from every property it gives to every faculty of man! In its fruitful soils; in its navigable sea; in its mountains of metal and stone; in its forests of all woods; in its animals;

in its chemical ingredients; in the powers and path of light, heat, attraction and life, it is well worth the pith and heart of great men to subdue and enjoy it. The planters, the mechanics, the inventors, the astronomers, the builders of cities, and the captains, history delights to honor.

But when the mind opens and reveals the laws which traverse the universe and make things what they are, then shrinks the great world at once into a mere illustration and fable of this mind. What am I? and What is? asks the human spirit with a curiosity new-kindled, but never to be quenched. Behold these outrunning laws, which our imperfect apprehension can see tend this way and that, but not come full circle. Behold these infinite relations, so like, so unlike; many, yet one. I would study, I would know, I would admire forever. These works of thought have been the entertainments of the human spirit in all ages.

A more secret, sweet, and overpowering beauty appears to man when his heart and mind open to the sentiment of virtue. Then he is instructed in what is above him. He learns that his being is without bound; that to the good, to the perfect, he is born, low as he now lies in evil and weakness. That which he venerates is still his own, though he has not realized it yet. *He ought.* He knows the sense of that grand word, though his analysis fails to render account of it. When in innocency or when by intellectual perception he attains to say, — " I love the Right ; Truth is beautiful within and without for evermore. Virtue, I am thine ; save me ; use me ; thee will I serve, day and night, in great, in small, that I may be not virtuous, but virtue ; " — then is the end of the creation answered, and God is well pleased.

The sentiment of virtue is a reverence and delight in the presence of certain divine laws. It perceives that this homely game of life we play, covers, under what seem foolish details, principles that astonish. The child amidst his baubles is learning the action of light, motion, gravity, muscular force ; and in the game of human life, love, fear, justice, appetite, man, and God, interact. These laws refuse to be adequately stated. They will not be written out on paper, or spoken by the tongue. They elude our persevering thought ; yet we read them hourly in each other's faces, in each other's actions, in our own remorse.[1] The moral traits which are all globed into every virtuous act and thought, — in speech we must sever, and describe or suggest by painful enumeration of many particulars. Yet, as this sentiment is the essence of all religion, let me guide your eye to the precise objects of the sentiment, by an enumeration of some of those classes of facts in which this element is conspicuous.

The intuition of the moral sentiment is an insight of the perfection of the laws of the soul. These laws execute themselves. They are out of time, out of space, and not subject to circumstance. Thus in the soul of man there is a justice whose retributions are instant and entire. He who does a good deed is instantly ennobled. He who does a mean deed is by the action itself contracted. He who puts off impurity, thereby puts on purity. If a man is at heart just, then in so far is he God ; the safety of God, the immortality of God, the majesty of God do enter into that man with justice.[1] If a man dissemble, deceive, he deceives himself, and goes out of acquaintance with his own being. A man in the view of absolute goodness, adores, with total humility. Every step so downward, is a step upward. The man who renounces himself, comes to himself.[2]

See how this rapid intrinsic energy worketh everywhere, righting wrongs, correcting appearances, and bringing up facts to a harmony with thoughts. Its operation in life, though slow to the senses, is at last as sure as in the soul. By it a man is made the Providence to himself, dispensing good to his goodness, and evil to his sin.' Character is always known. Thefts never enrich ; alms never impoverish ; murder will speak out of stone walls. The least admixture of a lie, — for example, the taint of vanity, any attempt to make a good impression, a favorable appearance, — will instantly vitiate the effect. But speak the truth, and all nature and all spirits help you with unexpected furtherance. Speak the truth, and all things alive or brute are vouchers, and the very roots of the grass underground there do seem to stir and move to bear you witness. See again the perfection of the Law as it applies itself to the affections, and becomes the law of society. As we are, so we associate. The good, by affinity, seek the good ; the vile, by affinity, the vile. Thus of their own volition, souls proceed into heaven, into hell.

These facts have always suggested to man the sublime creed that the world is not the product of manifold power, but of one will, of one mind ; and that one mind is everywhere active, in each ray of the star, in each wavelet of the pool ; and whatever opposes that will is everywhere balked and baffled, because things are made so, and not otherwise. Good is positive. Evil is merely privative, not absolute : it is like cold, which is the privation of heat. All evil is so much death or nonentity. Benevolence is absolute and real.' So much benevolence as a man hath, so much life hath he. For all things proceed out of this same spirit, which is differently named love, justice, temperance, in its different applications, just as the ocean receives different names on the several shores which it washes. All things proceed out of the same spirit, and all things conspire with it. Whilst a man seeks good ends, he is strong by the whole strength of nature. In so far as he roves from these ends, he bereaves himself of power, or auxiliaries ; his being shrinks out of all remote channels, he becomes less and less, a mote, a point, until absolute badness is absolute death.'

The perception of this law of laws awakens in the mind a sentiment which we call the religious sentiment, and which makes our highest happiness. Wonderful is its power to charm and to command. It is a mountain air. It is the embalmer of the world. It is myrrh and storax,

and chlorine and rosemary. It makes the sky
and the hills sublime, and the silent song of the
stars is it. By it is the universe made safe and
habitable, not by science or power.[1] Thought
may work cold and intransitive in things, and
find no end or unity; but the dawn of the sentiment of virtue on the heart, gives and is the
assurance that Law is sovereign over all natures;
and the worlds, time, space, eternity, do seem to
break out into joy.[2]

This sentiment is divine and deifying. It is
the beatitude of man. It makes him illimitable.
Through it, the soul first knows itself. It cor-
rects the capital mistake of the infant man, who
seeks to be great by following the great, and
hopes to derive advantages *from another*, — by
showing the fountain of all good to be in himself, and that he, equally with every man, is an
inlet into the deeps of Reason. When he says,
"I ought;" when love warms him; when he
chooses, warned from on high, the good and
great deed; then, deep melodies wander through
his soul from Supreme Wisdom. —Then he can
worship, and be enlarged by his worship; for he
can never go behind this sentiment. In the sub-
limest flights of the soul, rectitude is never sur-
mounted, love is never outgrown.

This sentiment lies at the foundation of society, and successively creates all forms of worship. The principle of veneration never dies out. Man fallen into superstition, into sensuality, is never quite without the visions of the moral sentiment. In like manner, all the expressions of this sentiment are sacred and permanent in proportion to their purity. The expressions of this sentiment affect us more than all other compositions. The sentences of the oldest time, which ejaculate this piety, are still fresh and fragrant. This thought dwelled always deepest in the minds of men in the devout and contemplative East; not alone in Palestine, where it reached its purest expression, but in Egypt, in Persia, in India, in China. Europe has always owed to oriental genius its divine impulses. What these holy bards said, all sane men found agreeable and true.[1] And the unique impression of Jesus upon mankind, whose name is not so much written as ploughed into the history of this world, is proof of the subtle virtue of this infusion.

Meantime, whilst the doors of the temple stand open, night and day, before every man, and the oracles of this truth cease never, it is guarded by one stern condition; this, namely;

it is an intuition. It cannot be received at second hand. Truly speaking, it is not instruction, but provocation, that I can receive from another soul. What he announces, I must find true in me, or reject; and on his word, or as his second, be he who he may, I can accept nothing. On the contrary, the absence of this primary faith is the presence of degradation. As is the flood, so is the ebb. Let this faith depart, and the very words it spake and the things it made become false and hurtful. Then falls the church, the state, art, letters, life. The doctrine of the divine nature [1] being forgotten, a sickness infects and dwarfs the constitution. Once man was all; now he is an appendage, a nuisance. And because the indwelling Supreme Spirit cannot wholly be got rid of, the doctrine of it suffers this perversion, that the divine nature is attributed to one or two persons, and denied to all the rest, and denied with fury. The doctrine of inspiration is lost; the base doctrine of the majority of voices usurps the place of the doctrine of the soul. Miracles, prophecy, poetry, the ideal life, the holy life, exist as ancient history merely; they are not in the belief, nor in the aspiration of society; but, when suggested, seem ridiculous. Life is comic or pitiful as soon as the high ends of being fade out of sight, and man becomes near-sighted, and can only attend to what addresses the senses.

These general views, which, whilst they are general, none will contest, find abundant illustration in the history of religion, and especially in the history of the Christian church. In that, all of us have had our birth and nurture. The truth contained in that, you, my young friends, are now setting forth to teach. As the Cultus, or established worship of the civilized world, it has great historical interest for us. Of its blessed words, which have been the consolation of humanity, you need not that I should speak. I shall endeavor to discharge my duty to you on this occasion, by pointing out two errors in its administration, which daily appear more gross from the point of view we have just now taken.

Jesus Christ belonged to the true race of prophets. He saw with open eye the mystery of the soul. Drawn by its severe harmony, ravished with its beauty, he lived in it, and had his being there. Alone in all history he estimated the greatness of man. One man was true to what is in you and me. He saw that God incarnates himself in man, and evermore goes forth anew to take possession of his World.

He said, in this jubilee of sublime emotion, ' I am divine. Through me, God acts; through me, speaks. Would you see God, see me; or see thee, when thou also thinkest as I now think.' But what a distortion did his doctrine and memory suffer in the same, in the next, and the following ages! There is no doctrine of the Reason which will bear to be taught by the Understanding. The understanding caught this high chant from the poet's lips, and said, in the next age, ' This was Jehovah come down out of heaven. I will kill you, if you say he was a man.' The idioms of his language and the figures of his rhetoric have usurped the place of his truth; and churches are not built on his principles, but on his tropes. Christianity became a Mythus, as the poetic teaching of Greece and of Egypt, before. He spoke of miracles; for he felt that man's life was a miracle, and all that man doth, and he knew that this daily miracle shines as the character ascends. But the word Miracle, as pronounced by Christian churches, gives a false impression; it is Monster. It is not one with the blowing clover and the falling rain.'

He felt respect for Moses and the prophets, but no unfit tenderness at postponing their ini-

tial revelations to the hour and the man that
now is ; to the eternal revelation in the heart.
Thus was he. a true man. Having seen that the
law in us is commanding, he would not suffer
it to be commanded. Boldly, with hand, and
heart, and life, he declared it was God.   Thus
is he, as I think, the only soul in history who
has appreciated the worth of man.

1. In this point of view we become sensible of the first defect of historical Christianity.
Historical Christianity has fallen into the error
that corrupts all attempts to communicate religion. As it appears to us, and as it has appeared for ages, it is not the doctrine of the
soul, but an exaggeration of the personal, the
positive, the ritual. It has dwelt, it dwells, with
noxious exaggeration about the *person* of Jesus.
The soul knows no persons. It invites every
man to expand to the full circle of the universe,
and will have no preferences but those of spontaneous love.   But by this eastern monarchy
of a Christianity, which indolence and fear have
built, the friend of man ' is made the injurer
of man. The manner in which his name is surrounded with expressions which were once sallies
of admiration and love, but are now petrified
into official titles, kills all generous sympathy

and liking. All who hear me, feel that the language that describes Christ to Europe and America is not the style of friendship and enthusiasm to a good and noble heart, but is appropriated and formal, — paints a demigod, as the Orientals or the Greeks would describe Osiris or Apollo. Accept the injurious impositions of our early catechetical instruction, and even honesty and self-denial were but splendid sins, if they did not wear the Christian name. One would rather be

" A pagan, suckled in a creed outworn," [1]

than to be defrauded of his manly right in coming into nature and finding not names and places, not land and professions, but even virtue and truth foreclosed and monopolized. You shall not be a man even. You shall not own the world ; you shall not dare and live after the infinite Law that is in you, and in company with the infinite Beauty which heaven and earth reflect to you in all lovely forms ; but you must subordinate your nature to Christ's nature ; you must accept our interpretations, and take his portrait as the vulgar draw it.

That is always best which gives me to myself. The sublime is excited in me by the great

stoical doctrine, Obey thyself. That which
shows God in me, fortifies me.¹ That which
shows God out of me, makes me a wart and
a wen. There is no longer a necessary reason
for my being. Already the long shadows of
untimely oblivion creep over me, and I shall
decease forever.

The divine bards are the friends of my virtue,
of my intellect, of my strength. They admonish me that the gleams which flash across my
mind are not mine, but God's; that they had
the like, and were not disobedient to the heavenly vision. So I love them. Noble provocations go out from them, inviting me to resist
evil; to subdue the world; and to Be. And
thus, by his holy thoughts, Jesus serves us, and
thus only. To aim to convert a man by miracles is a profanation of the soul. A true conversion, a true Christ, is now, as always, to be
made by the reception of beautiful sentiments.
It is true that a great and rich soul, like his,
falling among the simple, does so preponderate,
that, as his did, it names the world. The world
seems to them to exist for him, and they have not
yet drunk so deeply of his sense as to see that
only by coming again to themselves, or to God
in themselves, can they grow forevermore. It

is a low benefit to give me something; it is a
high benefit to enable me to do somewhat of
myself.[1] The time is coming when all men
will see that the gift of God to the soul is not a
vaunting, overpowering, excluding sanctity, but
a sweet, natural goodness, a goodness like thine
and mine, and that so invites thine and mine to
be and to grow.

The injustice of the vulgar tone of preaching
is not less flagrant to Jesus than to the souls
which it profanes. The preachers do not see
that they make his gospel not glad, and shear
him of the locks of beauty and the attributes
of heaven. When I see a majestic Epaminondas, or Washington; when I see among my
contemporaries a true orator, an upright judge,
a dear friend; when I vibrate to the melody
and fancy of a poem; I see beauty that is to be
desired. And so lovely, and with yet more entire consent of my human being, sounds in my
ear the severe music of the bards that have sung
of the true God in all ages.[2] Now do not degrade the life and dialogues of Christ out of the
circle of this charm, by insulation and peculiarity. Let them lie as they befell, alive and warm,
part of human life and of the landscape and of
the cheerful day.

2. The second defect of the traditionary and limited way of using the mind of Christ is a consequence of the first; this, namely; that the Moral Nature, that Law of laws whose revelations introduce greatness —yea, God himself— into the open soul, is not explored as the fountain of the established teaching in society. Men have come to speak of the revelation as somewhat long ago given and done, as if God were dead. The injury to faith throttles the preacher; and the goodliest of institutions becomes an uncertain and inarticulate voice.

It is very certain that it is the effect of conversation with the beauty of the soul, to beget a desire and need to impart to others the same knowledge and love. If utterance is denied, the thought lies like a burden on the man. Always the seer is a sayer. Somehow his dream is told; somehow he publishes it with solemn joy: sometimes with pencil on canvas, sometimes with chisel on stone, sometimes in towers and aisles of granite, his soul's worship is builded; sometimes in anthems of indefinite music; but clearest and most permanent, in words.[1]

The man enamored of this excellency becomes its priest or poet. The office is coeval with the world. But observe the condition, the spiritual limitation of the office. The spirit only can teach. Not any profane man, not any sensual, not any liar, not any slave can teach, but only he can give, who has; he only can create, who is. The man on whom the soul descends, through whom the soul speaks, alone can teach. Courage, piety, love, wisdom, can teach; and every man can open his door to these angels, and they shall bring him the gift of tongues. But the man who aims to speak as books enable, as synods use, as the fashion guides, and as interest commands, babbles. Let him hush.

To this holy office you propose to devote yourselves. I wish you may feel your call in throbs of desire and hope. The office is the first in the world. It is of that reality that it cannot suffer the deduction of any falsehood. And it is my duty to say to you that the need was never greater of new revelation than now. From the views I have already expressed, you will infer the sad conviction, which I share, I believe, with numbers, of the universal decay and now almost death of faith in society. The soul is not preached. The Church seems to totter to its fall, almost all life extinct.[1] On this occasion, any complaisance would be criminal which told you, whose hope and commission it is to preach the faith of Christ, that the faith of Christ is preached.

It is time that this ill-suppressed murmur of all thoughtful men against the famine of our churches ; — this moaning of the heart because it is bereaved of the consolation, the hope, the grandeur that come alone out of the culture of the moral nature, — should be heard through the sleep of indolence, and over the din of routine. This great and perpetual office of the preacher is not discharged. Preaching is the expression of the moral sentiment in application to the duties of life. In how many churches, by how many prophets, tell me, is man made sensible that he is an infinite Soul ; that the earth and heavens are passing into his mind ; that he is drinking forever the soul of God? Where now sounds the persuasion, that by its very melody imparadises my heart, and so affirms its own origin in heaven ? Where shall I hear words such as in elder ages drew men to leave all and follow, — father and mother, house and land, wife and child ? Where shall I hear these august laws of moral being so pronounced as to fill my ear, and I feel ennobled by the offer of my uttermost action and passion? The test

of the true faith, certainly, should be its power
to charm and command the soul, as the laws of
nature control the activity of the hands, — so
commanding that we find pleasure and honor in
obeying. The faith should blend with the light
of rising and of setting suns, with the flying cloud,
the singing bird, and the breath of flowers. But
now the priest's Sabbath has lost the splendor
of nature ; it is unlovely ; we are glad when it
is done ; we can make, we do make, even sitting
in our pews, a far better, holier, sweeter, for
ourselves.¹

Whenever the pulpit is usurped by a formal-
ist, then is the worshipper defrauded and dis-
consolate. We shrink as soon as the prayers
begin, which do not uplift, but smite and offend
us. We are fain to wrap our cloaks about us,
and secure, as best we can, a solitude that hears
not. I once heard a preacher who sorely tempted
me to say I would go to church no more. Men
go, thought I, where they are wont to go, else
had no soul entered the temple in the afternoon.
A snow-storm was falling around us. The snow-
storm was real, the preacher merely spectral, and
the eye felt the sad contrast in looking at him,
and then out of the window behind him into the
beautiful meteor of the snow. He had lived in

vain. He had no one word intimating that he
had laughed or wept, was married or in love, had
been commended, or cheated, or chagrined. If
he had ever lived and acted, we were none the
wiser for it. The capital secret of his profession,
namely, to convert life into truth, he had not
learned. Not one fact in all his experience had
he yet imported into his doctrine. This man
had ploughed and planted and talked and bought
and sold; he had read books; he had eaten and
drunken; his head aches, his heart throbs; he
smiles and suffers; yet was there not a surmise,
a hint, in all the discourse, that he had ever lived
at all. Not a line did he draw out of real history. The true preacher can be known by this,
that he deals out to the people his life, — life
passed through the fire of thought.[1] But of the
bad preacher, it could not be told from his sermon what age of the world he fell in; whether
he had a father or a child; whether he was a
freeholder or a pauper; whether he was a citizen
or a countryman; or any other fact of his biography. It seemed strange that the people should
come to church. It seemed as if their houses
were very unentertaining, that they should prefer this thoughtless clamor. It shows that there
is a commanding attraction in the moral senti-

ment, that can lend a faint tint of light to dulness and ignorance coming in its name and place. The good hearer is sure he has been touched sometimes; is sure there is somewhat to be reached, and some word that can reach it. When he listens to these vain words, he comforts himself by their relation to his remembrance of better hours, and so they clatter and echo unchallenged.

I am not ignorant that when we preach unworthily, it is not always quite in vain. There is a good ear, in some men, that draws supplies to virtue out of very indifferent nutriment. There is poetic truth concealed in all the commonplaces of prayer and of sermons, and though foolishly spoken, they may be wisely heard; for each is some select expression that broke out in a moment of piety from some stricken or jubilant soul, and its excellency made it remembered. The prayers and even the dogmas of our church are like the zodiac of Denderah and the astronomical monuments of the Hindoos, wholly insulated from anything now extant in the life and business of the people. They mark the height to which the waters once rose. But this docility is a check upon the mischief from the good and devout. In a large portion of the community, the religious service gives rise to quite other thoughts and emotions. We need not chide the negligent servant. We are struck with pity, rather, at the swift retribution of his sloth. Alas for the unhappy man that is called to stand in the pulpit, and *not* give bread of life. Everything that befalls, accuses him. Would he ask contributions for the missions, foreign or domestic? Instantly his face is suffused with shame, to propose to his parish that they should send money a hundred or a thousand miles, to furnish such poor fare as they have at home and would do well to go the hundred or the thousand miles to escape. Would he urge people to a godly way of living ; — and can he ask a fellow-creature to come to Sabbath meetings, when he and they all know what is the poor uttermost they can hope for therein ? Will he invite them privately to the Lord's Supper ? He dares not. If no heart warm this rite, the hollow, dry, creaking formality is too plain, than that he can face a man of wit and energy and put the invitation without terror. In the street, what has he to say to the bold village blasphemer? The village blasphemer sees fear in the face, form, and gait of the minister.

Let me not taint the sincerity of this plea by any oversight of the claims of good men. I

know and honor the purity and strict conscience
of numbers of the clergy. What life the public
worship retains, it owes to the scattered company of pious men, who minister here and there
in the churches, and who, sometimes accepting
with too great tenderness the tenet of the elders,
have not accepted from others, but from their
own heart, the genuine impulses of virtue, and so
still command our love and awe, to the sanctity
of character. Moreover, the exceptions are not
so much to be found in a few eminent preachers, as in the better hours, the truer inspirations
of all, — nay, in the sincere moments of every
man. But, with whatever exception, it is still true
that tradition characterizes the preaching of this
country ; that it comes out of the memory, and
not out of the soul ; that it aims at what is usual,
and not at what is necessary and eternal ; that
thus historical Christianity destroys the power
of preaching, by withdrawing it from the explo-
ration of the moral nature of man ; where the
sublime is, where are the resources of astonishment and power. What a cruel injustice it is to
that Law, the joy of the whole earth, which alone
can make thought dear and rich ; that Law whose
fatal sureness the astronomical orbits poorly
emulate ; — that it is travestied and depreciated,

that it is behooted and behowled, and not a trait, not a word of it articulated. The pulpit in losing sight of this Law, loses its reason, and gropes after it knows not what. And for want of this culture the soul of the community is sick and faithless. It wants nothing so much as a stern, high, stoical, Christian discipline, to make it know itself and the divinity that speaks through it. Now man is ashamed of himself; he skulks and sneaks through the world, to be tolerated, to be pitied,[1] and scarcely in a thousand years does any man dare to be wise and good, and so draw after him the tears and blessings of his kind.

Certainly there have been periods when, from the inactivity of the intellect on certain truths, a greater faith was possible in names and persons. The Puritans in England and America found in the Christ of the Catholic Church and in the dogmas inherited from Rome, scope for their austere piety and their longings for civil freedom. But their creed is passing away, and none arises in its room. I think no man can go with his thoughts about him into one of our churches, without feeling that what hold the public worship had on men is gone, or going. It has lost its grasp on the affection of the good and the fear of the

bad. In the country, neighborhoods, half par-
ishes are *signing off*, to use the local term. It is
already beginning to indicate character and religion to withdraw from the religious meetings.
I have heard a devout person, who prized the
Sabbath, say in bitterness of heart, "On Sundays, it seems wicked to go to church." And
the motive that holds the best there is now only
a hope and a waiting. What was once a mere
circumstance, that the best and the worst men in
the parish, the poor and the rich, the learned
and the ignorant, young and old, should meet
one day as fellows in one house, in sign of an
equal right in the soul, has come to be a paramount motive for going thither.

My friends, in these two errors, I think, I find
the causes of a decaying church and a wasting
unbelief. And what greater calamity can fall
upon a nation than the loss of worship? Then
all things go to decay. Genius leaves the temple to haunt the senate or the market. Literature becomes frivolous. Science is cold. The
eye of youth is not lighted by the hope of other
worlds, and age is without honor. Society lives
to trifles, and when men die we do not mention
them.

And now, my brothers, you will ask, What in

these desponding days can be done by us? The
remedy is already declared in the ground of our
complaint of the Church. We have contrasted
the Church with the Soul. In the soul then let
the redemption be sought. Wherever a man
comes, there comes revolution. The old is for
slaves. When a man comes, all books are legi-
ble, all things transparent, all religions are forms.
He is religious. Man is the wonderworker. He
is seen amid miracles. All men bless and curse.
He saith yea and nay, only. The stationari-
ness of religion; the assumption that the age of
inspiration is past, that the Bible is closed; the
fear of degrading the character of Jesus by representing him as a man; — indicate with sufficient clearness the falsehood of our theology.
It is the office of a true teacher to show us that
God is, not was; that He speaketh, not spake.
The true Christianity, — a faith like Christ's in
the infinitude of man, — is lost. None believeth
in the soul of man, but only in some man or person old and departed. Ah me! no man goeth
alone. All men go in flocks to this saint or
that poet, avoiding the God who seeth in secret.
They cannot see in secret; they love to be blind
in public. They think society wiser than their
soul, and know not that one soul, and their soul,

is wiser than the whole world.' See how nations
and races flit by on the sea of time and leave no
ripple to tell where they floated or sunk, and
one good soul shall make the name of Moses,
or of Zeno, or of Zoroaster, reverend forever.
None assayeth the stern ambition to be the Self
of the nation and of nature, but each would be
an easy secondary to some Christian scheme,
or sectarian connection, or some eminent man.
Once leave your own knowledge of God, your
own sentiment, and take secondary knowledge,
as St. Paul's, or George Fox's, or Swedenborg's,
and you get wide from God with every year this
secondary form lasts, and if, as now, for centuries, — the chasm yawns to that breadth, that
men can scarcely be convinced there is in them
anything divine.

Let me admonish you, first of all, to go alone;
to refuse the good models, even those which
are sacred in the imagination of men, and dare
to love God without mediator or veil. Friends
enough you shall find who will hold up to your
emulation Wesleys and Oberlins, Saints and
Prophets. Thank God for these good men, but
say, 'I also am a man.' Imitation cannot go
above its model. The imitator dooms himself
to hopeless mediocrity. The inventor did it be-

cause it was natural to him, and so in him it has
a charm. In the imitator something else is natural, and he bereaves himself of his own beauty,
to come short of another man's.

Yourself a newborn bard of the Holy Ghost,
cast behind you all conformity, and acquaint
men at first hand with Deity. Look to it first
and only, that fashion, custom, authority, pleasure, and money, are nothing to you, — are not
bandages over your eyes, that you cannot see,
— but live with the privilege of the immeasur-
able mind. Not too anxious to visit periodically
all families and each family in your parish connection, — when you meet one of these men or
women, be to them a divine man; be to them
thought and virtue; let their timid aspirations
find in you a friend; let their trampled instincts
be genially tempted out in your atmosphere; let
their doubts know that you have doubted, and
their wonder feel that you have wondered. By
trusting your own heart, you shall gain more
confidence in other men. For all our penny-
wisdom, for all our soul-destroying slavery to
habit, it is not to be doubted that all men have
sublime thoughts; that all men value the few
real hours of life; they love to be heard; they
love to be caught up into the vision of princi-

ples. We mark with light in the memory the few
interviews we have had, in the dreary years of
routine and of sin, with souls that made our
souls wiser; that spoke what we thought; that
told us what we knew; that gave us leave to
be what we inly were. Discharge to men the
priestly office, and, present or absent, you shall
be followed with their love as by an angel.

And, to this end, let us not aim at common
degrees of merit. Can we not leave, to such as
love it, the virtue that glitters for the commendation of society, and ourselves pierce the deep
solitudes of absolute ability and worth? We
easily come up to the standard of goodness in
society. Society's praise can be cheaply secured,
and almost all men are content with those easy
merits; but the instant effect of conversing with
God will be to put them away. There are persons who are not actors, not speakers, but influences; persons too great for fame, for display;
who disdain eloquence; to whom all we call art
and artist, seems too nearly allied to show and
by-ends, to the exaggeration of the finite and
selfish, and loss of the universal. The orators,
the poets, the commanders encroach on us only
as fair women do, by our allowance and homage.
Slight them by preoccupation of mind, slight

them, as you can well afford to do, by high and
universal aims, and they instantly feel that you
have right, and that it is in lower places that they
must shine. They also feel your right; for they
with you are open to the influx of the all-know-
ing Spirit, which annihilates before its broad
noon the little shades and gradations of intelligence in the compositions we call wiser and
wisest.   ·

In such high communion let us study the
grand strokes of rectitude: a bold benevolence,
an independence of friends, so that not the unjust wishes of those who love us shall impair
our freedom, but we shall resist for truth's sake
the freest flow of kindness, and appeal to sympathies far in advance; ' and,—what is the highest form in which we know this beautiful element, — a certain solidity of merit, that has
nothing to do with opinion, and which is so
essentially and manifestly virtue, that it is taken
for granted that the right, the brave, the generous step will be taken by it, and nobody thinks
of commending it. You would compliment a
coxcomb doing a good act, but you would not
praise an angel. The silence that accepts merit
as the most natural thing in the world, is the
highest applause. Such souls, when they appear,

are the Imperial Guard of Virtue, the perpetual reserve, the dictators of fortune. One needs
not praise their courage, — they are the heart
and soul of nature. O my friends, there are
resources in us on which we have not drawn.
There are men who rise refreshed on hearing a
threat; men to whom a crisis which intimidates
and paralyzes the majority,—demanding not the
faculties of prudence and thrift, but comprehension, immovableness, the readiness of sacrifice,
— comes graceful and beloved as a bride. Napoleon said of Massena, that he was not himself
until the battle began to go against him ; then,
when the dead began to fall in ranks around
him, awoke his powers of combination, and he
put on terror and victory as a robe. So it is in
rugged crises, in unweariable endurance, and in
aims which put sympathy out of question, that
the angel is shown. But these are heights that
we can scarce remember and look up to without
contrition and shame. Let us thank God that
such things exist.

And now let us do what we can to rekindle
the smouldering, nigh quenched fire on the
altar. The evils of the church that now is are
manifest. The question returns, What shall we
do ? I confess, all attempts to project and es-

tablish a Cultus with new rites and forms, seem
to me vain. Faith makes us, and not we it,
and faith makes its own forms. All attempts to
contrive a system are as cold as the new worship introduced by the French to the goddess
of Reason, — to-day, pasteboard and filigree,
and ending to-morrow in madness and murder.
Rather let the breath of new life be breathed by
you through the forms already existing. For
if once you are alive, you shall find they shall
become plastic and new. The remedy to their
deformity is first, soul, and second, soul, and
evermore, soul. A whole popedom of forms
one pulsation of virtue can uplift and vivify.
Two inestimable advantages Christianity has
given us ; first the Sabbath, the jubilee of the
whole world, whose light dawns welcome alike
into the closet of the philosopher, into the garret of toil, and into prison-cells, and everywhere
suggests, even to the vile, the dignity of spiritual being. Let it stand forevermore, a temple,
which new love, new faith, new sight shall restore to more than its first splendor to mankind.[1]
And secondly, the institution of preaching, —
the speech of man to men, — essentially the
most flexible of all organs, of all forms. What
hinders that now, everywhere, in pulpits, in

lecture-rooms, in houses, in fields, wherever the invitation of men or your own occasions lead you, you speak the very truth, as your life and conscience teach it, and cheer the waiting, fainting hearts of men with new hope and new revelation ? [1]

I look for the hour when that supreme Beauty which ravished the souls of those Eastern men, and chiefly of those Hebrews, and through their lips spoke oracles to all time, shall speak in the West also. The Hebrew and Greek Scriptures contain immortal sentences, that have been bread of life to millions. But they have no epical integrity ; are fragmentary ; are not shown in their order to the intellect. I look for the new Teacher that shall follow so far those shining laws that he shall see them come full circle ; shall see their rounding complete grace ; shall see the world to be the mirror of the soul ; [2] shall see the identity of the law of gravitation with purity of heart ; and shall show that the Ought, that Duty, is one thing with Science, with Beauty, and with Joy.

LITERARY ETHICS

AN ORATION DELIVERED BEFORE THE LITERARY
SOCIETIES OF DARTMOUTH COLLEGE,
JULY 24, 1838

LITERARY ETHICS

GENTLEMEN:

THE invitation to address you this day, with which you have honored me, was a call so welcome that I made haste to obey it. A summons to celebrate with scholars a literary festival, is so alluring to me as to overcome the doubts I might well entertain of my ability to bring you any thought worthy of your attention. I have reached the middle age of man; yet I believe I am not less glad or sanguine at the meeting of scholars, than when, a boy, I first saw the graduates of my own College assembled at their anniversary. Neither years nor books have yet availed to extirpate a prejudice then rooted in me, that a scholar is the favorite of Heaven and earth, the excellency of his country, the happiest of men.[1] His duties lead him directly into the holy ground where other men's aspirations only point. His successes are occasions of the purest joy to all men. Eyes is he to the blind; feet is he to the lame. His failures,[2] if he is worthy, are inlets to higher advantages. And because the scholar by every thought he thinks extends his dominion into the general mind of men, he is not one, but many. The few scholars in each country, whose genius I know, seem to me not individuals, but societies; and when events occur of great import, I count over these representatives of opinion, whom they will affect, as if I were counting nations. And even if his results were incommunicable; if they abode in his own spirit; the intellect hath somewhat so sacred in its possessions that the fact of his existence and pursuits would be a happy omen.

Meantime I know that a very different estimate of the scholar's profession prevails in this country, and the importunity, with which society presses its claim upon young men, tends to pervert the views of the youth in respect to the culture of the intellect. Hence the historical failure, on which Europe and America have so freely commented. This country has not fulfilled what seemed the reasonable expectation of mankind. Men looked, when all feudal straps and bandages were snapped asunder, that nature, too long the mother of dwarfs, should reimburse itself by a brood of Titans, who should laugh and leap in the continent, and run up the mountains of the West with the errand of genius and of love. But the mark of American merit in

painting, in sculpture, in poetry, in fiction, in
eloquence, seems to be a certain grace without
grandeur, and itself not new but derivative, a
vase of fair outline, but empty, — which whoso
sees may fill with what wit and character is in
him, but which does not, like the charged cloud,
overflow with terrible beauty, and emit light-
nings on all beholders.

I will not lose myself in the desultory questions, what are the limitations, and what the
causes of the fact. It suffices me to say, in general, that the diffidence of mankind in the soul
has crept over the American mind; that men
here, as elsewhere, are indisposed to innovation,
and prefer any antiquity, any usage, any livery
productive of ease or profit, to the unproductive
service of thought.

Yet in every sane hour the service of thought
appears reasonable, the despotism of the senses
insane. The scholar may lose himself in schools,
in words, and become a pedant; but when he
comprehends his duties he above all men is
a realist, and converses with things. For the
scholar is the student of the world; and of what
worth the world is, and with what emphasis it
accosts the soul of man, such is the worth, such
the call of the scholar.

The want of the times and the propriety of
this anniversary concur to draw attention to the
doctrine of Literary Ethics. What I have to.
say on that doctrine distributes itself under the
topics of the resources, the subject, and the discipline of the scholar.

I. The resources of the scholar are proportioned to his confidence in the attributes of the
Intellect. The resources of the scholar are coextensive with nature and truth, yet can never
be his unless claimed by him with an equal
greatness of mind. He cannot know them until
he has beheld with awe the infinitude and im-
personality of the intellectual power.[1] When he
has seen that it is not his, nor any man's, but
that it is the soul which made the world, and
that it is all accessible to him, he will know that
he, as its minister, may rightfully hold all things
subordinate and answerable to it. A divine pil-
grim in nature, all things attend his steps. Over
him stream the flying constellations ; over him
streams Time, as they, scarcely divided into
months and years. He inhales the year as a
vapor: its fragrant midsummer breath, its spar-
kling January heaven. And so pass into his mind,
in bright transfiguration, the grand events of

history, to take a new order and scale from him.
He is the world; and the epochs and heroes
of chronology are pictorial images, in which his
thoughts are told. There is no event but sprung
somewhere from the soul of man; and therefore there is none but the soul of man can
interpret. Every presentiment of the mind is
executed somewhere in a gigantic fact. What
else is Greece, Rome, England, France, St. He-
lena? What else are churches, literatures, and
empires? The new man must feel that he is
new, and has not come into the world mort-
gaged to the opinions and usages of Europe,
and Asia, and Egypt. The sense of spiritual
independence is like the lovely varnish of the
dew,' whereby the old, hard, peaked earth and
its old self-same productions are made new every
morning, and shining with the last touch of the
artist's hand. A false humility, a complaisance
to reigning schools or to the wisdom of antiquity,
must not defraud me of supreme possession of
this hour. If any person have less love of liberty and less jealousy to guard his integrity, shall
he therefore dictate to you and me? Say to such
doctors, We are thankful to you, as we are to
history, to the pyramids, and the authors; but
now our day is come; we have been born out

of the eternal silence ; and now will we live, —
live for ourselves, — and not as the pall-bearers
of a funeral, but as the upholders and creators of
our age ; and neither Greece nor Rome, nor the
three Unities of Aristotle, nor the three Kings
of Cologne, nor the College of the Sorbonne,
nor the Edinburgh Review is to command any
longer. Now that we are here we will put our
own interpretation on things, and our own things
for interpretation. Please himself with complaisance who will,[1] — for me, things must take my
scale, not I theirs. I will say with the warlike
king, " God gave me this crown, and the whole
world shall not take it away."

The whole value of history, of biography, is
to increase my self-trust, by demonstrating what
man can be and do.[2] This is the moral of the
Plutarchs, the Cudworths, the Tennemanns, who
give us the story of men or of opinions.[3] Any
history of philosophy fortifies my faith, by showing me that what high dogmas I had supposed
were the rare and late fruit of a cumulative culture, and only now possible to some recent Kant
or Fichte, — were the prompt improvisations of
the earliest inquirers ; of Parmenides, Heraclitus, and Xenophanes.[4] In view of these students,
the soul seems to whisper, ' There is a better way

than this indolent learning of another. Leave
me alone; do not teach me out of Leibnitz or
Schelling, and I shall find it all out myself.'

Still more do we owe to biography the forti-
fication of our hope. If you would know the
power of character, see how much you would
impoverish the world if you could take clean
out of history the lives of Milton, Shakspeare,
and Plato, — these three, and cause them not to
be. See you not how much less the power of
man would be? I console myself in the poverty
of my thoughts, in the paucity of great men, in
the malignity and dulness of the nations, by falling back on these sublime recollections, and seeing what the prolific soul could beget on actual
nature;—seeing that Plato was, and Shakspeare,
and Milton, — three irrefragable facts. Then I
dare; I also will essay to be.' The humblest,
the most hopeless, in view of these radiant facts,
may now theorize and hope. In spite of all the
rueful abortions that squeak and gibber in the
street, in spite of slumber and guilt, in spite of
the army, the bar-room, and the jail, *have been*
these glorious manifestations of the mind; and
I will thank my great brothers so truly for the
admonition of their being, as to endeavor also
to be just and brave, to aspire and to speak.

Plotinus too, and Spinoza, and the immortal bards of philosophy, — that which they have written out with patient courage, makes me bold. No more will I dismiss, with haste, the visions which flash and sparkle across my sky ; but observe them, approach them, domesticate them, brood on them, and draw out of the past, genuine life for the present hour.

To feel the full value of these lives, as occasions of hope and provocation, you must come to know that each admirable genius is but a successful diver in that sea whose floor of pearls is all your own. The impoverishing philosophy of ages has laid stress on the distinctions of the individual, and not on the universal attributes of man. The youth, intoxicated with his admiration of a hero, fails to see that it is only a projection of his own soul which he admires.¹ In solitude, in a remote village, the ardent youth loiters and mourns. With inflamed eye, in this sleeping wilderness, he has read the story of the Emperor Charles the Fifth, until his fancy has brought home to the surrounding woods the faint roar of cannonades in the Milanese, and marches in Germany. He is curious concerning that man's day. What filled it ? the crowded orders, the stern decisions, the foreign despatches,

the Castilian etiquette? The soul answers —
Behold his day here! In the sighing of these
woods, in the quiet of these gray fields, in the
cool breeze that sings out of these northern
mountains; in the workmen, the boys, the maidens you meet, — in the hopes of the morning, the ennui of noon, and sauntering of the
afternoon; in the disquieting comparisons; in
the regrets at want of vigor; in the great idea
and the puny execution ; — behold Charles the
Fifth's day ; another, yet the same; behold Chatham's, Hampden's, Bayard's, Alfred's, Scipio's,
Pericles's day, — day of all that are born of women. The difference of circumstance is merely
costume. I am tasting the self-same life, — its
sweetness, its greatness, its pain, which I so admire in other men. Do not foolishly ask of the
inscrutable, obliterated past, what it cannot tell,
— the details of that nature, of that day, called
Byron, or Burke ; — but ask it of the envelop-
ing Now; the more quaintly you inspect its
evanescent beauties, its wonderful details, its
spiritual causes, its astounding whole, — so much
the more you master the biography of this hero,
and that, and every hero. Be lord of a day,
through wisdom and justice, and you can put up
your history books.[1]

An intimation of these broad rights is familiar in the sense of injury which men feel in the assumption of any man to limit their possible progress. We resent all criticism which denies us anything that lies in our line of advance. Say to the man of letters that he cannot paint a Transfiguration, or build a steamboat, or be a grand-marshal, — and he will not seem to himself depreciated. But deny to him any quality of literary or metaphysical power, and he is piqued. Concede to him genius, which is a sort of Stoical *plenum* annulling the comparative, and he is content; but concede him talents never so rare, denying him genius, and he is aggrieved. What does this mean? Why simply that the soul has assurance, by instincts and presentiments, of *all* power in the direction of its ray, as well as of the special skills it has already acquired.

In order to a knowledge of the resources of the scholar, we must not rest in the use of slender accomplishments, — of faculties to do this and that other feat with words ; but we must pay our vows to the highest power, and pass, if it be possible, by assiduous love and watching, into the visions of absolute truth. The growth of the intellect is strictly analogous in all individuals. It is larger reception. Able men, in

general, have good dispositions, and a respect
for justice; because an able man is nothing else
than a good, free, vascular organization, where-
into the universal spirit freely flows; so that his
fund of justice is not only vast, but infinite. All
men, in the abstract, are just and good; what
hinders them in the particular is the momentary
predominance of the finite and individual over
the general truth. The condition of our incarnation in a private self seems to be a perpetual
tendency to prefer the private law, to obey the
private impulse, to the exclusion of the law of
universal being. The hero is great by means
of the predominance of the universal nature;
he has only to open his mouth, and it speaks;
he has only to be forced to act, and it acts. All
men catch the word, or embrace the deed, with
the heart, for it is verily theirs as much as his;
but in them this disease of an excess of organization cheats them of equal issues. Nothing is
more simple than greatness; indeed, to be simple is to be great. The vision of genius comes
by renouncing the too officious activity of the
understanding, and giving leave and amplest
privilege to the spontaneous sentiment. Out of
this must all that is alive and genial in thought
go. Men grind and grind in the mill of a tru-

ism, and nothing comes out but what was put
in. But the moment they desert the tradition
for a spontaneous thought, then poetry, wit,
hope, virtue, learning, anecdote, all flock to their
aid. Observe the phenomenon of extempore debate. A man of cultivated mind but reserved
habits, sitting silent, admires the miracle of free,
impassioned, picturesque speech, in the man
addressing an assembly ; — a state of being and
power how unlike his own ! [1] Presently his own
emotion rises to his lips, and overflows in speech.
He must also rise and say somewhat. Once embarked, once having overcome the novelty of
the situation, he finds it just as easy and natural to speak, — to speak with thoughts, with
pictures, with rhythmical balance of sentences,
— as it was to sit silent ; for it needs not to do,
but to suffer ; he only adjusts himself to the free
spirit which gladly utters itself through him ;
and motion is as easy as rest.

II. I pass now to consider the task offered
to the intellect of this country. The view I
have taken of the resources of the scholar, pre-
supposes a subject as broad. We do not seem
to have imagined its riches. We have not
heeded the invitation it holds out. To be as

good a scholar as Englishmen are, to have as
much learning as our contemporaries, to have
written a book that is read, satisfies us.   We
assume that all thought is already long ago
adequately set down in books, — all imagina-
tions in poems ; and what we say we only throw
in as confirmatory of this supposed complete
body of literature.   A very shallow assumption.
Say rather all literature is yet to be written.
Poetry has scarce chanted its first song.   The
perpetual admonition of nature to us, is, ' The
world is new, untried.   Do not believe the past.
I give you the universe a virgin to-day.'

By Latin and English poetry we were born
and bred in an oratorio of praises of nature, —
flowers, birds, mountains, sun, and moon ; — yet
the naturalist of this hour finds that he knows
nothing, by all their poems, of any of these fine
things ; that he has conversed with the mere
surface and show of them all ; and of their
essence, or of their history, knowing nothing.
Further inquiry will discover that nobody, —
that not these chanting poets themselves, knew
anything sincere of these handsome natures they
so commended ; that they contented themselves
with the passing chirp of a bird, that they saw
one or two mornings, and listlessly looked at

sunsets, and repeated idly these few glimpses in
their song. But go into the forest, you shall find
all new and undescribed. The honking of the
wild geese flying by night; the thin note of
the companionable titmouse in the winter day;
the fall of swarms of flies, in autumn, from com-
bats high in the air, pattering down on the leaves
like rain; the angry hiss of the wood-birds;
the pine throwing out its pollen for the benefit
of the next century; the turpentine exuding
from the tree;—and indeed any vegetation, any
animation, any and all, are alike unattempted.
The man who stands on the seashore, or who
rambles in the woods, seems to be the first man
that ever stood on the shore, or entered a grove,
his sensations and his world are so novel and
strange.[1] Whilst I read the poets, I think that
nothing new can be said about morning and
evening. But when I see the daybreak I am not
reminded of these Homeric, or Shakspearian,
or Miltonic, or Chaucerian pictures. No, but I
feel perhaps the pain of an alien world; a world
not yet subdued by the thought; or I am
cheered by the moist, warm, glittering, budding,
melodious hour, that takes down the narrow
walls of my soul, and extends its life and pulsation to the very horizon. *That* is morning, to

cease for a bright hour to be a prisoner of this sickly body, and to become as large as nature.

The noonday darkness of the American forest, the deep, echoing, aboriginal woods, where the living columns of the oak and fir tower up from the ruins of the trees of the last millennium; where, from year to year, the eagle and the crow see no intruder; the pines, bearded with savage moss, yet touched with grace by the violets at their feet; the broad, cold lowland which forms its coat of vapor with the stillness of subterranean crystallization; and where the traveller, amid the repulsive plants that are native in the swamp, thinks with pleasing terror of the distant town; this beauty, — haggard and desert beauty, which the sun and the moon, the snow and the rain, repaint and vary, has never been recorded by art, yet is not indifferent to any passenger. All men are poets at heart. They serve nature for bread, but her loveliness overcomes them sometimes. What mean these journeys to Niagara; these pilgrims to the White Hills? Men believe in the adaptations of utility, always: in the mountains, they may believe in the adaptations of the eye. Undoubtedly the changes of geology have a relation to the prosperous sprouting of the corn and peas in my kitchen garden ; but not less is there a relation of beauty between my soul and the dim crags of Agiochook up there in the clouds. Every man, when this is told, hearkens with joy, and yet his own conversation with nature is still unsung.

Is it otherwise with civil history ? Is it not the lesson of our experience that every man, were life long enough, would write history for himself ? What else do these volumes of extracts and manuscript commentaries, that every scholar writes, indicate ? Greek history is one thing to me ; another to you. Since the birth of Niebuhr and Wolf, Roman and Greek history have been written anew. Since Carlyle wrote French History, we see that no history that we have is safe, but a new classifier shall give it new and more philosophical arrangement. Thucydides, Livy, have only provided materials. The moment a man of genius pronounces the name of the Pelasgi, of Athens, of the Etrurian, of the Roman people, we see their state under a new aspect. As in poetry and history, so in the other departments. There are few masters or none. Religion is yet to be settled on its fast foundations in the breast of man ; and politics, and philosophy, and letters,

and art.   As yet we have nothing but tendency
and indication.

This starting, this warping of the best literary
works from the adamant of nature, is especially
observable in philosophy. Let it take what tone
of pretension it will, to this complexion must
it come, at last. Take for example the French
Eclecticism, which Cousin esteems so conclu-
sive ; there is an optical illusion in it. It avows
great pretensions. It looks as if they had all
truth, in taking all the systems, and had nothing
to do but to sift and wash and strain, and the
gold and diamonds would remain in the last
colander. But Truth is such a fly-away, such a
slyboots, so untransportable and unbarrelable
a commodity, that it is as bad to catch as light.
Shut the shutters never so quick to keep all the
light in, it is all in vain ; it is gone before you
can cry, Hold. And so it happens with our philosophy. Translate, collate, distil all the systems, it steads you nothing ; for truth will not
be compelled in any mechanical manner. But
the first observation you make, in the sincere
act of your nature, though on the veriest trifle,
may open a new view of nature and of man,
that, like a menstruum, shall dissolve all theories in it ; shall take up Greece, Rome, Stoi-

cism, Eclecticism, and what not, as mere data and food for analysis, and dispose of your world-containing system as a very little unit. A profound thought, anywhere, classifies all things : a profound thought will lift Olympus. The book of philosophy is only a fact, and no more inspiring fact than another, and no less ; but a wise man will never esteem it anything final and transcending. Go and talk with a man of genius, and the first word he utters, sets all your so-called knowledge afloat and at large. Then Plato, Bacon, Kant, and the Eclectic Cousin condescend instantly to be men and mere facts.[1]

I by no means aim in these remarks to disparage the merit of these or of any existing compositions ; I only say that any particular portraiture does not in any manner exclude or forestall a new attempt, but, when considered by the soul, warps and shrinks away. The inundation of the spirit sweeps away before it all our little architecture of wit and memory, as straws and straw-huts before the torrent.[2] Works of the intellect are great only by comparison with each other ; Ivanhoe and Waverley compared with Castle Radcliffe and the Porter novels ; but nothing is great, — not mighty Homer and Milton, — beside the infinite Reason. It carries them away as a flood. They are as a sleep.

Thus is justice done to each generation and individual, — wisdom teaching man that he shall not hate, or fear, or mimic his ancestors; that he shall not bewail himself, as if the world was old, and thought was spent, and he was born into the dotage of things; for, by virtue of the Deity, thought renews itself inexhaustibly every day, and the thing whereon it shines, though it were dust and sand, is a new subject with countless relations.

III. Having thus spoken of the resources and the subject of the scholar, out of the same faith proceeds also the rule of his ambition and life. Let him know that the world is his, but he must possess it by putting himself into harmony with the constitution of things. He must be a solitary, laborious, modest, and charitable soul.

He must embrace solitude as a bride. He must have his glees and his glooms alone. His own estimate must be measure enough, his own praise reward enough for him.[1] And why must the student be solitary and silent? That he may become acquainted with his thoughts. If he

pines in a lonely place, hankering for the crowd,
for display, he is not in the lonely place; his
heart is in the market; he does not see; he
does not hear; he does not think. But go cher-
ish your soul; expel companions; set your
habits to a life of solitude; then will the faculties rise fair and full within, like forest trees
and field flowers; you will have results, which,
when you meet your fellow-men, you can communicate, and they will gladly receive. Do not
go into solitude only that you may presently
come into public. Such solitude denies itself;
is public and stale. The public can get public
experience, but they wish the scholar to replace
to them those private, sincere, divine experiences of which they have been defrauded by
dwelling in the street. It is the noble, manlike,
just thought, which is the superiority demanded
of you, and not crowds but solitude confers this
elevation. Not insulation of place, but independence of spirit is essential, and it is only as
the garden, the cottage, the forest, and the rock,
are a sort of mechanical aids to this, that they
are of value. Think alone, and all places are
friendly and sacred. The poets who have lived
in cities have been hermits still. Inspiration
makes solitude anywhere. Pindar, Raphael,

Angelo, Dryden, De Staël, dwell in crowds it may be, but the instant thought comes the crowd grows dim to their eye; their eye fixes on the horizon, on vacant space; they forget the by-standers; they spurn personal relations; they deal with abstractions, with verities, with ideas. They are alone with the mind.

Of course I would not have any superstition about solitude. Let the youth study the uses of solitude and of society. Let him use both, not serve either. The reason why an ingenious soul shuns society, is to the end of finding soci-ety. It repudiates the false, out of love of the true. You can very soon learn all that society can teach you for one while.[1] Its foolish rou-tine, an indefinite multiplication of balls, con-certs, rides, theatres, can teach you no more than a few can. Then accept the hint of shame, of spiritual emptiness and waste which true na-ture gives you, and retire and hide; lock the door; shut the shutters; then welcome falls the imprisoning rain, — dear hermitage of nature. Re-collect the spirits. Have solitary prayer and praise. Digest and correct the past experience; and blend it with the new and divine life.

You will pardon me, Gentlemen, if I say I think that we have need of a more rigorous scholastic rule ; such an asceticism, I mean, as only the hardihood and devotion of the scholar himself can enforce. We live in the sun and on the surface, — a thin, plausible, superficial existence, and talk of muse and prophet, of art and creation. But out of our shallow and frivolous way of life, how can greatness ever grow? Come now, let us go and be dumb. Let us sit with our hands on our mouths, a long, austere, Pythagorean lustrum. Let us live in corners, and do chores, and suffer, and weep, and drudge, with eyes and hearts that love the Lord. Silence, seclusion, austerity, may pierce deep into the grandeur and secret of our being, and so diving, bring up out of secular darkness the sublimities of the moral constitution. How mean to go blazing, a gaudy butterfly, in fashionable or political *salons*, the fool of society, the fool of notoriety, a topic for newspapers, a piece of the street, and forfeiting the real prerogative of the russet coat, the privacy, and the true and warm heart of the citizen !

Fatal to the man of letters, fatal to man, is the lust of display, the seeming that unmakes our being. A mistake of the main end to which they labor is incident to literary men, who, dealing with the organ of language, — the subtlest,

strongest, and longest-lived of man's creations,
and only fitly used as the weapon of thought
and of justice, — learn to enjoy the pride of
playing with this splendid engine, but rob it of
its almightiness by failing to work with it. Ex-
tricating themselves from the tasks of the world,
the world revenges itself by exposing, at every
turn, the folly of these incomplete, pedantic,
useless, ghostly creatures. The scholar will feel
that the richest romance, the noblest fiction
that was ever woven, the heart and soul of
beauty, lies enclosed in human life. Itself of
surpassing value, it is also the richest material
for his creations. How shall he know its secrets of tenderness, of terror, of will, and of
fate? How can he catch and keep the strain
of upper music that peals from it? Its laws are
concealed under the details of daily action. All
action is an experiment upon them. He must
bear his share of the common load. He must
work with men in houses, and not with their
names in books. His needs, appetites, talents,
affections, accomplishments, are keys that open
to him the beautiful museum of human life.
Why should he read it as an Arabian tale, and
not know, in his own beating bosom, its sweet
and smart? Out of love and hatred, out of

earnings, and borrowings, and lendings, and losses ; out of sickness and pain ; out of wooing and worshipping ; out of travelling, and voting, and watching, and caring ; out of disgrace and contempt, comes our tuition in the serene and beautiful laws. Let him not slur his lesson ; let him learn it by heart. Let him endeavor exactly, bravely, and cheerfully, to solve the problem of that life which is set before *him*. And this by punctual action, and not by promises or dreams. Believing, as in God, in the presence and favor of the grandest influences, let him deserve that favor, and learn how to receive and use it, by fidelity also to the lower observances.

This lesson is taught with emphasis in the life of the great actor of this age, and affords the explanation of his success. Bonaparte represents truly a great recent revolution, which we in this country, please God, shall carry to its farthest consummation. Not the least instructive passage in modern history seems to me a trait of Napoleon exhibited to the English when he became their prisoner. On coming on board the Bellerophon, a file of English soldiers drawn up on deck gave him a military salute. Napoleon observed that their manner of handling their arms differed from the French exercise, and, putting aside the guns of those nearest him, walked up to a soldier, took his gun, and himself went through the motion in the French mode. The English officers and men looked on with astonishment, and inquired if such familiarity was usual with the Emperor.

In this instance, as always, that man, with whatever defects or vices, represented performance in lieu of pretension. Feudalism and Orientalism had long enough thought it majestic to do nothing; the modern majesty consists in work. He belonged to a class fast growing in the world, who think that what a man can do is his greatest ornament, and that he always consults his dignity by doing it. He was not a believer in luck; he had a faith, like sight, in the application of means to ends. Means to ends, is the motto of all his behavior. He believed that the great captains of antiquity performed their exploits only by correct combinations, and by justly comparing the relation between means and consequences, efforts and obstacles. The vulgar call good fortune that which really is produced by the calculations of genius. But Napoleon, thus faithful to facts, had also this crowning merit, that whilst he believed in number and

weight, and omitted no part of prudence, he believed also in the freedom and quite incalculable
force of the soul. A man of infinite caution, he
neglected never the least particular of preparation, of patient adaptation ; yet nevertheless he
had a sublime confidence, as in his all, in the
sallies of the courage, and the faith in his destiny,
which, at the right moment, repaired all losses,
and demolished cavalry, infantry, king, and kai-
sar, as with irresistible thunderbolts. As they
say the bough of the tree has the character of
the leaf, and the whole tree of the bough, so, it
is curious to remark, Bonaparte's army partook
of this double strength of the captain ; for, whilst
strictly supplied in all its appointments, and
everything expected from the valor and discipline of every platoon, in flank and centre, yet
always remained his total trust in the prodigious
revolutions of fortune which his reserved Imperial Guard were capable of working, if, in all else,
the day was lost. Here he was sublime. He no
longer calculated the chance of the cannon ball.
He was faithful to tactics to the uttermost, —
and when all tactics had come to an end then he
dilated and availed himself of the mighty salta-
tions of the most formidable soldiers in nature.

Let the scholar appreciate this combination

of gifts, which, applied to better purpose, make
true wisdom. He is a revealer of things. Let
him first learn the things. Let him not, too
eager to grasp some badge of reward, omit the
work to be done. Let him know that though
the success of the market is in the reward, true
success is the doing; that, in the private obedience to his mind; in the sedulous inquiry, day
after day, year after year, to know how the thing
stands; in the use of all means, and most in the
reverence of the humble commerce and humble
needs of life, — to hearken what *they* say, and
so, by mutual reaction of thought and life, to
make thought solid, and life wise; and in a contempt for the gabble of to-day's opinions the
secret of the world is to be learned, and the skill
truly to unfold it is acquired. Or, rather, is it
not, that, by this discipline, the usurpation of
the senses is overcome, and the lower faculties
of man are subdued to docility; through which
as an unobstructed channel the soul now easily
and gladly flows?

The good scholar will not refuse to bear the
yoke in his youth; to know, if he can, the uttermost secret of toil and endurance; to make
his own hands acquainted with the soil by which
he is fed, and the sweat that goes before comfort

and luxury. Let him pay his tithe and serve the world as a true and noble man; never forgetting to worship the immortal divinities who whisper to the poet and make him the utterer of melodies that pierce the ear of eternal time. If he have this twofold goodness, — the drill and the inspiration, — then he has health ; then he is a whole, and not a fragment; and the perfection of his endowment will appear in his compositions. Indeed, this twofold merit characterizes ever the productions of great masters. The man of genius should occupy the whole space between God or pure mind and the multitude of uneducated men. He must draw from the infinite Reason, on one side; and he must penetrate into the heart and sense of the crowd, on the other. From one, he must draw his strength ; to the other, he must owe his aim. The one yokes him to the real; the other, to the apparent. At one pole is Reason; at the other, Common Sense. If he be defective at either extreme of the scale, his philosophy will seem low and utilitarian, or it will appear too vague and indefinite for the uses of life.[1]

The student, as we all along insist, is great only by being passive to the superincumbent spirit. Let this faith then dictate all his ac-

tion. Snares and bribes abound to mislead him;
let him be true nevertheless. His success has
its perils too. There is somewhat inconven-
ient and injurious in his position. They whom
his thoughts have entertained or inflamed, seek
him before yet they have learned the hard conditions of thought. They seek him, that he may
turn his lamp on the dark riddles whose solution they think is inscribed on the walls of their
being. They find that he is a poor, ignorant
man, in a white-seamed, rusty coat, like themselves, nowise emitting a continuous stream of
light, but now and then a jet of luminous thought
followed by total darkness ; moreover, that he
cannot make of his infrequent illumination a
portable taper to carry whither he would, and
explain now this dark riddle, now that. Sorrow
ensues. The scholar regrets to damp the hope
of ingenuous boys; and the youth has lost a
star out of his new flaming firmament. Hence
the temptation to the scholar to mystify, to hear
the question, to sit upon it, to make an answer
of words in lack of the oracle of things. Not
the less let him be cold and true, and wait in
patience, knowing that truth can make even silence eloquent and memorable. Truth shall be
policy enough for him. Let him open his breast

to all honest inquiry, and be an artist superior
to tricks of art. Show frankly as a saint would
do, your experience, methods, tools, and means.
Welcome all comers to the freest use of the
same. And out of this superior frankness and
charity you shall learn higher secrets of your
nature, which gods will bend and aid you to
communicate.

If, with a high trust, he can thus submit himself, he will find that ample returns are poured
into his bosom out of what seemed hours of
obstruction and loss. Let him not grieve too
much on account of unfit associates. When he
sees how much thought he owes to the disagreeable antagonism of various persons who
pass and cross him, he can easily think that in
a society of perfect sympathy, no word, no act,
no record, would be. He will learn that it is
not much matter what he reads, what he does.
Be a scholar, and he shall have the scholar's
part of everything. As in the counting-room
the merchant cares little whether the cargo be
hides or barilla ; the transaction, a letter of credit
or a transfer of stocks ; be it what it may, his
commission comes gently out of it; so you shall
get your lesson out of the hour, and the object,
whether it be a concentrated or a wasteful em-

ployment, even in reading a dull book, or working off a stint of mechanical day-labor which
your necessities or the necessities of others impose.

Gentlemen, I have ventured to offer you these
considerations upon the scholar's place and hope,
because I thought that standing, as many of you
now do, on the threshold of this College, girt
and ready to go and assume tasks, public and
private, in your country, you would not be sorry
to be admonished of those primary duties of the
intellect whereof you will seldom hear from the
lips of your new companions. You will hear
every day the maxims of a low prudence. You
will hear that the first duty is to get land and
money, place and name. 'What is this Truth
you seek? what is this Beauty?' men will ask,
with derision. If nevertheless God have called
any of you to explore truth and beauty, be bold,
be firm, be true. When you shall say, 'As
others do, so will I: I renounce, I am sorry for it,
my early visions; I must eat the good of the land
and let learning and romantic expectations go,
until a more convenient season;' — then dies
the man in you; then once more perish the buds
of art, and poetry, and science, as they have died

already in a thousand thousand men. The hour
of that choice is the crisis of your history, and
see that you hold yourself fast by the intellect.
It is this domineering temper of the sensual
world that creates the extreme need of the priests
of science; and it is the office and right of the
intellect to make and not take its estimate.
Bend to the persuasion which is flowing to you
from every object in nature, to be its tongue to
the heart of man, and to show the besotted
world how passing fair is wisdom.¹ Forewarned
that the vice of the times and the country is
an excessive pretension, let us seek the shade,
and find wisdom in neglect. Be content with a
little light, so it be your own. Explore, and
explore. Be neither chided nor flattered out of
your position of perpetual inquiry. Neither dog-
matize, nor accept another's dogmatism. Why
should you renounce your right to traverse the
star-lit deserts of truth, for the premature comforts of an acre, house, and barn? Truth also
has its roof, and bed, and board. Make yourself necessary to the world, and mankind will
give you bread, and if not store of it, yet such
as shall not take away your property in all men's
possessions, in all men's affections, in art, in nature, and in hope.

You will not fear that I am enjoining too stern an asceticism. Ask not, Of what use is a scholarship that systematically retreats? or, Who is the better for the philosopher who conceals his accomplishments, and hides his thoughts from the waiting world? Hides his thoughts! Hide the sun and moon. Thought is all light, and publishes itself to the universe. It will speak, though you were dumb, by its own miraculous organ. It will flow out of your actions, your manners, and your face. It will bring you friendships. It will impledge you to truth by the love and expectation of generous minds. By virtue of the laws of that Nature which is one and perfect, it shall yield every sincere good that is in the soul to the scholar beloved of earth and heaven.

THE METHOD OF NATURE

AN ORATION DELIVERED BEFORE THE SOCIETY OF THE
ADELPHI, IN WATERVILLE COLLEGE, MAINE,
AUGUST 11, 1841.

THE METHOD OF NATURE

GENTLEMEN :

LET us exchange congratulations on the en-
joyments and the promises of this literary
anniversary. The land we live in has no interest
so dear, if it knew its want, as the fit consecra-
tion of days of reason and thought. Where
there is no vision, the people perish. The
scholars are the priests of that thought which
establishes the foundations of the earth. No
matter what is their special work or profession,
they stand for the spiritual interest of the world,
and it is a common calamity if they neglect their
post in a country where the material interest is
so predominant as it is in America. We hear
something too much of the results of machinery, commerce, and the useful arts. We are a
puny and a fickle folk. Avarice, hesitation, and
following, are our diseases. The rapid wealth
which hundreds in the community acquire in
trade, or by the incessant expansions of our population and arts, enchants the eyes of all the
rest; the luck of one is the hope of thousands,
and the bribe acts like the neighborhood of a

gold mine to impoverish the farm, the school, the church, the house, and the very body and feature of man.[1]

I do not wish to look with sour aspect at the industrious manufacturing village, or the mart of commerce. I love the music of the water-wheel; I value the railway; I feel the pride which the sight of a ship inspires; I look on trade and every mechanical craft as education also. But let me discriminate what is precious herein. There is in each of these works an act of invention, an intellectual step, or short series of steps, taken ; that act or step is the spiritual act ; all the rest is mere repetition of the same a thousand times. And I will not be deceived into admiring the routine of handicrafts and mechanics, how splendid soever the result, any more than I admire the routine of the scholars or clerical class. That splendid results ensue from the labors of stupid men, is the fruit of higher laws than their will, and the routine is not to be praised for it. I would not have the laborer sacrificed to the result, — I would not have the laborer sacrificed to my convenience and pride, nor to that of a great class of such as me. Let there be worse cotton and better men. The weaver should not be bereaved of his superiority to his work, and his knowledge that the product or the skill is of no value, except so far as it embodies his spiritual prerogatives.[1] If I see nothing to admire in the unit, shall I admire a million units?   Men stand in awe of the city, but do not honor any individual citizen; and are continually yielding to this dazzling result of numbers, that which they would never yield to the solitary example of any one.

Whilst the multitude of men degrade each other, and give currency to desponding doctrines, the scholar must be a bringer of hope, and must reinforce man against himself. I sometimes believe that our literary anniversaries will presently assume a greater importance, as the eyes of men open to their capabilities. Here, a new set of distinctions, a new order of ideas, prevail. Here, we set a bound to the respectability of wealth, and a bound to the pretensions of the law and the church. The bigot must cease to be a bigot to-day. Into our charmed circle, power cannot enter; and the sturdiest defender of existing institutions feels the terrific inflammability of this air which condenses heat in every corner that may restore to the elements the fabrics of ages. Nothing solid is secure; everything tilts and rocks. Even the scholar is not safe; he too is searched and revised. Is his learning dead? Is he living in his memory? The power of mind is not mortification, but life. But come forth, thou curious child! hither, thou loving, all-hoping poet! hither, thou tender, doubting heart, which hast not yet found any place in the world's market fit for thee; any wares which thou couldst buy or sell, — so large is thy love and ambition, — thine and not theirs is the hour. Smooth thy brow, and hope and love on, for the kind Heaven justifies thee, and the whole world feels that thou art in the right.

We ought to celebrate this hour by expressions of manly joy. Not thanks, not prayer seem quite the highest or truest name for our communication with the infinite, — but glad and conspiring reception, — reception that becomes giving in its turn, as the receiver is only the All-Giver in part and in infancy. I cannot, — nor can any man, — speak precisely of things so sublime, but it seems to me the wit of man, his strength, his grace, his tendency, his art, is the grace and the presence of God. It is beyond explanation. When all is said and done, the rapt saint is found the only logician. Not exhortation, not argument becomes our lips, but

pæans of joy and praise.¹   But not of adulation :
we are too nearly related in the deep of the
mind to that we honor.   It is God in us which
checks the language of petition by a grander
thought.   In the bottom of the heart it is said;
'I am, and by me, O child ! this fair body and
world of thine stands and grows.   I am: all
things are mine : and all mine are thine.'

The festival of the intellect and the return to
its source cast a strong light on the always interesting topics of Man and Nature.   We are
forcibly reminded of the old want.   There is no
man; there hath never been.   The Intellect still
asks that a man may be born.   The flame of
life flickers feebly in human breasts.   We demand
of men a richness and universality we do not
find.   Great men do not content us.   It is their
solitude, not their force, that makes them conspicuous.   There is somewhat indigent and tedious about them.   They are poorly tied to one
thought.   If they are prophets they are egotists;
if polite and various they are shallow.   How
tardily men arrive at any result ! how tardily
they pass from it to another !   The crystal sphere
of thought is as concentrical as the geologi-
cal structure of the globe.   As our soils and
rocks lie in strata, concentric strata, so do all

men's thinkings run laterally, never vertically. Here comes by a great inquisitor with auger and plumb-line, and will bore an Artesian well through our conventions and theories, and pierce to the core of things. But as soon as he probes the crust, behold gimlet, plumb-line, and philosopher take a lateral direction, in spite of all resistance, as if some strong wind took everything off its feet, and if you come month after month to see what progress our reformer has made, — not an inch has he pierced,— you still find him with new words in the old place, floating about in new parts of the same old vein or crust. The new book says, ' I will give you the key to nature,' and we expect to go like a thunderbolt to the centre. But the thunder is a surface phenomenon, makes a skin-deep cut, and so does the sage. The wedge turns out to be a rocket. Thus a man lasts but a very little while, for his monomania becomes insupportably tedious in a few months. It is so with every book and person : and yet — and yet — we do not take up a new book or meet a new man without a pulse-beat of expectation. And this invincible hope of a more adequate interpreter is the sure prediction of his advent.'

In the absence of man, we turn to nature,

which stands next. In the divine order, intellect is primary; nature, secondary; it is the memory of the mind. That which once existed in intellect as pure law, has now taken body as Nature. It existed already in the mind in solution; now, it has been precipitated, and the bright sediment is the world. We can never be quite strangers or inferiors in nature. It is flesh of our flesh, and bone of our bone. But we no longer hold it by the hand; we have lost our miraculous power; our arm is no more as strong as the frost, nor our will equivalent to gravity and the elective attractions. Yet we can use nature as a convenient standard, and the meter of our rise and fall. It has this advantage as a witness, it cannot be debauched. When man curses, nature still testifies to truth and love. We may therefore safely study the mind in nature, because we cannot steadily gaze on it in mind; as we explore the face of the sun in a pool, when our eyes cannot brook his direct splendors.

It seems to me therefore that it were some suitable pæan if we should piously celebrate this hour by exploring the *method of nature*. Let us see *that*, as nearly as we can, and try how far it is transferable to the literary life. Every earnest glance we give to the realities around us, with intent to learn, proceeds from a holy impulse, and is really songs of praise. What difference can it make whether it take the shape of exhortation, or of passionate exclamation, or of scientific statement? These are forms merely. Through them we express, at last, the fact that God has done thus or thus.

In treating a subject so large, in which we must necessarily appeal to the intuition, and aim much more to suggest than to describe, I know it is not easy to speak with the precision attainable on topics of less scope. I do not wish in attempting to paint a man, to describe an air-fed, unimpassioned, impossible ghost. My eyes and ears are revolted by any neglect of the physical facts, the limitations of man. And yet one who conceives the true order of nature, and beholds the visible as proceeding from the invisible, cannot state his thought without seeming to those who study the physical laws to do them some injustice. There is an intrinsic defect in the organ. Language overstates. Statements of the infinite are usually felt to be unjust to the finite, and blasphemous. Empedocles undoubtedly spoke a truth of thought, when he said, " I am God ; " but the moment it was out of his mouth it became a lie to the ear; and the world revenged itself for the seeming arrogance by the good story about his shoe. How can I hope for better hap in my attempts to enunciate spiritual facts? Yet let us hope that as far as we receive the truth, so far shall we be felt by every true person to say what is just.'

The method of nature: who could ever analyze it? That rushing stream will not stop to be observed. We can never surprise nature in a corner; never find the end of a thread; never tell where to set the first stone. The bird hastens to lay her egg: the egg hastens to be a bird. The wholeness we admire in the order of the world is the result of infinite distribution. Its smoothness is the smoothness of the pitch of the cataract. Its permanence is a perpetual inchoation. Every natural fact is an emanation, and that from which it emanates is an emanation also, and from every emanation is a new emanation. If anything could stand still, it would be crushed and dissipated by the torrent it resisted, and if it were a mind, would be crazed; as insane persons are those who hold fast to one thought and do not flow with the course of nature. Not the cause, but an ever novel effect, nature descends always from above. It is unbroken obedience. The beauty of these fair objects is imported into them from a metaphysical and eternal spring. In all animal and vegetable forms, the physiologist concedes that no chemistry, no mechanics, can account for the facts, but a mysterious principle of life must be assumed, which not only inhabits the organ but makes the organ.[1]

How silent, how spacious, what room for all, yet without place to insert an atom ; — in graceful succession, in equal fulness, in balanced beauty, the dance of the hours goes forward still. Like an odor of incense, like a strain of music, like a sleep, it is inexact and boundless. It will not be dissected, nor unravelled, nor shown. Away, profane philosopher! seekest thou in nature the cause? This refers to that, and that to the next, and the next to the third, and everything refers. Thou must ask in another mood, thou must feel it and love it, thou must behold it in a spirit as grand as that by which it exists, ere thou canst know the law. Known it will not be, but gladly beloved and enjoyed.

The simultaneous life throughout the whole body, the equal serving of innumerable ends without the least emphasis or preference to any, but the steady degradation of each to the success of all, allows the understanding no place to work. Nature can only be conceived as existing to a universal and not to a particular end; to a universe of ends, and not to one, — a work of *ecstasy*, to be represented by a circular movement, as intention might be signified by a straight line of definite length.[1] Each effect strengthens every other. There is no revolt in all the kingdoms from the commonweal: no detachment of an individual. Hence the catholic character which makes every leaf an exponent of the world. When we behold the landscape in a poetic spirit, we do not reckon individuals. Nature knows neither palm nor oak, but only vegetable life, which sprouts into forests, and festoons the globe with a garland of grasses and vines.

That no single end may be selected and nature judged thereby, appears from this, that if man himself be considered as the end, and it be assumed that the final cause of the world is to make holy or wise or beautiful men, we see that it has not succeeded. Read alternately in natural and in civil history, a treatise of astronomy, for example, with a volume of French *Mémoires pour servir*. When we have spent our wonder in computing this wasteful hospitality with

which boon Nature turns off new firmaments
without end into her wide common, as fast as
the madrepores make coral, — suns and planets
hospitable to souls, — and then shorten the sight
to look into this court of Louis Quatorze, and
see the game that is played there, — duke and
marshal, abbé and madame, — a gambling table
where each is laying traps for the other, where
the end is ever by some lie or fetch to outwit
your rival and ruin him with this solemn fop in
wig and stars, — the king ; — one can hardly
help asking if this planet is a fair specimen of
the so generous astronomy, and if so, whether
the experiment have not failed, and whether it
be quite worth while to make more, and glut
the innocent space with so poor an article.[1]

I think we feel not much otherwise if, instead
of beholding foolish nations, we take the great
and wise men, the eminent souls, and narrowly
inspect their biography. None of them seen by
himself, and his performance compared with his
promise or idea, will justify the cost of that
enormous apparatus of means by which this
spotted and defective person was at last procured.

To questions of this sort, Nature replies, ' I
grow.' All is nascent, infant. When we are

dizzied with the arithmetic of the savant toiling
to compute the length of her line, the return
of her curve, we are steadied by the perception
that a great deal is doing; that all seems just
begun; remote aims are in active accomplish-
ment. We can point nowhere to anything final;
but tendency appears on all hands: planet, system, constellation, total nature is growing like
a field of maize in July; is becoming somewhat
else; is in rapid metamorphosis. The embryo
does not more strive to be man, than yonder burr of light we call a nebula tends to be a
ring, a comet, a globe, and parent of new stars.
Why should not then these messieurs of Ver-
sailles strut and plot for tabourets and ribbons,
for a season, without prejudice to their faculty
to run on better errands by and by?

But Nature seems further to reply, 'I have
ventured so great a stake as my success, in no
single creature. I have not yet arrived at any
end. The gardener aims to produce a fine peach
or pear, but my aim is the health of the whole
tree, — root, stem, leaf, flower, and seed, — and
by no means the pampering of a monstrous
pericarp at the expense of all the other functions.'

In short, the spirit and peculiarity of that impression nature makes on us is this, that it does not exist to any one or to any number of particular ends, but to numberless and endless benefit; that there is in it no private will, no rebel leaf or limb, but the whole is oppressed by one superincumbent tendency, obeys that redundancy or excess of life which in conscious beings we call *ecstasy*.

With this conception of the genius or method of nature, let us go back to man. It is true he pretends to give account of himself to himself, but, at last, what has he to recite but the fact that there is a Life not to be described or known otherwise than by possession? What account can he give of his essence more than *so it was to be?* The *royal* reason, the Grace of God, seems the only description of our multiform but ever identical fact. There is virtue, there is genius, there is success, or there is not. There is the incoming or the receding of God: that is all we can affirm; and we can show neither how nor why. Self-accusation, remorse, and the didactic morals of self-denial and strife with sin, are in the view we are constrained by our constitution to take of the fact seen from the platform of action; but seen from the platform of intellection there is nothing for us but praise and wonder.

The termination of the world in a man appears to be the last victory of intelligence. The universal does not attract us until housed in an individual. Who heeds the waste abyss of possibility? The ocean is everywhere the same, but it has no character until seen with the shore or the ship. Who would value any number of miles of Atlantic brine bounded by lines of latitude and longitude? Confine it by granite rocks, let it wash a shore where wise men dwell, and it is filled with expression; and the point of greatest interest is where the land and water meet. So must we admire in man the form of the formless, the concentration of the vast, the house of reason, the cave of memory. See the play of thoughts! what nimble gigantic creatures are these! what saurians, what palaiotheria shall be named with these agile movers? The great Pan of old, who was clothed in a leopard skin to signify the beautiful variety of things, and the firmament, his coat of stars, — was but the representative of thee, O rich and various Man! thou palace of sight and sound, carrying in thy senses the morning and the night and the unfathomable galaxy; in thy brain, the geometry of the City of God; in thy heart, the bower of love and the realms of right and

wrong.¹ An individual man is a fruit which it
cost all the foregoing ages to form and ripen.
The history of the genesis or the old mytho-
logy repeats itself in the experience of every
child. He too is a demon or god thrown into
a particular chaos, where he strives ever to lead
things from disorder into order. Each individual soul is such in virtue of its being a power
to translate the world into some particular language of its own ; if not into a picture, a statue,
or a dance, — why, then, into a trade, an art, a
science, a mode of living, a conversation, a character, an influence. You admire pictures, but it
is as impossible for you to paint a right picture
as for grass to bear apples. But when the genius
comes, it makes fingers : it is pliancy, and the
power of transferring the affair in the street into
oils and colors. Raphael must be born, and Sal-
vator must be born.

There is no attractiveness like that of a new
man. The sleepy nations are occupied with their
political routine. England, France, and America
read Parliamentary Debates, which no high genius now enlivens ; and nobody will read them
who trusts his own eye: only they who are deceived by the popular repetition of distinguished
names. But when Napoleon unrolls his map,

the eye is commanded by original power. When Chatham leads the debate, men may well listen, because they must listen. A man, a personal ascendency, is the only great phenomenon. When Nature has work to be done, she creates a genius to do it. Follow the great man, and you shall see what the world has at heart in these ages. There is no omen like that.

But what strikes us in the fine genius is that which belongs of right to every one. A man should know himself for a necessary actor. A link was wanting between two craving parts of nature, and he was hurled into being as the bridge over that yawning need, the mediator betwixt two else unmarriageable facts. His two parents held each of them one of the wants, and the union of foreign constitutions in him enables him to do gladly and gracefully what the assembled human race could not have sufficed to do. He knows his materials; he applies himself to his work; he cannot read, or think, or look, but he unites the hitherto separated strands into a perfect cord. The thoughts he delights to utter are the reason of his incarnation. Is it for him to account himself cheap and superfluous, or to linger by the wayside for opportunities? Did he not come into being because

something must be done which he and no other
is and does? If only he *sees*, the world will be
visible enough. He need not study where to
stand, nor to put things in favorable lights;
in him is the light, from him all things are illuminated to their centre. What patron shall he
ask for employment and reward? Hereto was
he born, to deliver the thought of his heart
from the universe to the universe; to do an
office which nature could not forego, nor he be
discharged from rendering, and then immerge
again into the holy silence and eternity out of
which as a man he arose. God is rich, and many
more men than one he harbors in his bosom,
biding their time and the needs and the beauty
of all. Is not this the theory of every man's
genius or faculty? Why then goest thou as
some Boswell or listening worshipper to this
saint or to that? That is the only lese-majesty.
Here art thou with whom so long the universe
travailed in labor; darest thou think meanly
of thyself whom the stalwart Fate brought forth
to unite his ragged sides, to shoot the gulf, to
reconcile the irreconcilable?

Whilst a necessity so great caused the man
to exist, his health and erectness consist in the
fidelity with which he transmits influences from

the vast and universal to the point on which his genius can act. The ends are momentary; they are vents for the current of inward life which increases as it is spent. A man's wisdom is to know that all ends are momentary, that the best end must be superseded by a better. But there is a mischievous tendency in him to transfer his thought from the life to the ends, to quit his agency and rest in his acts: the tools run away with the workman, the human with the divine. I conceive a man as always spoken to from behind, and unable to turn his head and see the speaker. In all the millions who have heard the voice, none ever saw the face. As children in their play run behind each other, and seize one by the ears and make him walk before them, so is the spirit our unseen pilot. That well-known voice speaks in all languages, governs all men, and none ever caught a glimpse of its form. If the man will exactly obey it, it will adopt him, so that he shall not any longer separate it from himself in his thought; he shall seem to be it, he shall be it. If he listen with insatiable ears, richer and greater wisdom is taught him; the sound swells to a ravishing music, he is borne away as with a flood, he becomes careless of his food and of his house, he

is the fool of ideas, and leads a heavenly life.
But if his eye is set on the things to be done,
and not on the truth that is still taught, and for
the sake of which the things are to be done,
then the voice grows faint, and at last is but a
humming in his ears. His health and greatness
consist in his being the channel through which
heaven flows to earth, in short, in the fulness in
which an ecstatical state takes place in him. It
is pitiful to be an artist, when by forbearing to
be artists we might be vessels filled with the
divine overflowings, enriched by the circulations
of omniscience and omnipresence. Are there
not moments in the history of heaven when the
human race was not counted by individuals, but
was only the Influenced, was God in distribution, God rushing into multiform benefit? It
is sublime to receive, sublime to love, but this
lust of imparting as from *us*, this desire to be
loved, the wish to be recognized as individuals,
— is finite, comes of a lower strain.[1]

Shall I say then that as far as we can trace the
natural history of the soul, its health consists in
the fulness of its reception? — call it piety, call
it veneration, — in the fact that enthusiasm is
organized therein. What is best in any work of
art but that part which the work itself seems to

require and do; that which the man cannot do
again; that which flows from the hour and the
occasion, like the eloquence of men in a tu-
multuous debate?[1] It was always the theory of
literature that the word of a poet was authori-
tative and final. He was supposed to be the
mouth of a divine wisdom. We rather envied
his circumstance than his talent. We too could
have gladly prophesied standing in that place.
We so quote our Scriptures; and the Greeks so
quoted Homer, Theognis, Pindar, and the rest.
If the theory has receded out of modern criticism, it is because we have not had poets.
Whenever they appear, they will redeem their
own credit.[2]

This ecstatical state seems to direct a regard
to the whole and not to the parts; to the cause
and not to the ends; to the tendency and not
to the act. It respects genius and not talent;
hope, and not possession; the anticipation of all
things by the intellect, and not the history itself; art, and not works of art; poetry, and not
experiment; virtue, and not duties.

There is no office or function of man but is
rightly discharged by this divine method, and
nothing that is not noxious to him if detached
from its universal relations. Is it his work in

the world to study nature, or the laws of the
world? Let him beware of proposing to himself any end. Is it for use? nature is debased,
as if one looking at the ocean can remember
only the price of fish. Or is it for pleasure? he
is mocked; there is a certain infatuating air in
woods and mountains which draws on the idler
to want and misery. There is something social
and intrusive in the nature of all things; they
seek to penetrate and overpower each the nature of every other creature, and itself alone in
all modes and throughout space and spirit to
prevail and possess. Every star in heaven is
discontented and insatiable. Gravitation and
chemistry cannot content them. Ever they woo
and court the eye of every beholder. Every
man who comes into the world they seek to
fascinate and possess, to pass into his mind, for
they desire to republish themselves in a more
delicate world than that they occupy. It is not
enough that they are Jove, Mars, Orion, and
the North Star, in the gravitating firmament;
they would have such poets as Newton, Herschel and Laplace, that they may re-exist and
re-appear in the finer world of rational souls,
and fill that realm with their fame. So is it with
all immaterial objects. These beautiful basi-

lisks set their brute glorious eyes on the eye of
every child, and, if they can, cause their nature
to pass through his wondering eyes into him,
and so all things are mixed.[1]

Therefore man must be on his guard against
this cup of enchantments, and must look at nature with a supernatural eye. By piety alone,
by conversing with the cause of nature, is he
safe and commands it. And because all knowledge is assimilation to the object of knowledge,
as the power or genius of nature is ecstatic, so
must its science or the description of it be. The
poet must be a rhapsodist; his inspiration a sort
of bright casualty; his will in it only the sur-
render of will to the Universal Power, which
will not be seen face to face, but must be received and sympathetically known.[2] It is remarkable that we have, out of the deeps of
antiquity in the oracles ascribed to the half fab-
ulous Zoroaster, a statement of this fact which
every lover and seeker of truth will recognize.
" It is not proper," said Zoroaster, " to understand the Intelligible with vehemence, but if
you incline your mind, you will apprehend
it: not too earnestly, but bringing a pure and
inquiring eye. You will not understand it as
when understanding some particular thing, but

with the flower of the mind. Things divine are
not attainable by mortals who understand sensual things, but only the light-armed arrive at
the summit." [1]

And because ecstasy is the law and cause of
nature, therefore you cannot interpret it in too
high and deep a sense. Nature represents the
best meaning of the wisest man. Does the sunset landscape seem to you the place of Friendship, — those purple skies and lovely waters the
amphitheatre dressed and garnished only for the
exchange of thought and love of the purest
souls? It is that. All other meanings which
base men have put on it are conjectural and
false. You cannot bathe twice in the same river,
said Heraclitus; and I add, a man never sees
the same object twice: with his own enlargement the object acquires new aspects.

Does not the same law hold for virtue? It is
vitiated by too much will. He who aims at
progress should aim at an infinite, not at a special benefit. The reforms whose fame now fills
the land with Temperance, Anti-Slavery, Non-
Resistance, No Government, Equal Labor, fair
and generous as each appears, are poor bitter
things when prosecuted for themselves as an
end. To every reform, in proportion to its

energy, early disgusts are incident, so that the
disciple is surprised at the very hour of his first
triumphs with chagrins, and sickness, and a general distrust; so that he shuns his associates,
hates the enterprise which lately seemed so fair,
and meditates to cast himself into the arms of
that society and manner of life which he had
newly abandoned with so much pride and hope.
Is it that he attached the value of virtue to some
particular practices, as the denial of certain appetites in certain specified indulgences, and afterward found himself still as wicked and as far
from happiness in that abstinence as he had
been in the abuse? But the soul can be ap-
peased not by a deed but by a tendency. It is
in a hope that she feels her wings. You shall
love rectitude, and not the disuse of money or
the avoidance of trade; an unimpeded mind,
and not a monkish diet; sympathy and usefulness, and not hoeing or coopering. Tell me
not how great your project is, the civil libera-
tion of the world, its conversion into a Christian
church, the establishment of public education,
cleaner diet, a new division of labor and of land,
laws of love for laws of property; — I say to
you plainly there is no end to which your practical faculty can aim, so sacred or so large, that,

if pursued for itself, will not at last become car-
rion and an offence to the nostril. The imaginative faculty of the soul must be fed with objects immense and eternal. Your end should
be one inapprehensible to the senses ; then will
it be a god always approached, never touched ;
always giving health. A man adorns himself
with prayer and love, as an aim adorns an action. What is strong but goodness, and what is
energetic but the presence of a brave man? The
doctrine in vegetable physiology of the *presence*,
or the general influence of any substance over
and above its chemical influence, as of an alkali
or a living plant, is more predicable of man.
You need not speak to me, I need not go where
you are, that you should exert magnetism on
me. Be you only whole and sufficient, and I
shall feel you in every part of my life and fortune, and I can as easily dodge the gravitation
of the globe as escape your influence.

But there are other examples of this total and
supreme influence, besides Nature and the conscience. "From the poisonous tree, the world,"
say the Brahmins, "two species of fruit are produced, sweet as the waters of life ; Love or the
society of beautiful souls, and Poetry, whose
taste is like the immortal juice of Vishnu."

What is Love, and why is it the chief good, but because it is an overpowering enthusiasm? Never self-possessed or prudent, it is all abandonment. Is it not a certain admirable wisdom, preferable to all other advantages, and whereof all others are only secondaries and indemnities, because this is that in which the individual is no longer his own foolish master, but inhales an odorous and celestial air, is wrapped round with awe of the object, blending for the time that object with the real and only good, and consults every omen in nature with tremulous interest? When we speak truly,—is not he only unhappy who is not in love? his fancied freedom and self-rule — is it not so much death? He who is in love is wise and is becoming wiser, sees newly every time he looks at the object beloved, drawing from it with his eyes and his mind those virtues which it possesses. Therefore if the object be not itself a living and expanding soul, he presently exhausts it. But the love remains in his mind, and the wisdom it brought him; and it craves a new and higher object. And the reason why all men honor love is because it looks up and not down; aspires and not despairs.

And what is Genius but finer love, a love im-

personal, a love of the flower and perfection of
things, and a desire to draw a new picture or
copy of the same? It looks to the cause and
life: it proceeds from within outward, whilst
Talent goes from without inward. Talent finds
its models, methods, and ends, in society, exists
for exhibition, and goes to the soul only for
power to work. Genius is its own end, and
draws its means and the style of its architecture
from within, going abroad only for audience and
spectator, as we adapt our voice and phrase to
the distance and character of the ear we speak
to. All your learning of all literatures would
never enable you to anticipate one of its thoughts
or expressions, and yet each is natural and familiar as household words. Here about us coils
forever the ancient enigma, so old and so unut-
terable. Behold! there is the sun, and the rain,
and the rocks; the old sun, the old stones.
How easy were it to describe all this fitly; yet
no word can pass. Nature is a mute, and man,
her articulate, speaking brother, lo! he also is
a mute. Yet when Genius arrives, its speech
is like a river; it has no straining to describe,
more than there is straining in nature to exist.
When thought is best, there is most of it. Genius sheds wisdom like perfume, and advertises

us that it flows out of a deeper source than the foregoing silence, that it knows so deeply and speaks so musically, because it is itself a mutation of the thing it describes. It is sun and moon and wave and fire in music, as astronomy is thought and harmony in masses of matter.

What is all history but the work of ideas, a record of the incomputable energy which his infinite aspirations infuse into man? Has anything grand and lasting been done? Who did it? Plainly not any man, but all men: it was the prevalence and inundation of an idea. What brought the pilgrims here? One man says, civil liberty; another, the desire of founding a church; and a third discovers that the motive force was plantation and trade. But if the Puritans could rise from the dust they could not answer. It is to be seen in what they were, and not in what they designed; it was the growth and expansion of the human race, and resembled herein the sequent Revolution, which was not begun in Concord, or Lexington, or Virginia, but was the overflowing of the sense of natural right in every clear and active spirit of the period. Is a man boastful and knowing, and his own master? — we turn from him without hope: but let him be filled with awe and dread before the Vast and

the Divine, which uses him glad to be used, and
our eye is riveted to the chain of events. What
a debt is ours to that old religion which, in the
childhood of most of us, still dwelt like a sabbath morning in the country of New England,
teaching privation, self-denial and sorrow! A
man was born not for prosperity, but to suffer
for the benefit of others, like the noble rock-
maple which all around our villages bleeds for
the service of man. Not praise, not men's acceptance of our doing, but the spirit's holy
errand through us absorbed the thought. How
dignified was this! How all that is called talents
and success, in our noisy capitals, becomes buzz
and din before this man-worthiness![1] How our
friendships and the complaisances we use, shame
us now! Shall we not quit our companions, as
if they were thieves and pot-companions, and
betake ourselves to some desert cliff of Mount
Katahdin, some unvisited recess in Moosehead
Lake, to bewail our innocency and to recover it,
and with it the power to communicate again with
these sharers of a more sacred idea?

And what is to replace for us the piety of
that race? We cannot have theirs; it glides
away from us day by day; but we also can bask
in the great morning which rises forever out of

the eastern sea, and be ourselves the children
of the light. I stand here to say, Let us worship the mighty and transcendent Soul. It is
the office, I doubt not, of this age to annul that
adulterous divorce which the superstition of
many ages has effected between the intellect and
holiness. The lovers of goodness have been
one class, the students of wisdom another; as if
either could exist in any purity without the other.
Truth is always holy, holiness always wise. I
will that we keep terms with sin and a sinful
literature and society no longer, but live a life
of discovery and performance. Accept the intellect, and it will accept us. Be the lowly ministers of that pure omniscience, and deny it not
before men. It will burn up all profane literature, all base current opinions, all the false powers
of the world, as in a moment of time. I draw
from nature the lesson of an intimate divinity.
Our health and reason as men need our respect
to this fact, against the heedlessness and against
the contradiction of society. The sanity of man
needs the poise of this immanent force. His nobility needs the assurance of this inexhaustible
reserved power. How great soever have been
its bounties, they are a drop to the sea whence
they flow. If you say, 'The acceptance of the

vision is also the act of God:'—I shall not
seek to penetrate the mystery, I admit the force
of what you say. If you ask, 'How can any
rules be given for the attainment of gifts so
sublime?' I shall only remark that the solicitations of this spirit, as long as there is life, are
never forborne. Tenderly, tenderly, they woo
and court us from every object in nature, from
every fact in life, from every thought in the
mind. The one condition coupled with the gift
of truth is its use. That man shall be learned
who reduceth his learning to practice. Emanuel
Swedenborg affirmed that it was opened to him
"that the spirits who knew truth in this life, but
did it not, at death shall lose their knowledge."
"If knowledge," said Ali the Caliph,¹ "calleth
unto practice, well; if not, it goeth away." The
only way into nature is to enact our best insight.
Instantly we are higher poets, and can speak a
deeper law. Do what you know, and perception
is converted into character, as islands and con-
tinents were built by invisible infusories, or as
these forest leaves absorb light, electricity, and
volatile gases, and the gnarled oak to live a
thousand years is the arrest and fixation of the
most volatile and ethereal currents. The doctrine of this Supreme Presence is a cry of joy

and exultation. Who shall dare think he has
come late into nature, or has missed anything
excellent in the past, who seeth the admirable
stars of possibility, and the yet untouched continent of hope glittering with all its mountains
in the vast West? I praise with wonder this
great reality, which seems to drown all things in
the deluge of its light. What man seeing this,
can lose it from his thoughts, or entertain a
meaner subject? The entrance of this into his
mind seems to be the birth of man. We cannot describe the natural history of the soul, but
we know that it is divine. I cannot tell if these
wonderful qualities which house to-day in this
mortal frame shall ever re-assemble in equal
activity in a similar frame, or whether they have
before had a natural history like that of this
body you see before you; but this one thing I
know, that these qualities did not now begin to
exist, cannot be sick with my sickness, nor buried
in any grave; but that they circulate through
the Universe: before the world was, they were.
Nothing can bar them out, or shut them in, but
they penetrate the ocean and land, space and
time, form an essence, and hold the key to universal nature. I draw from this faith courage
and hope. All things are known to the soul. It

is not to be surprised by any communication. Nothing can be greater than it. Let those fear and those fawn who will. The soul is in her native realm, and it is wider than space, older than time, wide as hope, rich as love. Pusillanimity and fear she refuses with a beautiful scorn ; they are not for her who puts on her coronation robes, and goes out through universal love to universal power.

MAN THE REFORMER

A LECTURE READ BEFORE THE MECHANICS' APPREN-
TICES' LIBRARY ASSOCIATION, BOSTON,
JANUARY 25, 1841.

MAN THE REFORMER

MR. PRESIDENT, AND GENTLEMEN:

I WISH to offer to your consideration some
thoughts on the particular and general relations of man as a reformer. I shall assume that
the aim of each young man in this association is
the very highest that belongs to a rational mind.
Let it be granted that our life, as we lead it, is
common and mean; that some of those offices
and functions for which we were mainly created
are grown so rare in society that the memory
of them is only kept alive in old books and in
dim traditions; that prophets and poets, that
beautiful and perfect men we are not now, no,
nor have even seen such; that some sources of
human instruction are almost unnamed and unknown among us; that the community in which
we live will hardly bear to be told that every
man should be open to ecstacy or a divine illumination, and his daily walk elevated by intercourse with the spiritual world.[1] Grant all this,
as we must, yet I suppose none of my auditors
will deny that we ought to seek to establish
ourselves in such disciplines and courses as will
deserve that guidance and clearer communication

with the spiritual nature.   And further, I will
not dissemble my hope that each person whom
I address has felt his own call to cast aside all evil
customs, timidities, and limitations, and to be
in his place a free and helpful man, a reformer,
a benefactor, not content to slip along through
the world like a footman or a spy, escaping by
his nimbleness and apologies as many knocks
as he can, but a brave and upright man, who
must find or cut a straight road to everything
excellent in the earth, and not only go honorably
himself, but make it easier for all who follow
him to go in honor and with benefit.

In the history of the world the doctrine of Reform had never such scope as at the present hour.
Lutherans, Herrnhutters, Jesuits, Monks, Quakers, Knox, Wesley, Swedenborg, Bentham, in
their accusations of society, all respected something, — church or state, literature or history,
domestic usages, the market town, the dinner
table, coined money.   But now all these and all
things else hear the trumpet, and must rush to
judgment, — Christianity, the laws, commerce,
schools, the farm, the laboratory ; and not a
kingdom, town, statute, rite, calling, man, or
woman, but is threatened by the new spirit.

What if some of the objections whereby our

institutions are assailed are extreme and speculative, and the reformers tend to idealism? That
only shows the extravagance of the abuses which
have driven the mind into the opposite extreme.
It is when your facts and persons grow unreal
and fantastic by too much falsehood, that the
scholar flies for refuge to the world of ideas, and
aims to recruit and replenish nature from that
source.[1] Let ideas establish their legitimate
sway again in society, let life be fair and poetic,
and the scholars will gladly be lovers, citizens,
and philanthropists.

It will afford no security from the new ideas,
that the old nations, the laws of centuries, the
property and institutions of a hundred cities,
are built on other foundations. The demon of
reform has a secret door into the heart of every
lawmaker, of every inhabitant of every city.
The fact that a new thought and hope have
dawned in your breast, should apprize you that
in the same hour a new light broke in upon a
thousand private hearts. That secret which you
would fain keep, — as soon as you go abroad,
lo! there is one standing on the doorstep to
tell you the same. There is not the most
bronzed and sharpened money-catcher who does
not, to your consternation almost, quail and

shake the moment he hears a question prompted
by the new ideas. We thought he had some
semblance of ground to stand upon, that such
as he at least would die hard; but he trembles
and flees. Then the scholar says, 'Cities and
coaches shall never impose on me again; for
behold every solitary dream of mine is rushing
to fulfilment. That fancy I had, and hesitated to
utter because you would laugh,—the broker, the
attorney, the market-man are saying the same
thing. Had I waited a day longer to speak, I
had been too late. Behold, State Street thinks,
and Wall Street doubts, and begins to prophesy!'

It cannot be wondered at that this general
inquest into abuses should arise in the bosom
of society, when one considers the practical im-
pediments that stand in the way of virtuous
young men. The young man, on entering life,
finds the way to lucrative employments blocked
with abuses. The ways of trade are grown
selfish to the borders of theft, and supple to
the borders (if not beyond the borders) of fraud.
The employments of commerce are not intrin-
sically unfit for a man, or less genial to his
faculties; but these are now in their general
course so vitiated by derelictions and abuses at
which all connive, that it requires more vigor

and resources than can be expected of every
young man, to right himself in them; he is
lost in them; he cannot move hand or foot in
them. Has he genius and virtue? the less does
he find them fit for him to grow in, and if
he would thrive in them, he must sacrifice all
the brilliant dreams of boyhood and youth as
dreams; he must forget the prayers of his childhood and must take on him the harness of
routine and obsequiousness.   If not so minded,
nothing is left him but to begin the world anew,
as he does who puts the spade into the ground
for food.   We are all implicated of course in
this charge; it is only necessary to ask a few
questions as to the progress of the articles of
commerce from the fields where they grew, to
our houses, to become aware that we eat and
drink and wear perjury and fraud in a hundred
commodities.   How many articles of daily con-
sumption are furnished us from the West Indies; yet it is said that in the Spanish islands
the venality of the officers of the government
has passed into usage, and that no article passes
into our ships which has not been fraudulently
cheapened.   In the Spanish islands, every agent
or factor of the Americans, unless he be a con-
sul, has taken oath that he is a Catholic, or has

caused a priest to make that declaration for him.
The abolitionist has shown us our dreadful debt
to the southern negro. In the island of Cuba,
in addition to the ordinary abominations of
slavery, it appears only men are bought for the
plantations, and one dies in ten every year, of
these miserable bachelors, to yield us sugar. I
leave for those who have the knowledge the
part of sifting the oaths of our custom-houses;
I will not inquire into the oppression of the
sailors; I will not pry into the usages of our
retail trade. I content myself with the fact that
the general system of our trade (apart from the
blacker traits, which, I hope, are exceptions de-
nounced and unshared by all reputable men) is
a system of selfishness; is not dictated by the
high sentiments of human nature; is not measured by the exact law of reciprocity, much less
by the sentiments of love and heroism, but is a
system of distrust, of concealment, of superior
keenness, not of giving but of taking advantage.
It is not that which a man delights to unlock
to a noble friend; which he meditates on with
joy and self-approval in his hour of love and
aspiration; but rather what he then puts out
of sight, only showing the brilliant result, and
atoning for the manner of acquiring, by the

manner of expending it. I do not charge the
merchant or the manufacturer. The sins of our
trade belong to no class, to no individual. One
plucks, one distributes, one eats. Every body
partakes, every body confesses, — with cap and
knee volunteers his confession, yet none feels
himself accountable. He did not create the
abuse; he cannot alter it. What is he? an obscure private person who must get his bread.
That is the vice, — that no one feels himself
called to act for man, but only as a fraction of
man. It happens therefore that all such ingenuous souls as feel within themselves the irre-
pressible strivings of a noble aim, who by the
law of their nature must act simply, find these
ways of trade unfit for them, and they come
forth from it. Such cases are becoming more
numerous every year.

But by coming out of trade you have not
cleared yourself. The trail of the serpent
reaches into all the lucrative professions and
practices of man. Each has its own wrongs.
Each finds a tender and very intelligent conscience a disqualification for success. Each requires of the practitioner a certain shutting of
the eyes, a certain dapperness and compliance,
an acceptance of customs, a sequestration from

the sentiments of generosity and love, a compromise of private opinion and lofty integrity.
Nay, the evil custom reaches into the whole
institution of property, until our laws which
establish and protect it seem not to be the issue
of love and reason, but of selfishness. Suppose
a man is so unhappy as to be born a saint, with
keen perceptions but with the conscience and
love of an angel, and he is to get his living in
the world; he finds himself excluded from all
lucrative works; he has no farm, and he cannot
get one; for to earn money enough to buy one
requires a sort of concentration toward money,
which is the selling himself for a number of
years, and to him the present hour is as sacred
and inviolable as any future hour. Of course,
whilst another man has no land, my title to
mine, your title to yours, is at once vitiated.
Inextricable seem to be the twinings and ten-
drils of this evil, and we all involve ourselves
in it the deeper by forming connections, by
wives and children, by benefits and debts.[1]

Considerations of this kind have turned the
attention of many philanthropic and intelligent
persons to the claims of manual labor, as a part
of the education of every young man. If the
accumulated wealth of the past generation is

thus tainted, — no matter how much of it is offered to us, — we must begin to consider if it were not the nobler part to renounce it, and to put ourselves into primary relations with the soil and nature, and abstaining from whatever is dishonest and unclean, to take each of us bravely his part, with his own hands, in the manual labor of the world.

But it is said, ' What! will you give up the immense advantages reaped from the division of labor, and set every man to make his own shoes, bureau, knife, wagon, sails, and needle? This would be to put men back into barbarism by their own act.' I see no instant prospect of a virtuous revolution; yet I confess I should not be pained at a change which threatened a loss of some of the luxuries or conveniences of society, if it proceeded from a preference of the agricultural life out of the belief that our primary duties as men could be better discharged in that calling. Who could regret to see a high conscience and a purer taste exercising a sensible effect on young men in their choice of occupation, and thinning the ranks of competition in the labors of commerce, of law, and of state? It is easy to see that the inconvenience would last but a short time. This would be great

action, which always opens the eyes of men.
When many persons shall have done this, when
the majority shall admit the necessity of reform
in all these institutions, their abuses will be re-
dressed, and the way will be open again to the
advantages which arise from the division of
labor, and a man may select the fittest employment for his peculiar talent again, without compromise.[1]

But quite apart from the emphasis which the
times give to the doctrine that the manual labor
of society ought to be shared among all the
members, there are reasons proper to every individual why he should not be deprived of it.
The use of manual labor is one which never
grows obsolete, and which is inapplicable to no
person. A man should have a farm or a mechanical craft for his culture. We must have a
basis for our higher accomplishments, our delicate entertainments of poetry and philosophy,
in the work of our hands. We must have an
antagonism in the tough world for all the variety of our spiritual faculties, or they will not
be born. Manual labor is the study of the external world. The advantage of riches remains
with him who procured them, not with the
heir. When I go into my garden with a spade,

and dig a bed, I feel such an exhilaration and
health that I discover that I have been defraud-
ing myself all this time in letting others do for
me what I should have done with my own
hands. But not only health, but education is in
the work.[1] Is it possible that I, who get indefinite quantities of sugar, hominy, cotton, buck-
ets, crockery-ware, and letter-paper, by simply
signing my name once in three months to a
cheque in favor of John Smith & Co. traders,
get the fair share of exercise to my faculties by
that act which nature intended for me in making all these far-fetched matters important to
my comfort? It is Smith himself, and his car-
riers, and dealers, and manufacturers; it is the
sailor, the hide-drogher, the butcher, the negro,
the hunter, and the planter, who have inter-
cepted the sugar of the sugar, and the cotton
of the cotton. They have got the education, I
only the commodity. This were all very well
if I were necessarily absent, being detained by
work of my own, like theirs, work of the same
faculties; then should I be sure of my hands
and feet; but now I feel some shame before my
wood-chopper, my ploughman, and my cook,
for they have some sort of self-sufficiency, they
can contrive without my aid to bring the day

and year round, but I depend on them, and have not earned by use a right to my arms and feet.'

Consider further the difference between the first and second owner of property. Every species of property is preyed on by its own enemies, as iron by rust; timber by rot; cloth by moths; provisions by mould, putridity, or vermin; money by thieves; an orchard by insects; a planted field by weeds and the inroad of cattle; a stock of cattle by hunger; a road by rain and frost; a bridge by freshets. And whoever takes any of these things into his possession, takes the charge of defending them from this troop of enemies, or of keeping them in repair. A man who supplies his own want, who builds a raft or a boat to go a-fishing, finds it easy to caulk it, or put in a thole-pin, or mend the rudder. What he gets only as fast as he wants for his own ends, does not embarrass him, or take away his sleep with looking after. But when he comes to give all the goods he has year after year collected, in one estate to his son, —house, orchard, ploughed land, cattle, bridges, hardware, wooden-ware, carpets, cloths, provisions, books, money,—and cannot give him the skill and experience which made or collected

these, and the method and place they have in
his own life, the son finds his hands full, — not
to use these things, but to look after them and
defend them from their natural enemies. To
him they are not means, but masters. Their
enemies will not remit; rust, mould, vermin,
rain, sun, freshet, fire, all seize their own, fill
him with vexation, and he is converted from
the owner into a watchman or a watch-dog to
this magazine of old and new chattels. What
a change! Instead of the masterly good humor
and sense of power and fertility of resource in
himself; instead of those strong and learned
hands, those piercing and learned eyes, that
supple body, and that mighty and prevailing
heart which the father had, whom nature loved
and feared, whom snow and rain, water and
land, beast and fish seemed all to know and to
serve, — we have now a puny, protected person,
guarded by walls and curtains, stoves and down
beds, coaches, and men - servants and women-
servants from the earth and the sky, and who,
bred to depend on all these, is made anxious
by all that endangers those possessions, and is
forced to spend so much time in guarding them,
that he has quite lost sight of their original use,
namely, to help him to his ends, — to the pro-

secution of his love; to the helping of his friend,
to the worship of his God, to the enlargement
of his knowledge, to the serving of his country,
to the indulgence of his sentiment; and he is
now what is called a rich man, — the menial
and runner of his riches.[1]

Hence it happens that the whole interest of
history lies in the fortunes of the poor. Knowledge, Virtue, Power are the victories of man
over his necessities, his march to the dominion
of the world. Every man ought to have this
opportunity to conquer the world for himself.
Only such persons interest us, Spartans, Romans, Saracens, English, Americans, who have
stood in the jaws of need, and have by their
own wit and might extricated themselves, and
made man victorious.

I do not wish to overstate this doctrine of
labor, or insist that every man should be a
farmer, any more than that every man should
be a lexicographer. In general one may say that
the husbandman's is the oldest and most universal profession, and that where a man does
not yet discover in himself any fitness for one
work more than another, this may be preferred.
But the doctrine of the Farm is merely this,
that every man ought to stand in primary rela-

tions with the work of the world ; ought to do it himself, and not to suffer the accident of his having a purse in his pocket, or his having been bred to some dishonorable and injurious craft, to sever him from those duties ; and for this reason, that labor is God's education ; that he only is a sincere learner, he only can become a master, who learns the secrets of labor, and who by real cunning extorts from nature its sceptre.

Neither would I shut my ears to the plea of the learned professions, of the poet, the priest, the law - giver, and men of study generally ; namely, that in the experience of all men of that class, the amount of manual labor which is necessary to the maintenance of a family, indisposes and disqualifies for intellectual exertion. I know it often, perhaps usually, happens that where there is a fine organization, apt for poetry and philosophy, that individual finds himself compelled to wait on his thoughts ; to waste several days that he may enhance and glorify one ; and is better taught by a moderate and dainty exercise, such as rambling in the fields, rowing, skating, hunting, than by the downright drudgery of the farmer and the smith. I would not quite forget the venerable counsel of the Egyptian mysteries, which declared that

" there were two pairs of eyes in man, and it is requisite that the pair which are beneath should be closed, when the pair that are above them perceive, and that when the pair above are closed, those which are beneath should be opened." Yet I will suggest that no separation from labor can be without some loss of power and of truth to the seer himself; that, I doubt not, the faults and vices of our literature and philosophy, their too great fineness, effeminacy, and melancholy, are attributable to the enervated and sickly habits of the literary class. Better that the book should not be quite so good, and the book-maker abler and better, and not himself often a ludicrous contrast to all that he has written.

But granting that for ends so sacred and dear some relaxation must be had, I think that if a man find in himself any strong bias to poetry, to art, to the contemplative life, drawing him to these things with a devotion incompatible with good husbandry, that man ought to reckon early with himself, and, respecting the compensations of the Universe, ought to ransom himself from the duties of economy by a certain rigor and privation in his habits. For privileges so rare and grand, let him not stint to pay a great tax.

Let him be a cænobite, a pauper, and if need be, celibate also. Let him learn to eat his meals standing, and to relish the taste of fair water and black bread. He may leave to others the costly conveniences of housekeeping, and large hospitality, and the possession of works of art. Let him feel that genius is a hospitality, and that he who can create works of art needs not collect them. He must live in a chamber, and postpone his self-indulgence, forewarned and forearmed against that frequent misfortune of men of genius, — the taste for luxury. This is the tragedy of genius;—attempting to drive along the ecliptic with one horse of the heavens and one horse of the earth, there is only discord and ruin and downfall to chariot and charioteer.

The duty that every man should assume his own vows, should call the institutions of society to account, and examine their fitness to him, gains in emphasis if we look at our modes of living. Is our housekeeping sacred and honorable? Does it raise and inspire us, or does 't cripple us instead? I ought to be armed by every part and function of my household, by all my social function, by my economy, by my feasting, by my voting, by my traffic. Yet I am almost no party to any of these things. Custom does it for me, gives me no power therefrom, and runs me in debt to boot. We spend our incomes for paint and paper, for a hundred trifles, I know not what, and not for the things of a man. Our expense is almost all for conformity. It is for cake that we run in debt ; it is not the intellect, not the heart, not beauty, not worship, that costs so much. Why needs any man be rich ? Why must he have horses, fine garments, handsome apartments, access to public houses and places of amusement ? Only for want of thought. Give his mind a new image, and he flees into a solitary garden or garret to enjoy it, and is richer with that dream than the fee of a county could make him. But we are first thoughtless, and then find that we are moneyless. We are first sensual, and then must be rich. We dare not trust our wit for making our house pleasant to our friend, and so we buy ice-creams. He is accustomed to carpets, and we have not sufficient character to put floor cloths out of his mind whilst he stays in the house, and so we pile the floor with carpets. Let the house rather be a temple of the Furies of Lacedæmon, formidable and holy to all, which none but a Spartan may enter or so much as behold. As soon as there is faith, as soon as there is society, comfits

and cushions will be left to slaves. Expense
will be inventive and heroic. We shall eat hard
and lie hard, we shall dwell like the ancient
Romans in narrow tenements, whilst our public
edifices, like theirs, will be worthy for their proportion of the landscape in which we set them,
for conversation, for art, for music, for worship.
We shall be rich to great purposes; poor only
for selfish ones.

Now what help for these evils? How can the
man who has learned but one art, procure all the
conveniences of life honestly? Shall we say all
we think? — Perhaps with his own hands. Suppose he collects or makes them ill; — yet he
has learned their lesson. If he cannot do that?
— Then perhaps he can go without. Immense
wisdom and riches are in that. It is better to
go without, than to have them at too great a cost.
Let us learn the meaning of economy. Economy
is a high, humane office, a sacrament, when its
aim is grand; when it is the prudence of simple
tastes, when it is practised for freedom, or love, or
devotion. Much of the economy which we see in
houses is of a base origin, and is best kept out
of sight. Parched corn eaten to-day, that I may
have roast fowl to my dinner Sunday, is a base-
ness; but parched corn and a house with one

apartment, that I may be free of all perturbations, that I may be serene and docile to what the mind shall speak, and girt and road-ready for the lowest mission of knowledge or goodwill, is frugality for gods and heroes.

Can we not learn the lesson of self-help? Society is full of infirm people, who incessantly summon others to serve them. They contrive everywhere to exhaust for their single comfort the entire means and appliances of that luxury to which our invention has yet attained. Sofas, ottomans, stoves, wine, game-fowl, spices, perfumes, rides, the theatre, entertainments, — all these they want, they need, and whatever can be suggested more than these they crave also, as if it was the bread which should keep them from starving ; and if they miss any one, they represent themselves as the most wronged and most wretched persons on earth. One must have been born and bred with them to know how to prepare a meal for their learned stomach. Meantime they never bestir themselves to serve another person; not they ! they have a great deal more to do for themselves than they can possibly perform, nor do they once perceive the cruel joke of their lives, but the more odious they grow, the sharper is the tone of their complaining

and craving. Can anything be so elegant as to
have few wants and to serve them one's self, so
as to have somewhat left to give, instead of being
always prompt to grab? It is more elegant to
answer one's own needs than to be richly served;
inelegant perhaps it may look to-day, and to a
few, but it is an elegance forever and to all.

I do not wish to be absurd and pedantic in
reform. I do not wish to push my criticism on
the state of things around me to that extravagant mark that shall compel me to suicide, or
to an absolute isolation from the advantages of
civil society. If we suddenly plant our foot and
say, — I will neither eat nor drink nor wear nor
touch any food or fabric which I do not know
to be innocent, or deal with any person whose
whole manner of life is not clear and rational,
we shall stand still. Whose is so? Not mine;
not thine; not his. But I think we must clear
ourselves each one by the interrogation, whether
we have earned our bread to-day by the hearty
contribution of our energies to the common
benefit; and we must not cease to *tend* to the
correction of flagrant wrongs, by laying one
stone aright every day.

But the idea which now begins to agitate
society has a wider scope than our daily employ-

ments, our households, and the institutions of
property. We are to revise the whole of our
social structure, the State, the school, religion,
marriage, trade, science, and explore their foundations in our own nature; we are to see that
the world not only fitted the former men, but
fits us, and to clear ourselves of every usage
which has not its roots in our own mind.' What
is a man born for but to be a Reformer, a Re-
maker of what man has made; a renouncer of
lies; a restorer of truth and good, imitating
that great Nature which embosoms us all, and
which sleeps no moment on an old past, but
every hour repairs herself, yielding us▸ every
morning a new day, and with every pulsation a
new life? Let him renounce everything which
is not true to him, and put all his practices back
on their first thoughts, and do nothing for which
he has not the whole world for his reason. If
there are inconveniences and what is called ruin
in the way, because we have so enervated and
maimed ourselves, yet it would be like dying
of perfumes to sink in the effort to re-attach
the deeds of every day to the holy and mysterious recesses of life.

The power which is at once spring and regu-
lator in all efforts of reform is the conviction

that there is an infinite worthiness in man, which
will appear at the call of worth, and that all
particular reforms are the removing of some
impediment. Is it not the highest duty that
man should be honored in us ? I ought not
to allow any man, because he has broad lands, to
feel that he is rich in my presence. I ought to
make him feel that I can do without his riches,
that I cannot be bought, — neither by comfort,
neither by pride, — and though I be utterly pen-
niless, and receiving bread from him, that he
is the poor man beside me. And if, at the
same time, a woman or a child discovers a sentiment of piety, or a juster way of thinking than
mine, I ought to confess it by my respect and
obedience, though it go to alter my whole way
of life.[1]

The Americans have many virtues, but they
have not Faith and Hope. I know no two
words whose meaning is more lost sight of.
We use these words as if they were as obsolete
as Selah and Amen. And yet they have the
broadest meaning, and the most cogent application to Boston in this year. The Americans
have little faith. They rely on the power of a
dollar ; they are deaf to a sentiment. They
think you may talk the north wind down as

easily as raise society ; and no class more faithless than the scholars or intellectual men. Now
if I talk with a sincere wise man, and my friend,
with a poet, with a conscientious youth who is still
under the dominion of his own wild thoughts,
and not yet harnessed in the team of society to
drag with us all in the ruts of custom, I see at
once how paltry is all this generation of unbe-
lievers, and what a house of cards their institutions are, and I see what one brave man,
what one great thought executed might effect.
I see that the reason of the distrust of the practical man in all theory, is his inability to perceive the means whereby we work. Look, he
says, at the tools with which this world of yours
is to be built. As we cannot make a planet,
with atmosphere, rivers, and forests, by means
of the best carpenters' or engineers' tools, with
chemist's laboratory and smith's forge to boot,
— so neither can we ever construct that heavenly
society you prate of out of foolish, sick, selfish
men and women, such as we know them to be.
But the believer not only beholds his heaven
to be possible, but already to begin to exist, —
not by the men or materials the statesman uses,
but by men transfigured and raised above themselves by the power of principles. To princi-

ples something else is possible that transcends all the power of expedients.

Every great and commanding moment in the annals of the world is the triumph of some enthusiasm. The victories of the Arabs after Mahomet, who, in a few years, from a small and mean beginning, established a larger empire than that of Rome, is an example. They did they knew not what. The naked Derar, horsed on an idea, was found an overmatch for a troop of Roman cavalry. The women fought like men, and conquered the Roman men. They were miserably equipped, miserably fed. They were Temperance troops. There was neither brandy nor flesh needed to feed them. They conquered Asia, and Africa, and Spain, on barley. The Caliph Omar's walking-stick struck more terror into those who saw it than another man's sword.[1] His diet was barley bread; his sauce was salt; and oftentimes by way of abstinence he ate his bread without salt. His drink was water. His palace was built of mud; and when he left Medina to go to the conquest of Jerusalem, he rode on a red camel, with a wooden platter hanging at his saddle, with a bottle of water and two sacks, one holding barley and the other dried fruits.

But there will dawn ere long on our politics, on our modes of living, a nobler morning than that Arabian faith, in the sentiment of love. This is the one remedy for all ills, the panacea of nature. We must be lovers, and at once the impossible becomes possible. Our age and history, for these thousand years, has not been the history of kindness, but of selfishness. Our distrust is very expensive. The money we spend for courts and prisons is very ill laid out. We make, by distrust, the thief, and burglar, and incendiary, and by our court and jail we keep him so. An acceptance of the sentiment of love throughout Christendom for a season would bring the felon and the outcast to our side in tears, with the devotion of his faculties to our service. See this wide society of laboring men and women. We allow ourselves to be served by them, we live apart from them, and meet them without a salute in the streets.[1] We do not greet their talents, nor rejoice in their good fortune, nor foster their hopes, nor in the assembly · of the people vote for what is dear to them. Thus we enact the part of the selfish noble and king from the foundation of the world. See, this tree always bears one fruit. In every household, the peace of a pair is poi-

soned by the malice, slyness, indolence, and
alienation of domestics. Let any two matrons
meet, and observe how soon their conversation
turns on the troubles from their "*help,*" as our
phrase is. In every knot of laborers the rich
man does not feel himself among his friends, —
and at the polls he finds them arrayed in a mass
in distinct opposition to him. We complain
that the politics of masses of the people are
controlled by designing men, and led in opposition to manifest justice and the common weal,
and to their own interest. But the people do
not wish to be represented or ruled by the
ignorant and base. They only vote for these,
because they were asked with the voice and
semblance of kindness. They will not vote for
them long. They inevitably prefer wit and pro-
bity. To use an Egyptian metaphor, it is not
their will for any long time " to raise the nails
of wild beasts, and to depress the heads of the
sacred birds." ¹   Let our affection flow out to
our fellows ; it would operate in a day the greatest of all revolutions. It is better to work on
institutions by the sun than by the wind. The
State must consider the poor man, and all voices
must speak for him. Every child that is born
must have a just chance for his bread. Let the

amelioration in our laws of property proceed from the concession of the rich, not from the grasping of the poor. Let us begin by habitual imparting. Let us understand that the equitable rule is, that no one should take more than his share, let him be ever so rich. Let me feel that I am to be a lover. I am to see to it that the world is the better for me, and to find my reward in the act. Love would put a new face on this weary old world in which we dwell as pagans and enemies too long, and it would warm the heart to see how fast the vain diplomacy of statesmen, the impotence of armies, and navies, and lines of defence, would be superseded by this unarmed child. Love will creep where it cannot go, will accomplish that by imperceptible methods, — being its own lever, fulcrum, and power, — which force could never achieve. Have you not seen in the woods, in a late autumn morning, a poor fungus or mushroom, — a plant without any solidity, nay, that seemed nothing but a soft mush or jelly, — by its constant, total, and inconceivably gentle pushing, manage to break its way up through the frosty ground, and actually to lift a hard crust on its head ? It is the symbol of the power of kindness. The virtue of this principle in human society in application to great interests is obsolete and forgotten. Once or twice in history it has been tried in illustrious instances, with signal success. This great, overgrown, dead Christendom of ours still keeps alive at least the name of a lover of mankind. But one day all men will be lovers ; and every calamity will be dissolved in the universal sunshine.

Will you suffer me to add one trait more to this portrait of man the reformer ? The mediator between the spiritual and the actual world should have a great prospective prudence. An Arabian poet describes his hero by saying,

> Sunshine was he
> In the winter day;
> And in the midsummer
> Coolness and shade.

He who would help himself and others should not be a subject of irregular and interrupted impulses of virtue, but a continent, persisting, immovable person, — such as we have seen a few scattered up and down in time for the blessing of the world ; men who have in the gravity of their nature a quality which answers to the fly-wheel in a mill, which distributes the motion equably over all the wheels and hinders it from falling unequally and suddenly in destructive shocks. It is better that joy should be spread over all the day in the form of strength, than that it should be concentrated into ecstasies, full of danger and followed by reactions. There is a sublime prudence which is the very highest that we know of man, which, believing in a vast future, — sure of more to come than is yet seen, — postpones always the present hour to the whole life; postpones talent to genius, and special results to character. As the merchant gladly takes money from his income to add to his capital, so is the great man very willing to lose particular powers and talents, so that he gain in the elevation of his life. The opening of the spiritual senses disposes men ever to greater sacrifices, to leave their signal talents, their best means and skill of procuring a present success, their power and their fame, — to cast all things behind, in the insatiable thirst for divine communications. A purer fame, a greater power rewards the sacrifice. It is the conversion of our harvest into seed. As the farmer casts into the ground the finest ears of his grain, the time will come when we too shall hold nothing back, but shall eagerly convert more than we now possess into means and powers, when we shall be willing to sow the sun and the moon for seeds.[1]

LECTURE ON THE TIMES

READ AT THE MASONIC TEMPLE, BOSTON,
DECEMBER 2, 1841

.

LECTURE ON THE TIMES

THE TIMES, as we say — or the present
aspects of our social state, the Laws, Divinity, Natural Science, Agriculture, Art, Trade,
Letters, have their root in an invisible spiritual
reality. To appear in these aspects, they must
first exist, or have some necessary foundation.
Beside all the small reasons we assign, there is
a great reason for the existence of every extant
fact; a reason which lies grand and immovable,
often unsuspected, behind it in silence. The
Times are the masquerade of the Eternities;
trivial to the dull, tokens of noble and majestic
agents to the wise; the receptacle in which the
Past leaves its history; the quarry out of which
the genius of to-day is building up the Future.[1]
The Times — the nations, manners, institutions,
opinions, votes, are to be studied as omens, as
sacred leaves, whereon a weighty sense is inscribed, if we have the wit and the love to search
it out. Nature itself seems to propound to us
this topic, and to invite us to explore the meaning of the conspicuous facts of the day. Everything that is popular, it has been said, deserves
the attention of the philosopher: and this for the

obvious reason, that although it may not be of any worth in itself, yet it characterizes the people.

Here is very good matter to be handled, if we are skilful; an abundance of important practical questions which it behooves us to understand. Let us examine the pretensions of the attacking and defending parties. Here is this great fact of Conservatism, entrenched in its immense redoubts, with Himmaleh for its front, and Atlas for its flank, and Andes for its rear, and the Atlantic and Pacific seas for its ditches and trenches; which has planted its crosses, and crescents, and stars and stripes, and various signs and badges of possession, over every rood of the planet, and says, ' I will hold fast; and to whom I will, will I give; and whom I will, will I exclude and starve:' so says Conservatism; and all the children of men attack the colossus in their youth, and all, or all but a few, bow before it when they are old. A necessity not yet commanded, a negative imposed on the will of man by his condition, a deficiency in his force, is the foundation on which it rests. Let this side be fairly stated. Meantime, on the other part, arises Reform, and offers the sentiment of Love as an overmatch to this material might.¹ I wish to consider well this affirmative side, which has a loftier port and reason than heretofore, which encroaches on the other every day, puts it out of countenance, out of reason, and out of temper, and leaves it nothing but silence and possession.

The fact of aristocracy, with its two weapons of wealth and manners, is as commanding a feature of the nineteenth century and the American republic as of old Rome, or modern England. The reason and influence of wealth, the aspect of philosophy and religion, and the tendencies which have acquired the name of Transcendentalism in Old and New England; the aspect of poetry, as the exponent and interpretation of these things; the fuller development and the freer play of Character as a social and political agent; — these and other related topics will in turn come to be considered.

But the subject of the Times is not an abstract question. We talk of the world, but we mean a few men and women. If you speak of the age, you mean your own platoon of people, as Dante and Milton painted in colossal their platoons, and called them Heaven and Hell. In our idea of progress, we do not go out of this personal picture. We do not think the sky will be bluer, or honey sweeter, or our climate more temperate, but only that our relation to

our fellows will be simpler and happier. What
is the reason to be given for this extreme attraction which *persons* have for us, but that they are
the Age? they are the results of the Past; they
are the heralds of the Future. They indicate,
— these witty, suffering, blushing, intimidating
figures of the only race in which there are individuals or changes, how far on the Fate has gone,
and what it drives at.[1] As trees make scenery,
and constitute the hospitality of the landscape,
so persons are the world to persons, — a cunning
mystery by which the Great Desert of thoughts
and of planets takes this engaging form, to bring,
as it would seem, its meanings nearer to the mind.
Thoughts walk and speak, and look with eyes
at me, and transport me into new and magnificent scenes. These are the pungent instructors
who thrill the heart of each of us, and make all
other teaching formal and cold. How I follow
them with aching heart, with pining desire! I
count myself nothing before them. I would die
for them with joy. They can do what they will
with me. How they lash us with those tongues!
How they make the tears start, make us blush
and turn pale, and lap us in Elysium to sooth-
ing dreams and castles in the air! By tones of
triumph, of dear love, by threats, by pride that

freezes, these have the skill to make the world look bleak and inhospitable, or seem the nest of tenderness and joy. I do not wonder at the miracles which poetry attributes to the music of Orpheus, when I remember what I have experienced from the varied notes of the human voice. They are an incalculable energy which countervails all other forces in nature, because they are the channel of supernatural powers. There is no interest or institution so poor and withered, but if a new strong man could be born into it, he would immediately redeem and replace it. A personal ascendency,— that is the only fact much worth considering. I remember, some years ago, somebody shocked a circle of friends of order here in Boston, who supposed that our people were identified with their religious denominations, by declaring that an eloquent man,— let him be of what sect soever,—would be ordained at once in one of our metropolitan churches. To be sure he would ; and not only in ours but in any church, mosque, or temple on the planet ; but he must be eloquent, able to supplant our method and classification by the superior beauty of his own.¹ Every fact we have was brought here by some person ; and there is none that will not change and pass away before a person whose nature is broader than the person which the fact in question represents. And so I find the Age walking about in happy and hopeful natures, in strong eyes and pleasant thoughts, and think I read it nearer and truer so, than in the statute-book, or in the investments of capital, which rather celebrate with mournful music the obsequies of the last age. In the brain of a fanatic; in the wild hope of a mountain boy, called by city boys very ignorant, because they do not know what his hope has certainly apprized him shall be; in the love-glance of a girl; in the hair-splitting conscientiousness of some eccentric person who has found some new scruple to embarrass himself and his neighbors withal is to be found that which shall constitute the times to come, more than in the now organized and accredited oracles. For whatever is affirmative and now advancing, contains it. I think that only is real which men love and rejoice in; not what they tolerate, but what they choose; what they embrace and avow, and not the things which chill, benumb, and terrify them.

And so why not draw for these times a portrait gallery? Let us paint the painters. Whilst the Daguerreotypist, with camera-obscura and silver plate, begins now to traverse the land,

let us set up our Camera also, and let the sun
paint the people. Let us paint the agitator, and
the man of the old school, and the member of
Congress, and the college professor, the formidable editor, the priest and reformer, the contemplative girl, and the fair aspirant for fashion
and opportunities, the woman of the world who
has tried and knows; — let us examine how
well she knows. Could we indicate the indi-
cators, indicate those who most accurately represent every good and evil tendency of the
general mind, in the just order which they take
on this canvas of Time, so that all witnesses
should recognize a spiritual law as each well-
known form flitted for a moment across the
wall, we should have a series of sketches which
would report to the next ages the color and
quality of ours.

Certainly I think if this were done there
would be much to admire as well as to con-
demn; souls of as lofty a port as any in Greek
or Roman fame might appear; men of great
heart, of strong hand, and of persuasive speech;
subtle thinkers, and men of wide sympathy,
and an apprehension which looks over all history and everywhere recognizes its own. To
be sure, there will be fragments and hints of

men, more than enough : bloated promises, which end in nothing or little. And then truly great men, but with some defect in their composition which neutralizes their whole force. Here is a Damascus blade, such as you may search through nature in vain to parallel, laid up on the shelf in some village to rust and ruin. And how many seem not quite available for that idea which they represent? Now and then comes a bolder spirit, I should rather say, a more surrendered soul, more informed and led by God, which is much in advance of the rest, quite beyond their sympathy, but predicts what shall soon be the general fulness ; as when we stand by the seashore, whilst the tide is coming in, a wave comes up the beach far higher than any foregoing one, and recedes ; and for a long while none comes up to that mark ; but after some time the whole sea is there and beyond it.

But we are not permitted to stand as spectators of the pageant which the times exhibit ; we are parties also, and have a responsibility which is not to be declined. A little while this interval of wonder and comparison is permitted us, but to the end that we shall play a manly part. As the solar system moves forward in the heavens, certain stars open before us, and certain stars close up behind us; so is man's life. The reputations that were great and inaccessible change and tarnish. How great were once Lord Bacon's dimensions! he is now reduced almost to the middle height; and many another star has turned out to be a planet or an asteroid: only a few are the fixed stars which have no parallax, or none for us. The change and decline of old reputations are the gracious marks of our own growth. Slowly, like light of morning, it steals on us, the new fact, that we who were pupils or aspirants are now society: do compose a portion of that head and heart we are wont to think worthy of all reverence and heed. We are the representatives of religion and intellect, and stand in the light of Ideas, whose rays stream through us to those younger and more in the dark. What further relations we sustain, what new lodges we are entering, is now unknown. To-day is a king in disguise. To-day always looks mean to the thoughtless, in the face of an uniform experience that all good and great and happy actions are made up precisely of these blank to-days.[1] Let us not be so deceived. Let us unmask the king as he passes. Let us not inhabit times of wonderful and various promise without divining their tendency. Let us not see the foundations of nations, and of a new and better order of things laid, with roving eyes, and an attention preoccupied with trifles.

The two omnipresent parties of History, the party of the Past and the party of the Future, divide society to-day as of old. Here is the innumerable multitude of those who accept the state and the church from the last generation, and stand on no argument but possession. They have reason also, and, as I think, better reason than is commonly stated. No Burke, no Metternich has yet done full justice to the side of conservatism. But this class, however large, relying not on the intellect but on the instinct, blends itself with the brute forces of nature, is respectable only as nature is ; but the individuals have no attraction for us. It is the dissenter, the theorist, the aspirant, who is quitting this ancient domain to embark on seas of adventure, who engages our interest. Omitting then for the present all notice of the stationary class, we shall find that the movement party divides itself into two classes, the actors, and the students.

The actors constitute that great army of martyrs who, at least in America, by their con-

science and philanthropy, occupy the ground
which Calvinism occupied in the last age, and
compose the visible church of the existing generation. The present age will be marked by its
harvest of projects for the reform of domestic, civil, literary, and ecclesiastical institutions.
The leaders of the crusades against War, Negro
slavery, Intemperance, Government based on
force, Usages of trade, Court and Custom-house
Oaths, and so on to the agitators on the system of Education and the laws of Property, are
the right successors of Luther, Knox, Robinson,
Fox, Penn, Wesley, and Whitefield. They have
the same virtues and vices; the same noble
impulse, and the same bigotry. These movements are on all accounts important; they not
only check the special abuses, but they educate
the conscience and the intellect of the people.
How can such a question as the Slave-trade
be agitated for forty years by all the Christian
nations, without throwing great light on ethics
into the general mind? The fury with which
the slave-trader defends every inch of his bloody
deck and his howling auction - platform, is a
trumpet to alarm the ear of mankind, to wake
the dull, and drive all neutrals to take sides and
to listen to the argument and the verdict. The

Temperance-question, which rides the conversation of ten thousand circles, and is tacitly recalled at every public and at every private table, drawing with it all the curious ethics of the Pledge, of the Wine-question, of the equity of the manufacture and the trade, is a gymnastic training to the casuistry and conscience of the time. Anti-masonry had a deep right and wrong, which gradually emerged to sight out of the turbid controversy. The political questions touching the Banks; the Tariff; the limits of the executive power; the right of the constituent to instruct the representative; the treatment of the Indians; the Boundary wars; the Congress of nations; are all pregnant with ethical conclusions; and it is well if government and our social order can extricate themselves from these alembics and find themselves still government and social order. The student of history will hereafter compute the singular value of our endless discussion of questions to the mind of the period.

Whilst each of these aspirations and attempts of the people for the Better is magnified by the natural exaggeration of its advocates, until it excludes the others from sight, and repels discreet persons by the unfairness of the plea, the

movements are in reality all parts of one movement.   There is a perfect chain, — see it, or
see it not, — of reforms emerging from the surrounding darkness, each cherishing some part
of the general idea, and all must be seen in order
to do justice to any one.   Seen in this their
natural connection, they are sublime.[1] The conscience of the Age demonstrates itself in this
effort to raise the life of man by putting it in
harmony with his idea of the Beautiful and the
Just.   The history of reform is always identical,
it is the comparison of the idea with the fact.
Our modes of living are not agreeable to our
imagination.   We suspect they are unworthy.
We arraign our daily employments. They appear to us unfit, unworthy of the faculties we
spend on them.   In conversation with a wise
man, we find ourselves apologizing for our employments ; we speak of them with shame.
Nature, literature, science, childhood, appear to
us beautiful ; but not our own daily work, not
the ripe fruit and considered labors of man.
This beauty which the fancy finds in everything
else, certainly accuses the manner of life we lead.
Why should it be hateful?   Why should it
contrast thus with all natural beauty?   Why
should it not be poetic, and invite and raise us?

Is there a necessity that the works of man
should be sordid ? Perhaps not. — Out of this
fair Idea in the mind springs the effort at the
Perfect. It is the interior testimony to a fairer
possibility of life and manners which agitates
society every day with the offer of some new
amendment. If we would make more strict inquiry concerning its origin, we find ourselves
rapidly approaching the inner boundaries of
thought, that term where speech becomes silence, and science conscience. For the origin
of all reform is in that mysterious fountain
of the moral sentiment in man, which, amidst
the natural, ever contains the supernatural for
men. That is new and creative. That is alive.
That alone can make a man other than he is.
Here or nowhere resides unbounded energy,
unbounded power.

The new voices in the wilderness crying "Re-
pent," have revived a hope, which had well-
nigh perished out of the world, that the thoughts
of the mind may yet, in some distant age, in
some happy hour, be executed by the hands.
That is the hope, of which all other hopes are
parts. For some ages, these ideas have been
consigned to the poet and musical composer, to
the prayers and the sermons of churches; but

the thought that they can ever have any foot-
ing in real life, seems long since to have been
exploded by all judicious persons.   Milton, in
his best tract, describes a relation between religion and the daily occupations, which is true
until this time.

" A wealthy man, addicted to his pleasure
and to his profits, finds religion to be a traffic
so entangled, and of so many piddling accounts,
that of all mysteries he cannot skill to keep a
stock going upon that trade.   What should
he do ?   Fain he would have the name to be
religious ; fain he would bear up with his neighbors in that.   What does he therefore, but resolve to give over toiling, and to find himself
out some factor, to whose care and credit he
may commit the whole managing of his religious
affairs ; some divine of note and estimation that
must be.   To him he adheres, resigns the whole
warehouse of his religion, with all the locks and
keys, into his custody ; and indeed makes the
very person of that man his religion ; esteems
his associating with him a sufficient evidence and
commendatory of his own piety.   So that a man
may say his religion is now no more within himself, but is become a dividual moveable, and
goes and comes near him, according as that good

man frequents the house. He entertains him, gives him gifts, feasts him, lodges him; his religion comes home at night, prays, is liberally supped, and sumptuously laid to sleep; rises, is saluted, and after the malmsey, or some well spiced bruage, and better breakfasted than he whose morning appetite would have gladly fed on green figs between Bethany and Jerusalem, his religion walks abroad at eight, and leaves his kind entertainer in the shop, trading all day without his religion." [1]

This picture would serve for our times. Religion was not invited to eat or drink or sleep with us, or to make or divide an estate, but was a holiday guest. Such omissions judge the church; as the compromise made with the slaveholder, not much noticed at first, every day appears more flagrant mischief to the American constitution. But now the purists are looking into all these matters. The more intelligent are growing uneasy on the subject of Marriage. They wish to see the character represented also in that covenant. There shall be nothing brutal in it, but it shall honor the man and the woman, as much as the most diffusive and universal action. Grimly the same spirit looks into the law of Property, and accuses men of driving a trade in the great boundless providence which had given the air, the water, and the land to men, to use and not to fence in and monopolize. It casts its eye on Trade, and Day Labor, and so it goes up and down, paving the earth with eyes, destroying privacy and making thorough-lights. Is all this for nothing? Do you suppose that the reforms which are preparing will be as superficial as those we know?

By the books it reads and translates, judge what books it will presently print. A great deal of the profoundest thinking of antiquity, which had become as good as obsolete for us, is now re-appearing in extracts and allusions, and in twenty years will get all printed anew. See how daring is the reading, the speculation, the experimenting of the time. If now some genius shall arise who could unite these scattered rays! And always such a genius does embody the ideas of each time. Here is great variety and richness of mysticism, each part of which now only disgusts whilst it forms the sole thought of some poor Perfectionist or " Comer out," yet when it shall be taken up as the garniture of some profound and all-reconciling thinker, will appear the rich and appropriate decoration of his robes.

These reforms are our contemporaries ; they
are ourselves ; our own light, and sight, and
conscience ; they only name the relation which
subsists between us and the vicious institutions
which they go to rectify. They are the simplest
statements of man in these matters ; the plain
right and wrong. I cannot choose but allow
and honor them. The impulse is good, and
the theory ; the practice is less beautiful. The
Reformers affirm the inward life, but they do
not trust it, but use outward and vulgar means.
They do not rely on precisely that strength
which wins me to their cause ; not on love, not
on a principle, but on men, on multitudes, on
circumstances, on money, on party ; that is, on
fear, on wrath, and pride. The love which lifted
men to the sight of these better ends was the
true and best distinction of this time, the disposition to trust a principle more than a material
force. I think *that* the soul of reform ; the conviction that not sensualism, not slavery, not war,
not imprisonment, not even government, are
needed, — but in lieu of them all, reliance on
the sentiment of man, which will work best the
more it is trusted; not reliance on numbers, but,
contrariwise, distrust of numbers and the feeling
that then are we strongest when most private

and alone. The young men who have been vexing society for these last years with regenerative methods seem to have made this mistake; they all exaggerated some special means, and all failed to see that the Reform of Reforms must be accomplished without means.

The Reforms have their high origin in an ideal justice, but they do not retain the purity of an idea. They are quickly organized in some low, inadequate form, and present no more poetic image to the mind than the evil tradition which they reprobated. They mix the fire of the moral sentiment with personal and party heats, with measureless exaggerations, and the blindness that prefers some darling measure to justice and truth. Those who are urging with most ardor what are called the greatest benefits of mankind, are narrow, self-pleasing, conceited men, and affect us as the insane do. They bite us, and we run mad also.[1] I think the work of the reformer as innocent as other work that is done around him ; but when I have seen it near, I do not like it better. It is done in the same way, it is done profanely, not piously ; by management, by tactics and clamor. It is a buzz in the ear. I cannot feel any pleasure in sacrifices which display to me such partiality of character.

We do not want actions, but men ; not a chemical drop of water, but rain ; the spirit that sheds
and showers actions, countless, endless actions.
You have on some occasion played a bold part.
You have set your heart and face against society when you thought it wrong, and returned it
frown for frown. Excellent : now can you afford
to forget, it, reckoning all your action no more
than the passing of your hand through the air,
or a little breath of your mouth ? The world
leaves no track in space, and the greatest action
of man no mark in the vast idea.[1] To the youth
diffident of his ability and full of compunction
at his unprofitable existence, the temptation is
always great to lend himself to public movements, and as one of a party accomplish what
he cannot hope to effect alone. But he must
resist the degradation of a man to a measure.
I must get with truth, though I should never
come to act, as you call it, with effect. I must
consent to inaction. A patience which is grand ;
a brave and cold neglect of the offices which
prudence exacts, so it be done in a deep upper
piety ; a consent to solitude and inaction which
proceeds out of an unwillingness to violate
character, is the century which makes the gem.
Whilst therefore I desire to express the respect

and joy I feel before this sublime connection
of reforms now in their infancy around us, I
urge the more earnestly the paramount duties
of self-reliance. I cannot find language of sufficient energy to convey my sense of the sacredness of private integrity. All men, all things,
the state, the church, yea, the friends of the heart
are phantasms and unreal beside the sanctuary
of the heart. With so much awe, with so much
fear, let it be respected.

The great majority of men, unable to judge
of any principle until its light falls on a fact, are
not aware of the evil that is around them until
they see it in some gross form, as in a class of
intemperate men, or slaveholders, or soldiers,
or fraudulent persons. Then they are greatly
moved; and magnifying the importance of that
wrong, they fancy that if that abuse were re-
dressed all would go well, and they fill the land
with clamor to correct it. Hence the mission-
ary, and other religious efforts. If every island
and every house had a Bible, if every child
was brought into the Sunday School, would the
wounds of the world heal, and man be upright?

But the man of ideas, accounting the circumstance nothing, judges of the commonwealth
from the state of his own mind. 'If,' he says,

'I am selfish, then is there slavery, or the effort
to establish it, wherever I go. But if I am just,
then is there no slavery, let the laws say what
they will. For if I treat all men as gods, how
to me can there be any such thing as a slave?'
But how frivolous is your war against circumstances. This denouncing philanthropist is himself a slaveholder in every word and look. Does
he free me? Does he cheer me? He is the
state of Georgia, or Alabama, with their san-
guinary slave-laws, walking here on our north-
eastern shores. We are all thankful he has no
more political power, as we are fond of liberty
ourselves. I am afraid our virtue is a little geo-
graphical. I am not mortified by our vice; that
is obduracy; it colors and palters, it curses and
swears, and I can see to the end of it; but I
own our virtue makes me ashamed; so sour and
narrow, so thin and blind, virtue so vice-like.'
Then again, how trivial seem the contests of the
abolitionist, whilst he aims merely at the circumstance of the slave. Give the slave the least
elevation of religious sentiment, and he is no
slave; you are the slave; he not only in his
humility feels his superiority, feels that much
deplored condition of his to be a fading trifle,
but he makes you feel it too. He is the mas-

ter. The exaggeration which our young people make of his wrongs, characterizes themselves. What are no trifles to them, they naturally think are no trifles to Pompey.

We say then that the reforming movement is sacred in its origin; in its management and details, timid and profane. These benefactors hope to raise man by improving his circumstances: by combination of that which is dead they hope to make something alive. In vain. By new infusions alone of the spirit by which he is made and directed, can he be re-made and reinforced. The sad Pestalozzi, who shared with all ardent spirits the hope of Europe on the outbreak of the French Revolution, after witnessing its sequel, recorded his conviction that "the amelioration of outward circumstances will be the effect but can never be the means of mental and moral improvement." Quitting now the class of actors, let us turn to see how it stands with the other class of which we spoke, namely, the students.

A new disease has fallen on the life of man. Every Age, like every human body, has its own distemper. Other times have had war, or famine, or a barbarism, domestic or bordering, as their antagonism. Our forefathers walked in the

world and went to their graves tormented with
the fear of Sin and the terror of the Day of
Judgment. These terrors have lost their force,
and our torment is Unbelief, the Uncertainty
as to what we ought to do; the distrust of the
value of what we do, and the distrust that the
Necessity (which we all at last believe in) is fair
and beneficent. Our Religion assumes the negative form of rejection. Out of love of the true,
we repudiate the false; and the Religion is an
abolishing criticism. A great perplexity hangs
like a cloud on the brow of all cultivated persons, a certain imbecility in the best spirits,
which distinguishes the period. We do not find
the same trait in the Arabian, in the Hebrew, in
Greek, Roman, Norman, English periods; no,
but in other men a natural firmness. The men
did not see beyond the need of the hour. They
planted their foot strong, and doubted nothing.
We mistrust every step we take. We find it the
worst thing about time that we know not what
to do with it.[1]   We are so sharp-sighted that we
can neither work nor think, neither read Plato
nor not read him.

Then there is what is called a too intellectual
tendency. Can there be too much intellect?
We have never met with any such excess. But

the criticism which is levelled at the laws and manners, ends in thought, without causing a new method of life. The genius of the day does not incline to a deed, but to a beholding. It is not that men do not wish to act; they pine to be employed, but are paralyzed by the uncertainty what they should do. The inadequacy of the work to the faculties is the painful perception which keeps them still. This happens to the best. ˙ Then, talents bring their usual temptations, and the current literature and poetry with perverse ingenuity draw us away from life to solitude and meditation. This could well be borne, if it were great and involuntary; if the men were ravished by their thought, and hurried into ascetic extravagances. Society could then manage to release their shoulder from its wheel and grant them for a time this privilege of sabbath. But they are not so. Thinking, which was a rage, is become an art. The thinker gives me results, and never invites me to be present with him at his invocation of truth, and to enjoy with him its proceeding into his mind.

So little action amidst such audacious and yet sincere profession, that we begin to doubt if that great revolution in the art of war, which has made it a game of posts instead of a game of battles, has not operated on Reform; whether this be not also a war of posts, a paper blockade, in which each party is to display the utmost resources of his spirit and belief, and no conflict occur, but the world shall take that course which the demonstration of the truth shall indicate.

But we must pay for being too intellectual, as they call it. People are not as light-hearted for it. I think men never loved life less. I question if care and doubt ever wrote their names so legibly on the faces of any population. This *Ennui*, for which we Saxons had no name, this word of France has got a terrific significance. It shortens life, and bereaves the day of its light. Old age begins in the nursery, and before the young American is put into jacket and trowsers, he says, ' I want something which I never saw before;' and ' I wish I was not I.' I have seen the same gloom on the brow even of those adventurers from the intellectual class who had dived deepest and with most success into active life. I have seen the authentic sign of anxiety and perplexity on the greatest forehead of the State. The canker worms have crawled to the topmost bough of the wild elm, and swing down from that. Is there less oxygen in the atmosphere? What has checked in this age the animal spirits which gave to our forefathers their bounding pulse?

But have a little patience with this melancholy humor. Their unbelief arises out of a greater Belief; their inaction out of a scorn of inadequate action. By the side of these men, the hot agitators have a certain cheap and ridiculous air; they even look smaller than the others. Of the two, I own I like the speculators best. They have some piety which looks with faith to a fair Future, unprofaned by rash and unequal attempts to realize it. And truly we shall find much to console us, when we consider the cause of their uneasiness. It is the love of greatness, it is the need of harmony, the contrast of the dwarfish Actual with the exorbitant Idea. No man can compare the ideas and aspirations of the innovators of the present day with those of former periods, without feeling how great and high this criticism is. The revolutions that impend over society are not now from ambition and rapacity, from impatience of one or another form of government, but from new modes of thinking, which shall recompose society after a new order, which shall animate labor by love and science, which shall destroy the value of

many kinds of property and replace all property within the dominion of reason and equity.
There was never so great a thought laboring in
the breasts of men as now. It almost seems as
if what was aforetime spoken fabulously and
hieroglyphically, was now spoken plainly, the
doctrine, namely, of the indwelling of the Creator in man. The spiritualist wishes this only,
that the spiritual principle should be suffered
to demonstrate itself to the end, in all possible
applications to the state of man, without the
admission of anything unspiritual, that is, anything positive, dogmatic, or personal. The excellence of this class consists in this, that they
have believed ; that, affirming the need of new
and higher modes of living and action, they
have abstained from the recommendation of low
methods. Their fault is that they have stopped
at the intellectual perception ; that their will is
not yet inspired from the Fountain of Love.
But whose fault is this? and what a fault, and
to what inquiry does it lead ! We have come
to that which is the spring of all power, of
beauty and virtue, of art and poetry ; and who
shall tell us according to what law its inspirations and its informations are given or with-
holden ?

I do not wish to be guilty of the narrowness and pedantry of inferring the tendency and genius of the Age from a few and insufficient facts or persons. Every age has a thousand sides and signs and tendencies, and it is only when surveyed from inferior points of view that great varieties of character appear. Our time too is full of activity and performance. Is there not something comprehensive in the grasp of a society which to great mechanical invention and the best institutions of property adds the most daring theories; which explores the subtlest and most universal problems? At the manifest risk of repeating what every other Age has thought of itself, we might say we think the Genius of this Age more philosophical than any other has been, righter in its aims, truer, with less fear, less fable, less mixture of any sort.

But turn it how we will, as we ponder this meaning of the times, every new thought drives us to the deep fact that the Time is the child of the Eternity. The main interest which any aspects of the Times can have for us, is the great spirit which gazes through them, the light which they can shed on the wonderful questions, What we are? and Whither we tend? We do not wish to be deceived. Here we drift,

like white sail across the wild ocean, now bright
on the wave, now darkling in the trough of
the sea ; — but from what port did we sail?
Who knows? Or to what port are we bound?
Who knows! There is no one to tell us but
such poor weather-tossed mariners as ourselves,
whom we speak as we pass, or who have hoisted
some signal, or floated to us some letter in a
bottle from far.   But what know they more
than we?   They also found themselves on this
wondrous sea.   No; from the older sailors, nothing.   Over all their speaking-trumpets, the
gray sea and the loud winds answer, Not in us ;
not in Time.¹ Where then but in Ourselves,
where but in that Thought through which we
communicate with absolute nature, and are made
aware that whilst we shed the dust of which we
are built, grain by grain, till it is all gone, the
law which clothes us with humanity remains
anew? where but in the intuitions which are
vouchsafed us from within, shall we learn the
Truth?   Faithless, faithless, we fancy that with
the dust we depart and are not, and do not
know that the law and the perception of the law
are at last one; that only as much as the law
enters us, becomes us, we are living men, — immortal with the immortality of this law.   Under-

neath all these appearances lies that which is, that which lives, that which causes. This ever renewing generation of appearances rests on a reality, and a reality that is alive.[1]

To a true scholar the attraction of the aspects of nature, the departments of life, and the passages of his experience, is simply the information they yield him of this supreme nature which lurks within all. That reality, that causing force is moral. The Moral Sentiment is but its other name. It makes by its presence or absence right and wrong, beauty and ugliness, genius or depravation. As the granite comes to the surface and towers into the highest mountains, and, if we dig down, we find it below the superficial strata, so in all the details of our domestic or civil life is hidden the elemental reality, which ever and anon comes to the surface, and forms the grand men, who are the leaders and examples, rather than the companions of the race. The granite is curiously concealed under a thousand formations and surfaces, under fertile soils, and grasses, and flowers, under well - manured, arable fields, and large towns and cities, but it makes the foundation of these, and is always indicating its presence by slight but sure signs. So is it with the Life of our life ; so close does

that also hide. I read it in glad and in weeping
eyes ; I read it in the pride and in the humility
of people ; it is recognized in every bargain and
in every complaisance, in every criticism, and in
all praise; it is voted for at elections ; it wins
the cause with juries ; it rides the stormy eloquence of the senate, sole victor ; histories are
written of it, holidays decreed to it ; statues,
tombs, churches, built to its honor ; yet men
seem to fear and to shun it when it comes barely
to view in our immediate neighborhood.

For that reality let us stand; that let us serve,
and for that speak. Only as far as *that* shines
through them are these times or any times
worth consideration. I wish to speak of the politics, education, business, and religion around us
without ceremony or false deference. You will
absolve me from the charge of flippancy, or malignity, or the desire to say smart things at the
expense of whomsoever, when you see that reality is all we prize, and that we are bound on our
entrance into nature to speak for that. Let it
not be recorded in our own memories that in
this moment of the Eternity, when we who were
named by our names flitted across the light, we
were afraid of any fact, or disgraced the fair
Day by a pusillanimous preference of our bread

to our freedom. What is the scholar, what is
the man *for*, but for hospitality to every new
thought of his time? Have you leisure, power,
property, friends? You shall be the asylum and
patron of every new thought, every unproven
opinion, every untried project which proceeds
out of good will and honest seeking.[1] All the
newspapers, all the tongues of to-day will of
course at first defame what is noble; but you
who hold not of to-day, not of the times, but
of the Everlasting, are to stand for it: and
the highest compliment man ever receives from
heaven is the sending to him its disguised and
discredited angels.

THE CONSERVATIVE

A LECTURE DELIVERED AT THE MASONIC TEMPLE,
BOSTON, DECEMBER 9, 1841

THE CONSERVATIVE

THE two parties which divide the state, the party of Conservatism and that of Innovation, are very old, and have disputed the possession of the world ever since it was made. This quarrel is the subject of civil history. The conservative party established the reverend hierarchies and monarchies of the most ancient world. The battle of patrician and plebeian, of parent state and colony, of old usage and accommodation to new facts, of the rich and the poor, reappears in all countries and times. The war rages not only in battle-fields, in national councils and ecclesiastical synods, but agitates every man's bosom with opposing advantages every hour. On rolls the old world meantime, and now one, now the other gets the day, and still the fight renews itself as if for the first time, under new names and hot personalities.

Such an irreconcilable antagonism of course must have a correspondent depth of seat in the human constitution. It is the opposition of Past and Future, of Memory and Hope, of the Understanding and the Reason. It is the primal antagonism, the appearance in trifles of the two poles of nature.'

There is a fragment of old fable which seems somehow to have been dropped from the current mythologies, which may deserve attention, as it appears to relate to this subject.

Saturn grew weary of sitting alone, or with none but the great Uranus or Heaven beholding him, and he created an oyster. Then he would act again, but he made nothing more, but went on creating the race of oysters. Then Uranus cried, 'A new work, O Saturn! the old is not good again.'

Saturn replied, ' I fear. There is not only the alternative of making and not making, but also of unmaking. Seest thou the great sea, how it ebbs and flows? so is it with me; my power ebbs; and if I put forth my hands, I shall not do, but undo. Therefore I do what I have done; I hold what I have got; and so I resist Night and Chaos.'

' O Saturn,' replied Uranus, ' thou canst not hold thine own but by making more. Thy oysters are barnacles and cockles, and with the next flowing of the tide they will be pebbles and seafoam.'

' I see,' rejoins Saturn, ' thou art in league

with Night, thou art become an evil eye; thou
spakest from love; now thy words smite me
with hatred. I appeal to Fate, must there not
be rest?'—'I appeal to Fate also,' said Uranus, 'must there not be motion?'— But Saturn
was silent, and went on making oysters for a
thousand years.

After that, the word of Uranus came into
his mind like a ray of the sun, and he made
Jupiter; and then he feared again; and nature
froze, the things that were made went backward, and to save the world, Jupiter slew his
father Saturn.

This may stand for the earliest account of a
conversation on politics between a Conservative and a Radical which has come down to us.
It is ever thus. It is the counteraction of the cen-
tripetal and the centrifugal forces. Innovation is
the salient energy; Conservatism the pause on
the last movement. 'That which is was made by
God,' saith Conservatism. 'He is leaving that,
he is entering this other,' rejoins Innovation.'

There is always a certain meanness in the
argument of conservatism, joined with a certain superiority in its fact. It affirms because
it holds. Its fingers clutch the fact, and it will
not open its eyes to see a better fact. The cas-

tle which conservatism is set to defend is the actual state of things, good and bad. The project of innovation is the best possible state of things. Of course conservatism always has the worst of the argument, is always apologizing, pleading a necessity, pleading that to change would be to deteriorate: it must saddle itself with the mountainous load of the violence and vice of society, must deny the possibility of good, deny ideas, and suspect and stone the prophet; whilst innovation is always in the right, triumphant, attacking, and sure of final success. Conservatism stands on man's confessed limitations, reform on his indisputable infinitude; conservatism on circumstance, liberalism on power; one goes to make an adroit member of the social frame, the other to postpone all things to the man himself; conservatism is debonair and social, reform is individual and imperious. We are reformers in spring and summer, in autumn and winter we stand by the old; reformers in the morning, conservers at night. Reform is affirmative, conservatism negative; conservatism goes for comfort, reform for truth. Conservatism is more candid to behold another's worth; reform more disposed to maintain and increase its own. Conservatism

makes no poetry, breathes no prayer, has no
invention ; it is all memory. Reform has no
gratitude, no prudence, no husbandry. It makes
a great difference to your figure and to your
thought whether your foot is advancing or receding. Conservatism never puts the foot forward; in the hour when it does that, it is not
establishment, but reform. Conservatism tends
to universal seeming and treachery, believes in
a negative fate; believes that men's temper
governs them; that for me it avails not to trust
in principles, they will fail me, I must bend a
little; it distrusts nature; it thinks there is a
general law without a particular application, —
law for all that does not include any one. Reform in its antagonism inclines to asinine resistance, to kick with hoofs ; it runs to egotism
and bloated self-conceit; it runs to a bodiless
pretension, to unnatural refining and elevation
which ends in hypocrisy and sensual reaction.

And so, whilst we do not go beyond general
statements, it may be safely affirmed of these
two metaphysical antagonists, that each is a good
half, but an impossible whole. Each exposes
the abuses of the other, but in a true society, in
a true man, both must combine.[1] Nature does
not give the crown of its approbation, namely

beauty, to any action or emblem or actor but to one which combines both these elements; not to the rock which resists the waves from age to age, nor to the wave which lashes incessantly the rock, but the superior beauty is with the oak which stands with its hundred arms against the storms of a century, and grows every year like a sapling; or the river which ever flowing, yet is found in the same bed from age to age; or, greatest of all, the man who has subsisted for years amid the changes of nature, yet has distanced himself, so that when you remember what he was, and see what he is, you say, What strides! what a disparity is here!

Throughout nature the past combines in every creature with the present. Each of the convolutions of the sea - shell, each node and spine marks one year of the fish's life; what was the mouth of the shell for one season, with the addition of new matter by the growth of the animal, becoming an ornamental node. The leaves and a shell of soft wood are all that the vegetation of this summer has made; but the solid columnar stem, which lifts that bank of foliage into the air, to draw the eye and to cool us with its shade, is the gift and legacy of dead and buried years.

In nature, each of these elements being always present, each theory has a natural support. As we take our stand on Necessity, or on Ethics, shall we go for the conservative, or for the reformer. If we read the world historically, we shall say, Of all the ages, the present hour and circumstance is the cumulative result; this is the best throw of the dice of nature that has yet been, or that is yet possible. If we see it from the side of Will, or the Moral Sentiment, we shall accuse the Past and the Present, and require the impossible of the Future.

But although this bifold fact lies thus united in real nature, and so united that no man can continue to exist in whom both these elements do not work, yet men are not philosophers, but are rather very foolish children, who, by reason of their partiality, see everything in the most absurd manner, and are the victims at all times of the nearest object. There is even no philosopher who is a philosopher at all times. Our experience, our perception is conditioned by the need to acquire in parts and in succession, that is, with every truth a certain falsehood. As this is the invariable method of our training, we must give it allowance, and suffer men to learn as they have done for six millenniums, a word at

a time; to pair off into insane parties, and learn
the amount of truth each knows by the denial
of an equal amount of truth. For the present,
then, to come at what sum is attainable to us, we
must even hear the parties plead as parties.

That which is best about conservatism, that
which, though it cannot be expressed in detail, inspires reverence in all, is the Inevitable.
There is the question not only what the conservative says for himself, but, why must he say
it? What insurmountable fact binds him to that
side? Here is the fact which men call Fate, and
fate in dread degrees, fate behind fate, not to be
disposed of by the consideration that the Conscience commands this or that, but necessitating
the question whether the faculties of man will
play him true in resisting the facts of universal
experience? For although the commands of
the Conscience are *essentially* absolute, they are
historically limitary. Wisdom does not seek a
literal rectitude, but an useful, that is a conditioned one, such a one as the faculties of man
and the constitution of things will warrant. The
reformer, the partisan, loses himself in driving
to the utmost some specialty of right conduct,
until his own nature and all nature resist him :
but Wisdom attempts nothing enormous and

disproportioned to its powers, nothing which it cannot perform or nearly perform. We have all a certain intellection or presentiment of reform existing in the mind, which does not yet descend into the character, and those who throw themselves blindly on this lose themselves. Whatever they attempt in that direction, fails, and reacts suicidally on the actor himself. This is the penalty of having transcended nature. For the existing world is not a dream, and cannot with impunity be treated as a dream; neither is it a disease; but it is the ground on which you stand, it is the mother of whom you were born. Reform converses with possibilities, perchance with impossibilities; but here is sacred fact. This also was true, or it could not be : it had life in it, or it could not have existed; it has life in it, or it could not continue. Your schemes may be feasible, or may not be, but this has the endorsement of nature and a long friendship and cohabitation with the powers of nature. This will stand until a better cast of the dice is made. The contest between the Future and the Past is one between Divinity entering and Divinity departing. You are welcome to try your experiments, and, if you can, to displace the actual order by that ideal republic you announce, for nothing but God will expel God. But plainly the burden of proof must lie with the projector. We hold to this, until you can demonstrate something better.

The system of property and law goes back for its origin to barbarous and sacred times; it is the fruit of the same mysterious cause as the mineral or animal world. There is a natural sentiment and prepossession in favor of age, of ancestors, of barbarous and aboriginal usages, which is a homage to the element of necessity and divinity which is in them. The respect for the old names of places, of mountains and streams, is universal. The Indian and barbarous name can never be supplanted without loss. The ancients tell us that the gods loved the Ethiopians for their stable customs; and the Egyptians and Chaldeans, whose origin could not be explored, passed among the junior tribes of Greece and Italy for sacred nations.[1]

Moreover, so deep is the foundation of the existing social system, that it leaves no one out of it. We may be partial, but Fate is not. All men have their root in it. You who quarrel with the arrangements of society, and are willing to embroil all, and risk the indisputable good that exists, for the chance of better, live, move, and have your being in this, and your deeds contradict your words every day. For as you cannot jump from the ground without using the resistance of the ground, nor put out the boat to sea without shoving from the shore, nor attain liberty without rejecting obligation, so you are under the necessity of using the Actual order of things, in order to disuse it ; to live by it, whilst you wish to take away its life. The past has baked your loaf, and in the strength of its bread you would break up the oven. But you are betrayed by your own nature. You also are conservatives. However men please to style themselves, I see no other than a conservative party. You are not only identical with us in your needs, but also in your methods and aims. You quarrel with my conservatism, but it is to build up one of your own ; it will have a new beginning, but the same course and end, the same trials, the same passions; among the lovers of the new I observe that there is a jealousy of the newest, and that the seceder from the seceder is as damnable as the pope himself.

On these and the like grounds of general statement, conservatism plants itself without danger of being displaced. Especially before this *personal* appeal, the innovator must confess his weakness, must confess that no man is to be found good enough to be entitled to stand champion for the principle. But when this great tendency comes to practical encounters, and is challenged by young men, to whom it is no abstraction, but a fact of hunger, distress, and exclusion from opportunities, it must needs seem injurious. The youth, of course, is an innovator by the fact of his birth. There he stands, newly born on the planet, a universal beggar, with all the reason of things, one would say, on his side. In his first consideration how to feed, clothe, and warm himself, he is met by warnings on every hand that this thing and that thing have owners, and he must go elsewhere. Then he says, ' If I am born in the earth, where is my part ? have the goodness, gentlemen of this world, to show me my wood-lot, where I may fell my wood, my field where to plant my corn, my pleasant ground where to build my cabin.'

' Touch any wood, or field, or house-lot, on your peril,' cry all the gentlemen of this world ; ' but you may come and work in ours, for us, and we will give you a piece of bread.'   .

' And what is that peril ? '

' Knives and muskets, if we meet you in the act ; imprisonment, if we find you afterward.'

' And by what authority, kind gentlemen?'

' By our law.'

' And your law, — is it just?'

'As just for you as it was for us. We wrought for others under this law, and got our lands so.'

' I repeat the question, Is your law just?'

' Not quite just, but necessary. Moreover, it is juster now than it was when we were born ; we have made it milder and more equal.'

' I will none of your law,' returns the youth ; 'it encumbers me. I cannot understand, or so much as spare time to read that needless library of your laws. Nature has sufficiently provided me with rewards and sharp penalties, to bind me not to transgress. Like the Persian noble of old, I ask "that I may neither command nor obey." I do not wish to enter into your complex social system. I shall serve those whom I can, and they who can will serve me. I shall seek those whom I love, and shun those whom I love not, and what more can all your laws render me?'

With equal earnestness and good faith, replies to this plaintiff an upholder of the establishment, a man of many virtues :

'Your opposition is feather-brained and over-fine. Young man, I have no skill to talk with you, but look at me ; I have risen early and sat

late, and toiled honestly and painfully for very
many years. I never dreamed about methods ;
I laid my bones to, and drudged for the good
I possess ; it was not got by fraud, nor by luck,
but by work, and you must show me a warrant
like these stubborn facts in your own fidelity
and labor, before I suffer you, on the faith of a
few fine words, to ride into my estate, and claim
to scatter it as your own.'

' Now you touch the heart of the matter,' replies the reformer. ' To that fidelity and labor
I pay homage. I am unworthy to arraign your
manner of living, until I too have been tried.
But I should be more unworthy if I did not
tell you why I cannot walk in your steps. I
find this vast network, which you call property,
extended over the whole planet. I cannot occupy the bleakest crag of the White Hills or the
Alleghany Range, but some man or corporation
steps up to me to show me that it is his. Now,
though I am very peaceable, and on my private account could well enough die, since it appears there was some mistake in my creation, and
that I have been *mis*sent to this earth, where all
the seats were already taken, — yet I feel called
upon in behalf of rational nature, which I represent, to declare to you my opinion that if the

Earth is yours so also is it mine. All your aggregate existences are less to me a fact than is my
own; as I am born to the Earth, so the Earth
is given to me, what I want of it to till and to
plant; nor could I, without pusillanimity, omit
to claim so much. I must not only have a
name to live, I must live. My genius leads me
to build a different manner of life from any
of yours. I cannot then spare you the whole
world. I love you better. I must tell you the
truth practically; and take that which you call
yours. It is God's world and mine; yours as
much as you want, mine as much as I want.
Besides, I know your ways; I know the symp-
toms of the disease. To the end of your power
you will serve this lie which cheats you. Your
want is a gulf which the possession of the broad
earth would not fill. Yonder sun in heaven you
would pluck down from shining on the universe,
and make him a property and privacy, if you
could; and the moon and the north star you
would quickly have occasion for in your closet
and bed-chamber. What you do not want for
use, you crave for ornament, and what your
convenience could spare, your pride cannot.'

On the other hand, precisely the defence
which was set up for the British Constitution,

namely that with all its admitted defects, rotten
boroughs and monopolies, it worked well, and
substantial justice was somehow done ; the wisdom and the worth did get into parliament, and
every interest did by right, or might, or sleight,
get represented ; — the same defence is set up
for the existing institutions. They are not the
best ; they are not just ; and in respect to you,
personally, O brave young man ! they cannot be
justified. They have, it is most true, left you
no acre for your own, and no law but our law,
to the ordaining of which you were no party.
But they do answer the end, they are really
friendly to the good, unfriendly to the bad ;
they second the industrious and the kind ; they
foster genius. They really have so much flexi-
bility as to afford your talent and character, on
the whole, the same chance of demonstration
and success which they might have if there was
no law and no property.

It is trivial and merely superstitious to say
that nothing is given you, no outfit, no exhibition ; for in this institution of *credit*, which is
as universal as honesty and promise in the human countenance, always some neighbor stands
ready to be bread and land and tools and stock
to the young adventurer. And if in any one

respect they have come short, see what ample retribution of good they have made. They have lost no time and spared no expense to collect libraries, museums, galleries, colleges, palaces, hospitals, observatories, cities. The ages have not been idle, nor kings slack, nor the rich niggardly. Have we not atoned for this small offence (which we could not help) of leaving you no right in the soil, by this splendid indemnity of ancestral and national wealth? Would you have been born like a gipsy in a hedge, and preferred your freedom on a heath, and the range of a planet which had no shed or boscage to cover you from sun and wind,— to this towered and citied world? to this world of Rome, and Memphis, and Constantinople, and Vienna, and Paris, and London, and New York? For thee Naples, Florence, and Venice; for thee the fair Mediterranean, the sunny Adriatic; for thee both Indies smile; for thee the hospitable North opens its heated palaces under the polar circle; for thee roads have been cut in every direction across the land, and fleets of floating palaces with every security for strength and provision for luxury, swim by sail and by steam through all the waters of this world. Every island for thee has a town; every town a hotel.

Though thou wast born landless, yet to thy industry and thrift and small condescension to the established usage, — scores of servants are swarming in every strange place with cap and knee to thy command; scores, nay hundreds and thousands, for thy wardrobe, thy table, thy chamber, thy library, thy leisure; and every whim is anticipated and served by the best ability of the whole population of each country. The king on the throne governs for thee, and the judge judges; the barrister pleads, the farmer tills, the joiner hammers, the postman rides. Is it not exaggerating a trifle to insist on a formal acknowledgment of your claims, when these substantial advantages have been secured to you? Now can your children be educated, your labor turned to their advantage, and its fruits secured to them after your death. It is frivolous to say you have no acre, because you have not a mathematically measured piece of land. Providence takes care that you shall have a place, that you are waited for, and come accredited; and as soon as you put your gift to use, you shall have acre or acre's worth according to your exhibition of desert, — acre, if you need land; — acre's worth, if you prefer to draw, or carve, or make shoes or wheels, to the tilling of the soil.[1]

Besides, it might temper your indignation at the supposed wrong which society has done you, to keep the question before you, how society got into this predicament? Who put things on this false basis? No single man, but all men. No man voluntarily and knowingly; but it is the result of that degree of culture there is in the planet. The order of things is as good as the character of the population permits. Consider it as the work of a great and beneficent and progressive necessity, which, from the first pulsation in the first animal life, up to the present high culture of the best nations, has advanced thus far. Thank the rude foster-mother, though she has taught you a better wisdom than her own, and has set hopes in your heart which shall be history in the next ages. You are yourself the result of this manner of living, this foul compromise, this vituperated Sodom. It nourished you with care and love on its breast, as it had nourished many a lover of the right and many a poet, and prophet, and teacher of men. Is it so irremediably bad? Then again, if the mitigations are considered, do not all the mischiefs virtually vanish? The form is bad, but see you not how every personal character reacts on the form, and makes it new? A strong person makes the law and custom null before his own will. Then the principle of love and truth reappears in the strictest courts of fashion and property. Under the richest robes, in the darlings of the selectest circles of European or American aristocracy, the strong heart will beat with love of mankind, with impatience of accidental distinctions, with the desire to achieve its own fate and make every ornament it wears authentic and real.

Moreover, as we have already shown that there is no pure reformer, so it is to be considered that there is no pure conservative, no man who from the beginning to the end of his life maintains the defective institutions; but he who sets his face like a flint against every novelty, when approached in the confidence of conversation, in the presence of friendly and generous persons, has also his gracious and relenting moments, and espouses for the time the cause of man; and even if this be a shortlived emotion, yet the remembrance of it in private hours mitigates his selfishness and compliance with custom.

The Friar Bernard lamented in his cell on Mount Cenis the crimes of mankind, and rising one morning before day from his bed of moss and dry leaves, he gnawed his roots and berries, drank of the spring, and set forth to go to Rome to reform the corruption of mankind. On his way he encountered many travellers who greeted him courteously, and the cabins of the peasants and the castles of the lords supplied his few wants. When he came at last to Rome, his piety and good will easily introduced him to many families of the rich, and on the first day he saw and talked with gentle mothers with their babes at their breasts, who told him how much love they bore their children, and how they were perplexed in their daily walk lest they should fail in their duty to them. 'What!' he said, 'and this on rich embroidered carpets, on marble floors, with cunning sculpture, and carved wood, and rich pictures, and piles of books about you?' — 'Look at our pictures and books,' they said, 'and we will tell you, good Father, how we spent the last evening. These are stories of godly children and holy families and romantic sacrifices made in old or in recent times by great and not mean persons; and last evening our family was collected and our husbands and brothers discoursed sadly on what we could save and give in the hard times.' Then came in the men, and they said, 'What cheer,

brother ? Does thy convent want gifts ? ' Then
the Friar Bernard went home swiftly with other
thoughts than he brought, saying, ' This way
of life is wrong, yet these Romans, whom I
prayed God to destroy, are lovers, they are
lovers ; what can I do ? '

The reformer concedes that these mitigations
exist, and that if he proposed comfort, he should
take sides with the establishment. Your words
are excellent, but they do not tell the whole.
Conservatism is affluent and open-handed, but
there is a cunning juggle in riches. I observe
that they take somewhat for everything they
give. I look bigger, but am less ; I have more
clothes, but am not so warm ; more armor, but
less courage ; more books, but less wit. What
you say of your planted, builded and decorated
world is true enough, and I gladly avail myself
of its convenience ; yet I have remarked that
what holds in particular, holds in general, that
the plant Man does not require for his most
glorious flowering this pomp of preparation and
convenience, but the thoughts of some beggarly
Homer who strolled, God knows when, in the
infancy and barbarism of the old world ; the
gravity and sense of some slave Moses who
leads away his fellow slaves from their masters ;

the contemplation of some Scythian Anachar-
sis ; the erect, formidable valor of some Dorian
townsmen in the town of Sparta; the vigor of
Clovis the Frank, and Alfred the Saxon, and
Alaric the Goth, and Mahomet, Ali and Omar
the Arabians, Saladin the Kurd, and Othman
the Turk, sufficed to build what you call society
on the spot and in the instant when the sound
mind in a sound body appeared. Rich and
fine is your dress, O conservatism ! your horses
are of the best blood ; your roads are well cut
and well paved; your pantry is full of meats and
your cellar of wines, and a very good state and
condition are you for gentlemen and ladies to
live under ; but every one of these goods steals
away a drop of my blood. I want the necessity
of supplying my own wants. All this costly
culture of yours is not necessary. Greatness
does not need it. Yonder peasant, who sits neglected there in a corner, carries a whole revolution of man and nature in his head, which shall
be a sacred history to some future ages. For
man is the end of nature ; nothing so easily
organizes itself in every part of the universe as
he ; no moss, no lichen is so easily born ; and
he takes along with him and puts out from
himself the whole apparatus of society and con-

dition *extempore*, as an army encamps in a desert, and where all was just now blowing sand, creates a white city in an hour, a government, a market, a place for feasting, for conversation, and for love.

These considerations, urged by those whose characters and whose fortunes are yet to be formed, must needs command the sympathy of all reasonable persons. But beside that charity which should make all adult persons interested for the youth, and engage them to see that he has a free field and fair play on his entrance into life, we are bound to see that the society of which we compose a part, does not permit the formation or continuance of views and practices injurious to the honor and welfare of mankind. The objection to conservatism, when embodied in a party, is that in its love of acts it hates principles; it lives in the senses, not in truth; it sacrifices to despair; it goes for availableness in its candidate, not for worth; and for expediency in its measures, and not for the right. Under pretence of allowing for friction, it makes so many additions and supplements to the machine of society that it will play smoothly and softly, but will no longer grind any grist.

The conservative party in the universe concedes that the radical would talk sufficiently to the purpose, if we were still in the garden of Eden ; he legislates for man as he ought to be ; his theory is right, but he makes no allowance for friction ; and this omission makes his whole doctrine false. The idealist retorts that the conservative falls into a far more noxious error in the other extreme. The conservative assumes sickness as a necessity, and his social frame is a hospital, his total legislation is for the present distress, a universe in slippers and flannels, with bib and pap-spoon, swallowing pills and herb-tea. Sickness gets organized as well as health, the vice as well as the virtue. Now that a vicious system of trade has existed so long, it has stereotyped itself in the human generation, and misers are born. And now that sickness has got such a foothold, leprosy has grown cunning, has got into the ballot-box ; the lepers outvote the clean ; society has resolved itself into a Hospital Committee, and all its laws are quarantine. If any man resist and set up a foolish hope he has entertained as good against the general despair, Society frowns on him, shuts him out of her opportunities, her granaries, her refectories, her water and bread, and will serve him a sexton's turn. Conservatism takes as low a view of every part of human action and passion. Its religion is just as bad ; a lozenge for the sick ; a dolorous tune to beguile the distemper ; mitigations of pain by pillows and anodynes ; always mitigations, never remedies ; pardons for sin, funeral honors, — never self-help, renovation, and virtue. Its social and political action has no better aim ; to keep out wind and weather, to bring the week and year about, and make the world last our day ; not to sit on the world and steer it ; not to sink the memory of the past in the glory of a new and more excellent creation ; a timid cobbler and patcher, it degrades whatever it touches. The cause of education is urged in this country with the utmost earnestness, — on what ground ? Why on this, that the people have the power, and if they are not instructed to sympathize with the intelligent, reading, trading, and governing class ; inspired with a taste for the same competitions and prizes, they will upset the fair pageant of Judicature, and perhaps lay a hand on the sacred muniments of wealth itself, and new distribute the land. Religion is taught in the same spirit. The contractors who were building a road out of Baltimore, some years ago, found the Irish laborers

quarrelsome and refractory to a degree that embarrassed the agents and seriously interrupted
the progress of the work. The corporation were
advised to call off the police and build a Catholic chapel, which they did ; the priest presently
restored order, and the work went on prosper-
ously. Such hints, be sure, are too valuable to be
lost. If you do not value the Sabbath, or other
religious institutions, give yourself no concern
about maintaining them. They have already
acquired a market value as conservators of property ; and if priest and church-member should
fail, the chambers of commerce and the presi-
dents of the banks, the very innholders and
landlords of the county, would muster with fury
to their support.

Of course, religion in such hands loses its
essence. Instead of that reliance which the soul
suggests, on the eternity of truth and duty, men
are misled into a reliance on institutions, which,
the moment they cease to be the instantaneous
creations of the devout sentiment, are worthless.
Religion among the low becomes low. As it
loses its truth, it loses credit with the sagacious.
They detect the falsehood of the preaching, but
when they say so, all good citizens cry, Hush ;
do not weaken the State, do not take off the

strait jacket from dangerous persons. Every honest fellow must keep up the hoax the best he can; must patronize Providence and piety, and wherever he sees anything that will keep men amused, schools or churches or poetry or picture-galleries or music, or what not, he must cry 'Hist-a-boy,' and urge the game on. What a compliment we pay to the good SPIRIT with our superserviceable zeal!

But not to balance reasons for and against the establishment any longer, and if it still be asked in this necessity of partial organization, which party on the whole has the highest claims on our sympathy, — I bring it home to the private heart, where all such questions must have their final arbitrament. How will every strong and generous mind choose its ground, —with the defenders of the old? or with the seekers of the new? Which is that state which promises to edify a great, brave, and beneficent man; to throw him on his resources, and tax the strength of his character? On which part will each of us find himself in the hour of health and of aspiration?

I understand well the respect of mankind for war, because that breaks up the Chinese stagnation of society, and demonstrates the personal merits of all men. A state of war or anarchy, in which law has little force, is so far valuable that it puts every man on trial. The man of principle is known as such, and even in the fury of faction is respected. In the civil wars of France, Montaigne alone, among all the French gentry, kept his castle gates unbarred, and made his personal integrity as good at least as a regiment. The man of courage and resources is shown, and the effeminate and base person. Those who rise above war, and those who fall below it, it easily discriminates, as well as those who, accepting its rude conditions, keep their own head by their own sword.

But in peace and a commercial state we depend, not as we ought, on our knowledge and all men's knowledge that we are honest men, but we cowardly lean on the virtue of others. For it is always at last the virtue of some men in the society, which keeps the law in any reverence and power. Is there not something shameful that I should owe my peaceful occupancy of my house and field, not to the knowledge of my countrymen that I am useful, but to their respect for sundry other reputable persons, I know not whom, whose joint virtue still keeps the law in good odor?

It will never make any difference to a hero what the laws are. His greatness will shine and accomplish itself unto the end, whether they second him or not. If he have earned his bread by drudgery, and in the narrow and crooked ways which were all an evil law had left him, he will make it at least honorable by his expenditure. Of the past he will take no heed; for its wrongs he will not hold himself responsible: he will say, All the meanness of my progenitors shall not bereave me of the power to make this hour and company fair and fortunate. Whatsoever streams of power and commodity flow to me, shall of me acquire healing virtue, and become fountains of safety. Cannot I too descend a Redeemer into nature? Whosoever hereafter shall name my name, shall not record a malefactor but a benefactor in the earth. If there be power in good intention, in fidelity, and in toil, the north wind shall be purer, the stars in heaven shall glow with a kindlier beam, that I have lived. I am primarily engaged to myself to be a public servant of all the gods, to demonstrate to all men that there is intelligence and good will at the heart of things, and ever higher and yet higher leadings. These are my engagements; how can your law further or hin-

der me in what I shall do to men? On the
other hand, these dispositions establish their
relations to me. Wherever there is worth, I
shall be greeted. Wherever there are men, are
the objects of my study and love. Sooner or
later all men will be my friends, and will testify in all methods the energy of their regard.
I cannot thank your law for my protection. I
protect it. It is not in its power to protect me.
It is my business to make myself revered. I
depend on my honor, my labor, and my dispositions for my place in the affections of mankind, and not on any conventions or parchments
of yours.[1]

But if I allow myself in derelictions and become idle and dissolute, I quickly come to love
the protection of a strong law, because I feel no
title in myself to my advantages. To the intemperate and covetous person no love flows;
to him mankind would pay no rent, no dividend, if force were once relaxed; nay, if they
could give their verdict, they would say that
his self-indulgence and his oppression deserved
punishment from society, and not that rich
board and lodging he now enjoys. The law
acts then as a screen of his unworthiness, and
makes him worse the longer it protects him.

In conclusion, to return from this alternation of partial views to the high platform of universal and necessary history, it is a happiness for mankind that innovation has got on so far and has so free a field before it. The boldness of the hope men entertain transcends all former experience. It calms and cheers them with the picture of a simple and equal life of truth and piety. And this hope flowered on what tree? It was not imported from the stock of some celestial plant, but grew here on the wild crab of conservatism. It is much that this old and vituperated system of things has borne so fair a child. It predicts that amidst a planet peopled with conservatives, one Reformer may yet be born.

THE TRANSCENDENTALIST

A LECTURE READ AT THE MASONIC TEMPLE,
BOSTON, JANUARY, 1842

THE
TRANSCENDENTALIST

THE first thing we have to say respecting
what are called *new views* here in New
England, at the present time, is, that they are
not new, but the very oldest of thoughts cast
into the mould of these new times. The light
is always identical in its composition, but it falls
on a great variety of objects, and by so falling
is first revealed to us, not in its own form, for
it is formless, but in theirs; in like manner,
thought only appears in the objects it classifies.
What is popularly called Transcendentalism
among us, is Idealism; Idealism as it appears in
1842. As thinkers, mankind have ever divided
into two sects, Materialists and Idealists; the
first class founding on experience, the second
on consciousness; the first class beginning to
think from the data of the senses, the second
class perceive that the senses are not final, and
say, The senses give us representations of
things, but what are the things themselves, they
cannot tell. The materialist insists on facts, on
history, on the force of circumstances and the
animal wants of man; the idealist on the power

of Thought and of Will, on inspiration, on miracle, on individual culture. These two modes of thinking are both natural, but the idealist contends that his way of thinking is in higher nature. He concedes all that the other affirms, admits the impressions of sense, admits their coherency, their use and beauty, and then asks the materialist for his grounds of assurance that things are as his senses represent them. But I, he says, affirm facts not affected by the illusions of sense, facts which are of the same nature as the faculty which reports them, and not liable to doubt; facts which in their first appearance to us assume a native superiority to material facts, degrading these into a language by which the first are to be spoken; facts which it only needs a retirement from the senses to discern. Every materialist will be an idealist; but an idealist can never go backward to be a materialist.[1]

The idealist, in speaking of events, sees them as spirits. He does not deny the sensuous fact: by no means; but he will not see that alone. He does not deny the presence of this table, this chair, and the walls of this room, but he looks at these things as the reverse side of the tapestry, as the *other end*, each being a sequel or completion of a spiritual fact which nearly concerns him.   This manner of looking at things transfers every object in nature from an independent and anomalous position without there, into the consciousness.   Even the materialist Condillac, perhaps the most logical expounder of materialism, was constrained to say, "Though we should soar into the heavens, though we should sink into the abyss, we never go out of ourselves; it is always our own thought that we perceive."   What more could an idealist say?

The materialist, secure in the certainty of sensation, mocks at fine-spun theories, at star-gazers and dreamers, and believes that his life is solid, that he at least takes nothing for granted, but knows where he stands, and what he does. Yet how easy it is to show him that he also is a phantom walking and working amid phantoms, and that he need only ask a question or two beyond his daily questions to find his solid universe growing dim and impalpable before his sense.   The sturdy capitalist, no matter how deep and square on blocks of Quincy granite he lays the foundations of his banking-house or Exchange, must set it, at last, not on a cube corresponding to the angles of his structure, but on a mass of unknown materials and solidity, red-hot or white-hot perhaps at the core, which rounds off to an almost perfect sphericity, and lies floating in soft air, and goes spinning away, dragging bank and banker with it at a rate of thousands of miles the hour, he knows not whither, — a bit of bullet, now glimmering, now darkling through a small cubic space on the edge of an unimaginable pit of emptiness. And this wild balloon, in which his whole venture is embarked, is a just symbol of his whole state and faculty. One thing at least, he says, is certain, and does not give me the headache, that figures do not lie; the multiplication table has been hitherto found unimpeachable truth; and, moreover, if I put a gold eagle in my safe, I find it again to-morrow; — but for these thoughts, I know not whence they are. They change and pass away. But ask him why he believes that an uniform experience will continue uniform, or on what grounds he founds his faith in his figures, and he will perceive that his mental fabric is built up on just as strange and quaking foundations as his proud edifice of stone.

In the order of thought, the materialist takes his departure from the external world, and esteems a man as one product of that. The idealist takes his departure from his consciousness,

and reckons the world an appearance.¹ The
materialist respects sensible masses, Society,
Government, social art and luxury, every establishment, every mass, whether majority of
numbers, or extent of space, or amount of objects, every social action. The idealist has another measure, which is metaphysical, namely
the *rank* which things themselves take in his
consciousness; not at all the size or appearance.
Mind is the only reality, of which men and all
other natures are better or worse reflectors.
Nature, literature, history, are only subjective
phenomena. Although in his action overpowered by the laws of action, and so, warmly co-
operating with men, even preferring them to
himself, yet when he speaks scientifically, or
after the order of thought, he is constrained to
degrade persons into representatives of truths.
He does not respect labor, or the products of
labor, namely property, otherwise than as a
manifold symbol, illustrating with wonderful
fidelity of details the laws of being; he does not
respect government, except as far as it reiterates
the law of his mind; nor the church, nor charities, nor arts, for themselves; but hears, as at a
vast distance, what they say, as if his consciousness would speak to him through a pantomimic

scene. His thought,—that is the Universe. His experience inclines him to behold the procession of facts you call the world, as flowing perpetually outward from an invisible, unsounded centre in himself, centre alike of him and of them, and necessitating him to regard all things as having a subjective or relative existence, relative to that aforesaid Unknown Centre of him.

From this transfer of the world into the consciousness, this beholding of all things in the mind, follow easily his whole ethics. It is simpler to be self-dependent. The height, the deity of man is to be self-sustained, to need no gift, no foreign force. Society is good when it does not violate me, but best when it is likest to solitude. Everything real is self-existent. Everything divine shares the self-existence of Deity. All that you call the world is the shadow of that substance which you are, the perpetual creation of the powers of thought, of those that are dependent and of those that are independent of your will. Do not cumber yourself with fruitless pains to mend and remedy remote effects; let the soul be erect, and all things will go well. You think me the child of my circumstances: I make my circumstance. Let any thought or motive of mine be different from that they are, the difference will transform my condition and economy. I — this thought which is called I — is the mould into which the world is poured like melted wax. The mould is invisible, but the world betrays the shape of the mould. You call it the power of circumstance, but it is the power of me. Am I in harmony with myself? my position will seem to you just and commanding. Am I vicious and insane? my fortunes will seem to you obscure and descending. As I am, so shall I associate, and so shall I act; Cæsar's history will paint out Cæsar. Jesus acted so, because he thought so. I do not wish to overlook or to gainsay any reality; I say I make my circumstance; but if you ask me, Whence am I? I feel like other men my relation to that Fact which cannot be spoken, or defined, nor even thought, but which exists, and will exist.

The Transcendentalist adopts the whole connection of spiritual doctrine. He believes in miracle, in the perpetual openness of the human mind to new influx of light and power; he believes in inspiration, and in ecstasy.[1] He wishes that the spiritual principle should be suffered to demonstrate itself to the end, in all possible

applications to the state of man, without the
admission of anything unspiritual; that is, anything positive, dogmatic, personal. Thus the
spiritual measure of inspiration is the depth of
the thought, and never, who said it? And so
he resists all attempts to palm other rules and
measures on the spirit than its own.

In action he easily incurs the charge of anti-
nomianism by his avowal that he, who has the
Law-giver, may with safety not only neglect,
but even contravene every written command-
ment. In the play of Othello, the expiring Desdemona absolves her husband of the murder, to
her attendant Emilia. Afterwards, when Emilia
charges him with the crime, Othello exclaims,

> "You heard her say herself it was not I."

Emilia replies,

> "The more angel she, and thou the blacker devil."

Of this fine incident, Jacobi, the Transcendental moralist, makes use, with other parallel
instances, in his reply to Fichte. Jacobi, refus-
ing all measure of right and wrong except the
determinations of the private spirit, remarks that
there is no crime but has sometimes been a virtue. " I," he says, " am that atheist, that god-
less person who, in opposition to an imaginary

doctrine of calculation, would lie as the dying Desdemona lied ; would lie and deceive, as Pylades when he personated Orestes; would assassinate like Timoleon ; would perjure my-self like Epaminondas and John de Witt ; I would resolve on suicide like Cato; I would commit sacrilege with David ; yea, and pluck ears of corn on the Sabbath, for no other reason than that I was fainting for lack of food. For I have assurance in myself that in pardoning these faults according to the letter, man exerts the sovereign right which the majesty of his being confers on him ; he sets the seal of his divine nature to the grace he accords." [1]

In like manner, if there is anything grand and daring in human thought or virtue, any re-liance on the vast, the unknown ; any presenti-ment, any extravagance of faith, the spiritualist adopts it as most in nature. The oriental mind has always tended to this largeness. Buddhism is an expression of it. The Buddhist, who thanks no man, who says, " Do not flatter your bene-factors," but who, in his conviction that every good deed can by no possibility escape its re-ward, will not deceive the benefactor by pre-tending that he has done more than he should, is a Transcendentalist.

You will see by this sketch that there is no such thing as a Transcendental *party*; that there is no pure Transcendentalist; that we know of none but prophets and heralds of such a philosophy; that all who by strong bias of nature have leaned to the spiritual side in doctrine, have stopped short of their goal. We have had many harbingers and forerunners; but of a purely spiritual life, history has afforded no example. I mean we have yet no man who has leaned entirely on his character, and eaten angels' food; who, trusting to his sentiments, found life made of miracles; who, working for universal aims, found himself fed, he knew not how; clothed, sheltered, and weaponed, he knew not how, and yet it was done by his own hands.[1] Only in the instinct of the lower animals we find the suggestion of the methods of it, and something higher than our understanding. The squirrel hoards nuts and the bee gathers honey, without knowing what they do, and they are thus provided for without selfishness or disgrace.

Shall we say then that Transcendentalism is the Saturnalia or excess of Faith; the presentiment of a faith proper to man in his integrity, excessive only when his imperfect obedience hinders the satisfaction of his wish? Nature is transcendental, exists primarily, necessarily, ever works and advances, yet takes no thought for the morrow. Man owns the dignity of the life which throbs around him, in chemistry, and tree, and animal, and in the involuntary functions of his own body ; yet he is balked when he tries to fling himself into this enchanted circle, where all is done without degradation. Yet genius and virtue predict in man the same absence of private ends and of condescension to circumstances, united with every trait and talent of beauty and power.

This way of thinking, falling on Roman times, made Stoic philosophers; falling on despotic times, made patriot Catos and Brutuses ; falling on superstitious times, made prophets and apostles ; on popish times, made protestants and ascetic monks, preachers of Faith against the preachers of Works ; on prelatical times, made Puritans and Quakers ; and falling on Unitarian and commercial times, makes the peculiar shades of Idealism which we know.

It is well known to most of my audience that the Idealism of the present day acquired the name of Transcendental from the use of that term by Immanuel Kant, of Königsberg, who replied to the skeptical philosophy of Locke, which insisted that there was nothing in the intellect which was not previously in the experience of the senses, by showing that there was a very important class of ideas or imperative forms, which did not come by experience, but through which experience was acquired; that these were intuitions of the mind itself; and he denominated them *Transcendental* forms. The extraordinary profoundness and precision of that man's thinking have given vogue to his nomenclature, in Europe and America, to that extent that whatever belongs to the class of intuitive thought is popularly called at the present day *Transcendental*.

Although, as we have said, there is no pure Transcendentalist, yet the tendency to respect the intuitions and to give them, at least in our creed, all authority over our experience, has deeply colored the conversation and poetry of the present day ; and the history of genius and of religion in these times, though impure, and as yet not incarnated in any powerful individual, will be the history of this tendency.

It is a sign of our times, conspicuous to the coarsest observer, that many intelligent and religious persons withdraw themselves from the common labors and competitions of the market and the caucus, and betake themselves to a certain solitary and critical way of living, from which no solid fruit has yet appeared to justify their separation. They hold themselves aloof: they feel the disproportion between their faculties and the work offered them, and they prefer to ramble in the country and perish of ennui, to the degradation of such charities and such ambitions as the city can propose to them. They are striking work, and crying out for somewhat worthy to do! What they do is done only because they are overpowered by the humanities that speak on all sides; and they consent to such labor as is open to them, though to their lofty dream the writing of Iliads or Hamlets, or the building of cities or empires seems drudgery.

Now every one must do after his kind, be he asp or angel, and these must. The question which a wise man and a student of modern history will ask, is, what that kind is? And truly, as in ecclesiastical history we take so much pains to know what the Gnostics, what the Essenes, what the Manichees, and what the Reformers believed, it would not misbecome us to inquire nearer home, what these companions and contemporaries of ours think and do, at least so far as these thoughts and actions appear to be not accidental and personal, but common to many, and the inevitable flower of the Tree of Time. Our American literature and spiritual history are, we confess, in the optative mood; but whoso knows these seething brains, these admirable radicals, these unsocial worshippers, these talkers who talk the sun and moon away, will believe that this heresy cannot pass away without leaving its mark.[1]

They are lonely; the spirit of their writing and conversation is lonely; they repel influences; they shun general society; they incline to shut themselves in their chamber in the house, to live in the country rather than in the town, and to find their tasks and amusements in solitude. Society, to be sure, does not like this very well; it saith, Whoso goes to walk alone, accuses the whole world; he declares all to be unfit to be his companions; it is very uncivil, nay, insulting; Society will retaliate.[2] Meantime, this retirement does not proceed from any whim on the part of these separators; but if any one will take pains to talk with them, he will find that this part is chosen both from temperament and from principle; with some unwillingness too, and as a choice of the less of two evils; for these per-

sons are not by nature melancholy, sour, and
unsocial, — they are not stockish or brute, —
but joyous, susceptible, affectionate; they have
even more than others a great wish to be loved.
Like the young Mozart, they are rather ready
to cry ten times a day, " But are you sure you
love me?" Nay, if they tell you their whole
thought, they will own that love seems to them
the last and highest gift of nature; that there
are persons whom in their hearts they daily
thank for existing, — persons whose faces are
perhaps unknown to them, but whose fame and
spirit have penetrated their solitude, — and for
whose sake they wish to exist. To behold the
beauty of another character, which inspires a
new interest in our own ; to behold the beauty
lodged in a human being, with such vivacity of
apprehension that I am instantly forced home
to inquire if I am not deformity itself; to behold
in another the expression of a love so high that
it assures itself,— assures itself also to me against
every possible casualty except my unworthiness;
— these are degrees on the scale of human happiness to which they have ascended; and it is a
fidelity to this sentiment which has made common association distasteful to them. They wish
a just and even fellowship, or none. They can-

not gossip with you, and they do not wish, as they are sincere and religious, to gratify any mere curiosity which you may entertain. Like fairies, they do not wish to be spoken of. Love me, they say, but do not ask who is my cousin and my uncle. If you do not need to hear my thought, because you can read it in my face and behavior, then I will tell it you from sunrise to sunset. If you cannot divine it, you would not understand what I say. I will not molest myself for you. I do not wish to be profaned.

And yet, it seems as if this loneliness, and not this love, would prevail in their circumstances, because of the extravagant demand they make on human nature. That, indeed, constitutes a new feature in their portrait, that they are the most exacting and extortionate critics. Their quarrel with every man they meet is not with his kind, but with his degree. There is not enough of him, — that is the only fault. They prolong their privilege of childhood in this wise; of doing nothing, but making immense demands on all the gladiators in the lists of action and fame. They make us feel the strange disappointment which overcasts every human youth. So many promising youths, and never a finished man! The profound nature will have

a savage rudeness; the delicate one will be
shallow, or the victim of sensibility; the richly
accomplished will have some capital absurdity;
and so every piece has a crack. 'T is strange,
but this masterpiece is the result of such an extreme delicacy that the most unobserved flaw in
the boy will neutralize the most aspiring genius,
and spoil the work. Talk with a seaman of the
hazards to life in his profession and he will ask
you, ' Where are the old sailors? Do you not
see that all are young men?' And we, on this
sea of human thought, in like manner inquire,
Where are the old idealists? where are they
who represented to the last generation that extravagant hope which a few happy aspirants
suggest to ours? In looking at the class of
counsel, and power, and wealth, and at the ma-
tronage of the land, amidst all the prudence
and all the triviality, one asks, Where are they
who represented genius, virtue, the invisible and
heavenly world, to these? Are they dead, —
taken in early ripeness to the gods, — as ancient wisdom foretold their fate? Or did the
high idea die out of them, and leave their un-
perfumed body as its tomb and tablet, announcing to all that the celestial inhabitant, who once
gave them beauty, had departed? Will it be

better with the new generation? We easily predict a fair future to each new candidate who
enters the lists, but we are frivolous and volatile, and by low aims and ill example do what
we can to defeat this hope. Then these youths
bring us a rough but effectual aid. By their
unconcealed dissatisfaction they expose our poverty and the insignificance of man to man. A
man is a poor limitary benefactor. He ought
to be a shower of benefits — a great influence,
which should never let his brother go, but
should refresh old merits continually with new
ones; so that though absent he should never
be out of my mind, his name never far from
my lips; but if the earth should open at my
side, or my last hour were come, his name
should be the prayer I should utter to the Universe. But in our experience, man is cheap and
friendship wants its deep sense. We affect to
dwell with our friends in their absence, but we
do not; when deed, word, or letter comes not,
they let us go. These exacting children adver-
tise us of our wants. There is no compliment,
no smooth speech with them; they pay you
only this one compliment, of insatiable expectation; they aspire, they severely exact, and if
they only stand fast in this watch-tower, and

persist in demanding unto the end, and without
end, then are they terrible friends, whereof poet
and priest cannot choose but stand in awe ; and
what if they eat clouds, and drink wind, they
have not been without service to the race of
man.[1]

With this passion for what is great and extraordinary, it cannot be wondered at that they
are repelled by vulgarity and frivolity in people.
They say to themselves, It is better to be alone
than in bad company. And it is really a wish
to be met, — the wish to find society for their
hope and religion,— which prompts them to
shun what is called society. They feel that they
are never so fit for friendship as when they have
quitted mankind and taken themselves to friend.
A picture, a book, a favorite spot in the hills
or the woods which they can people with the
fair and worthy creation of the fancy, can give
them often forms so vivid that these for the
time shall seem real, and society the illusion.

But their solitary and fastidious manners not
only withdraw them from the conversation, but
from the labors of the world ; they are not
good citizens, not good members of society ;
unwillingly they bear their part of the public
and private burdens ; they do not willingly

share in the public charities, in the public religious rites, in the enterprises of education, of
missions foreign and domestic, in the abolition
of the slave-trade, or in the temperance society. They do not even like to vote. The philanthropists inquire whether Transcendentalism
does not mean sloth : they had as lief hear that
their friend is dead, as that he is a Transcendentalist; for then is he paralyzed, and can
never do anything for humanity. What right,
cries the good world, has the man of genius to
retreat from work, and indulge himself? The
popular literary creed seems to be, 'I am a sublime genius ; I ought not therefore to labor.'
But genius is the power to labor better and
more availably. Deserve thy genius : exalt it.
The good, the illuminated, sit apart from the
rest, censuring their dulness and vices, as if they
thought that by sitting very grand in their chairs,
the very brokers, attorneys, and congressmen
would see the error of their ways, and flock to
them. But the good and wise must learn to act,
and carry salvation to the combatants and de-
magogues in the dusty arena below.

   On the part of these children it is replied that
life and their faculty seem to them gifts too rich
to be squandered on such trifles as you propose

to them. What you call your fundamental
institutions, your great and holy causes, seem
to them great abuses, and, when nearly seen,
paltry matters. Each ' cause ' as it is called, —
say Abolition, Temperance, say Calvinism, or
Unitarianism, — becomes speedily a little shop,
where the article, let it have been at first never
so subtle and ethereal, is now made up into
portable and convenient cakes, and retailed in
small quantities to suit purchasers. You make
very free use of these words 'great ' and ' holy,'
but few things appear to them such. Few persons have any magnificence of nature to inspire
enthusiasm, and the philanthropies and charities have a certain air of quackery. As to the
general course of living, and the daily employments of men, they cannot see much virtue in
these, since they are parts of this vicious circle ;
and as no great ends are answered by the men,
there is nothing noble in the arts by which they
are maintained. Nay, they have made the experiment and found that from the liberal professions to the coarsest manual labor, and from
the courtesies of the academy and the college
to the conventions of the cotillon-room and the
morning call, there is a spirit of cowardly compromise and seeming which intimates a frightful

skepticism, a life without love, and an activity without an aim.

Unless the action is necessary, unless it is adequate, I do not wish to perform it. I do not wish to do one thing but once.[1] I do not love routine. Once possessed of the principle, it is equally easy to make four or forty thousand applications of it. A great man will be content to have indicated in any the slightest manner his perception of the reigning Idea of his time, and will leave to those who like it the multiplication of examples. When he has hit the white, the rest may shatter the target. Every thing admonishes us how needlessly long life is. Every moment of a hero so raises and cheers us that a twelvemonth is an age. All that the brave Xanthus brings home from his wars is the recollection that at the storming of Samos, " in the heat of the battle, Pericles smiled on me, and passed on to another detachment."[2] It is the quality of the moment, not the number of days, of events, or of actors, that imports.

New, we confess, and by no means happy, is our condition : if you want the aid of our labor, we ourselves stand in greater want of the labor. We are miserable with inaction. We perish of rest and rust : but we do not like your work.

' Then,' says the world, ' show me your own.'

' We have none.'

' What will you do, then ? ' cries the world.

' We will wait.'

' How long ? '

' Until the Universe beckons and calls us to work.'

' But whilst you wait, you grow old and useless.'

' Be it so : I can sit in a corner and *perish* (as you call it), but I will not move until I have the highest command. If no call should come for years, for centuries, then I know that the want of the Universe is the attestation of faith by my abstinence. Your virtuous projects, so called, do not cheer me. I know that which shall come will cheer me. If I cannot work, at least I need not lie. All that is clearly due to-day is not to lie. In other places other men have encountered sharp trials, and have behaved themselves well. The martyrs were sawn asunder, or hung alive on meat-hooks. Cannot we screw our courage to patience and truth, and without complaint, or even with good-humor, await our turn of action in the Infinite Counsels ? '

But to come a little closer to the secret of

these persons, we must say that to them it
seems a very easy matter to answer the objections of the man of the world, but not so easy
to dispose of the doubts and objections that occur to themselves. They are exercised in their
own spirit with queries which acquaint them
with all adversity, and with the trials of the
bravest heroes. When I asked them concerning
their private experience, they answered somewhat in this wise: It is not to be denied that
there must be some wide difference between
my faith and other faith; and mine is a certain
brief experience, which surprised me in the highway or in the market, in some place, at some
time, — whether in the body or out of the body,
God knoweth, — and made me aware that I had
played the fool with fools all this time, but that
law existed for me and for all; that to me belonged trust, a child's trust and obedience, and
the worship of ideas, and I should never be fool
more. Well, in the space of an hour probably,
I was let down from this height; I was at my
old tricks, the selfish member of a selfish society.
My life is superficial, takes no root in the deep
world; I ask, When shall I die and be relieved
of the responsibility of seeing an Universe which
I do not use? I wish to exchange this flash-

of-lightning faith for continuous daylight, this fever-glow for a benign climate.

These two states of thought diverge every moment, and stand in wild contrast. To him who looks at his life from these moments of illumination, it will seem that he skulks and plays a mean, shiftless and subaltern part in the world. That is to be done which he has not skill to do, or to be said which others can say better, and he lies by, or occupies his hands with some plaything, until his hour comes again. Much of our reading, much of our labor, seems mere waiting : it was not that we were born for. Any other could do it as well or better. So little skill enters into these works, so little do they mix with the divine life, that it really signifies little what we do, whether we turn a grindstone, or ride, or run, or make fortunes, or govern the state. The worst feature of this double consciousness is, that the two lives, of the understanding and of the soul, which we lead, really show very little relation to each other ; never meet and measure each other : one prevails now, all buzz and din ; and the other prevails then, all infinitude and paradise ; and, with the progress of life, the two discover no greater disposition to reconcile themselves. Yet, what is my faith? What am I? What but a thought of serenity and independence, an abode in the deep blue sky? Presently the clouds shut down again; yet we retain the belief that this petty web we weave will at last be overshot and reticulated with veins of the blue, and that the moments will characterize the days. Patience, then, is for us, is it not? Patience, and still patience. When we pass, as presently we shall, into some new infinitude, out of this Iceland of negations, it will please us to reflect that though we had few virtues or consolations, we bore with our indigence, nor once strove to repair it with hypocrisy or false heat of any kind.

But this class are not sufficiently characterized if we omit to add that they are lovers and worshippers of Beauty. In the eternal trinity of Truth, Goodness, and Beauty, each in its perfection including the three, they prefer to make Beauty the sign and head.[1] Something of the same taste is observable in all the moral movements of the time, in the religious and benevolent enterprises. They have a liberal, even an aesthetic spirit. A reference to Beauty in action sounds, to be sure, a little hollow and ridiculous in the ears of the old church. In politics, it has often sufficed, when they treated of justice, if they kept the bounds of selfish calculation. If they granted restitution, it was prudence which granted it. But the justice which is now claimed for the black, and the pauper, and the drunkard, is for Beauty, — is for a necessity to the soul of the agent, not of the beneficiary. I say this is the tendency, not yet the realization. Our virtue totters and trips, does not yet walk firmly. Its representatives are austere ; they preach and denounce ; their rectitude is not yet a grace. They are still liable to that slight taint of burlesque which in our strange world attaches to the zealot. A saint should be as dear as the apple of the eye. Yet we are tempted to smile, and we flee from the working to the speculative reformer, to escape that same slight ridicule. Alas for these days of derision and criticism ! We call the Beautiful the highest, because it appears to us the golden mean, escaping the dowdiness of the good and the heartlessness of the true. They are lovers of nature also, and find an indemnity in the inviolable order of the world for the violated order and grace of man.

There is, no doubt, a great deal of well-founded objection to be spoken or felt against the sayings and doings of this class, some of

whose traits we have selected; no doubt they
will lay themselves open to criticism and to lam-
poons, and as ridiculous stories will be to be
told of them as of any. There will be cant and
pretension; there will be subtilty and moon-
shine. These persons are of unequal strength,
and do not all prosper. They complain that
everything around them must be denied; and
if feeble, it takes all their strength to deny, before they can begin to lead their own life.[1]
Grave seniors insist on their respect to this institution and that usage; to an obsolete history;
to some vocation, or college, or etiquette, or
beneficiary, or charity, or morning or evening
call, which they resist as what does not concern
them. But it costs such sleepless nights, alien-
ations and misgivings, — they have so many
moods about it; these old guardians never
change *their* minds; they have but one mood
on the subject, namely, that Antony is very perverse, — that it is quite as much as Antony can
do to assert his rights, abstain from what he
thinks foolish, and keep his temper. He cannot
help the reaction of this injustice in his own
mind. He is braced-up and stilted; all freedom
and flowing genius, all sallies of wit and frolic
nature are quite out of the question; it is well

if he can keep from lying, injustice, and suicide. This is no time for gaiety and grace. His
strength and spirits are wasted in rejection.
But the strong spirits overpower those around
them without effort. Their thought and emotion comes in like a flood, quite withdraws them
from all notice of these carping critics; they sur-
render themselves with glad heart to the heavenly guide, and only by implication reject the
clamorous nonsense of the hour. Grave seniors
talk to the deaf,—church and old book mumble
and ritualize to an unheeding, preoccupied and
advancing mind, and thus they by happiness of
greater momentum lose no time, but take the
right road at first.

But all these of whom I speak are not pro-
ficients ; they are novices ; they only show the
road in which man should travel, when the soul
has greater health and prowess. Yet let them
feel the dignity of their charge, and deserve a
larger power. Their heart is the ark in which
the fire is concealed which shall burn in a broader
and universal flame. Let them obey the Genius
then most when his impulse is wildest; then
most when he seems to lead to uninhabitable
deserts of thought and life; for the path which
the hero travels alone is the highway of health

and benefit to mankind. What is the privilege and nobility of our nature but its persistency, through its power to attach itself to what is permanent?

Society also has its duties in reference to this class, and must behold them with what charity it can. Possibly some benefit may yet accrue from them to the state. In our Mechanics' Fair, there must be not only bridges, ploughs, carpenters' planes, and baking troughs, but also some few finer instruments, — rain-gauges, thermometers, and telescopes; and in society, besides farmers, sailors, and weavers, there must be a few persons of purer fire kept specially as gauges and meters of character; persons of a fine, detecting instinct, who note the smallest accumulations of wit and feeling in the bystander. Perhaps too there might be room for the exciters and monitors; collectors of the heavenly spark, with power to convey the electricity to others. Or, as the storm-tossed vessel at sea speaks the frigate or 'line packet' to learn its longitude, so it may not be without its advantage that we should now and then encounter rare and gifted men, to compare the points of our spiritual compass, and verify our bearings from superior chronometers.[1]

Amidst the downward tendency and prone-
ness of things, when every voice is raised for a
new road or another statute or a subscription
of stock; for an improvement in dress, or in
dentistry; for a new house or a larger business;
for a political party, or the division of an estate;
— will you not tolerate one or two solitary voices
in the land, speaking for thoughts and principles not marketable or perishable? Soon these
improvements and mechanical inventions will
be superseded; these modes of living lost out
of memory; these cities rotted, ruined by war,
by new inventions, by new seats of trade, or
the geologic changes: — all gone, like the shells
which sprinkle the sea-beach with a white colony
to-day, forever renewed to be forever destroyed.
But the thoughts which these few hermits strove
to proclaim by silence as well as by speech, not
only by what they did, but by what they for-
bore to do, shall abide in beauty and strength,
to reorganize themselves in nature, to invest
themselves anew in other, perhaps higher en-
dowed and happier mixed clay than ours, in
fuller union with the surrounding system.[1]

THE YOUNG AMERICAN

A LECTURE READ BEFORE THE MERCANTILE
LIBRARY ASSOCIATION, BOSTON,
FEBRUARY 7, 1844.

THE YOUNG AMERICAN

GENTLEMEN :

IT is remarkable that our people have their intellectual culture from one country and their duties from another.[1] This false state of things is newly in a way to be corrected. America is beginning to assert herself to the senses and to the imagination of her children, and Europe is receding in the same degree. This their reaction on education gives a new importance to the internal improvements and to the politics of the country. Who has not been stimulated to reflection by the facilities now in progress of construction for travel and the transportation of goods in the United States ?[2]

This rage of road building is beneficent for America, where vast distance is so main a consideration in our domestic politics and trade, inasmuch as the great political promise of the invention is to hold the Union staunch, whose days seemed already numbered by the mere inconvenience of transporting representatives, judges, and officers across such tedious distances of land and water. Not only is distance annihilated, but when, as now, the locomotive and the steamboat, like enormous shuttles, shoot every day across the thousand various threads of national descent and employment and bind them fast in one web, an hourly assimilation goes forward, and there is no danger that local peculiarities and hostilities should be preserved.[1]

1. But I hasten to speak of the utility of these improvements in creating an American sentiment. An unlooked-for consequence of the railroad is the increased acquaintance it has given the American people with the boundless resources of their own soil. If this invention has reduced England to a third of its size, by bringing people so much nearer, in this country it has given a new celerity to *time*, or anticipated by fifty years the planting of tracts of land, the choice of water privileges, the working of mines, and other natural advantages. Railroad iron is a magician's rod, in its power to evoke the sleeping energies of land and water.

The railroad is but one arrow in our quiver, though it has great value as a sort of yard-stick and surveyor's line. The bountiful continent is ours, state on state, and territory on territory, to the waves of the Pacific sea;

> " Our garden is the immeasurable earth,
> The heaven's blue pillars are Medea's house." [2]

The task of surveying, planting, and building upon this immense tract requires an education and a sentiment commensurate thereto. A consciousness of this fact is beginning to take the place of the purely trading spirit and education which sprang up whilst all the population lived on the fringe of sea-coast. And even on the coast, prudent men have begun to see that every American should be educated with a view to the values of land. The arts of engineering and of architecture are studied; scientific agriculture is an object of growing attention; the mineral riches are explored; limestone, coal, slate, and iron; and the value of timber-lands is enhanced.

Columbus alleged as a reason for seeking a continent in the West, that the harmony of nature required a great tract of land in the western hemisphere, to balance the known extent of land in the eastern; and it now appears that we must estimate the native values of this broad region to redress the balance of our own judgments, and appreciate the advantages opened to the human race in this country which is our fortunate home. The land is the appointed remedy for whatever is false and fantastic in our culture. The continent we inhabit is to be physic and food for our mind, as well as our body. The land, with its tranquillizing, sanative influences, is to repair the errors of a scholastic and traditional education, and bring us into just relations with men and things.[1]

The habit of living in the presence of these invitations of natural wealth is not inoperative; and this habit, combined with the moral sentiment which, in the recent years, has interrogated every institution, usage, and law, has naturally given a strong direction to the wishes and aims of active young men, to withdraw from cities and cultivate the soil. This inclination has appeared in the most unlooked-for quarters, in men supposed to be absorbed in business, and in those connected with the liberal professions.[2] And since the walks of trade were crowded, whilst that of agriculture cannot easily be, inasmuch as the farmer who is not wanted by others can yet grow his own bread, whilst the manufacturer or the trader, who is not wanted, cannot,—this seemed a happy tendency. For beside all the moral benefit which we may expect from the farmer's profession, when a man enters it considerately; this promised the conquering of the soil, plenty, and beyond this the adorning of the country with every advantage and ornament which labor, ingenuity, and affection for a man's home could suggest.

Meantime, with cheap land, and the pacific disposition of the people, everything invites to the arts of agriculture, of gardening, and domestic architecture. Public gardens, on the scale of such plantations in Europe and Asia, are now unknown to us. There is no feature of the old countries that strikes an American with more agreeable surprise than the beautiful gardens of Europe; such as the Boboli in Florence, the Villa Borghese in Rome, the Villa d' Este' in Tivoli, the gardens at Munich and at Frankfort on the Main: works easily imitated here, and which might well make the land dear to the citizen, and inflame patriotism. It is the fine art which is left for us, now that sculpture, painting, and religious and civil architecture have become effete, and have passed into second childhood. We have twenty degrees of latitude wherein to choose a seat, and the new modes of travelling enlarge the opportunity of selection, by making it easy to cultivate very distant tracts and yet remain in strict intercourse with the centres of trade and population. And the whole force of all the arts goes to facilitate the decoration of lands and dwellings. A garden has this advantage, that it makes it indifferent where you live. A well-laid garden makes the face of the country

of no account; let that be low or high, grand or
mean, you have made a beautiful abode worthy
of man. If the landscape is pleasing, the garden
shows it,—if tame, it excludes it. A little grove,
which any farmer can find or cause to grow near
his house, will in a few years make cataracts and
chains of mountains quite unnecessary to his
scenery; and he is so contented with his alleys,
woodlands, orchards and river, that Niagara, and
the Notch of the White Hills, and Nantasket
Beach, are superfluities.[1] And yet the selection
of a fit house-lot has the same advantage over
an indifferent one, as the selection to a given
employment of a man who has a genius for that
work. In the last case the culture of years will
never make the most painstaking apprentice his
equal: no more will gardening give the advantage of a happy site to a house in a hole or on a
pinnacle. In America we have hitherto little to
boast in this kind. The cities drain the country
of the best part of its population: the flower of
the youth, of both sexes, goes into the towns,
and the country is cultivated by a so much inferior class.[2] The land, — travel a whole day together, — looks poverty-stricken, and the buildings plain and poor. In Europe, where society
has an aristocratic structure, the land is full of

men of the best stock and the best culture,
whose interest and pride it is to remain half the
year on their estates, and to fill them with every
convenience and ornament. Of course these
make model farms, and model architecture, and
are a constant education to the eye of the surrounding population. Whatever events in progress shall go to disgust men with cities' and
infuse into them the passion for country life and
country pleasures, will render a service to the
whole face of this continent, and will further the
most poetic of all the occupations of real life,
the bringing out by art the native but hidden
graces of the landscape.

I look on such improvements also as directly
tending to endear the land to the inhabitant.
Any relation to the land, the habit of tilling it,
or mining it, or even hunting on it, generates
the feeling of patriotism. He who keeps shop
on it, or he who merely uses it as a support to
his desk and ledger, or to his manufactory, values
it less. The vast majority of the people of this
country live by the land, and carry its quality in
their manners and opinions.[1] We in the Atlantic states, by position, have been commercial,
and have, as I said, imbibed easily an European
culture. Luckily for us, now that steam has nar-

rowed the Atlantic to a strait, the nervous, rocky West is intruding a new and continental element into the national mind, and we shall yet have an American genius. How much better when the whole land is a garden, and the people have grown up in the bowers of a paradise. Without looking then to those extraordinary social influences which are now acting in precisely this direction, but only at what is inevitably doing around us, I think we must regard the *land* as a commanding and increasing power on the citizen, the sanative and Americanizing influence, which promises to disclose new virtues for ages to come.

2. In the second place, the uprise and culmination of the new and anti-feudal power of Commerce is the political fact of most significance to the American at this hour.

We cannot look on the freedom of this country, in connexion with its youth, without a presentiment that here shall laws and institutions exist on some scale of proportion to the majesty of nature. To men legislating for the area betwixt the two oceans, betwixt the snows and the tropics, somewhat of the gravity of nature will infuse itself into the code. A heterogeneous population crowding on all ships from all corners of the world to the great gates of North America, namely Boston, New York, and New Orleans, and thence proceeding inward to the prairie and the mountains, and quickly contributing their private thought to the public opinion, their toll to the treasury, and their vote to the election, it cannot be doubted that the legislation of this country should become more catholic and cosmopolitan than that of any other. It seems so easy for America to inspire and express the most expansive and humane spirit; new-born, free, healthful, strong, the land of the laborer, of the democrat, of the philanthropist, of the believer, of the saint, she should speak for the human race. It is the country of the Future. From Washington, proverbially 'the city of magnificent distances,' through all its cities, states, and territories, it is a country of beginnings, of projects, of designs, of expectations.[1]

Gentlemen, there is a sublime and friendly Destiny by which the human race is guided, — the race never dying, the individual never spared, — to results affecting masses and ages. Men are narrow and selfish, but the Genius or Destiny is not narrow, but beneficent. It is not discovered in their calculated and voluntary activity, but in what befalls, with or without their design.

Only what is inevitable interests us, and it turns out that love and good are inevitable, and in the course of things. That Genius has infused itself into nature. It indicates itself by a small excess of good, a small balance in brute facts always favoreble to the side of reason. All the facts in any part of nature shall be tabulated and the results shall indicate the same security and benefit; so slight as to be hardly observable, and yet it is there.[1] The sphere is flattened at the poles and swelled at the equator; a form flowing necessarily from the fluid state, yet *the* form, the mathematician assures us, required to prevent the protuberances of the continent, or even of lesser mountains cast up at any time by earthquakes, from continually deranging the axis of the earth. The census of the population is found to keep an invariable equality in the sexes, with a trifling predominance in favor of the male, as if to counterbalance the necessarily increased exposure of male life in war, navigation, and other accidents. Remark the unceasing effort throughout nature at somewhat better than the actual creatures: *amelioration in nature*, which alone permits and authorizes amelioration in mankind.[2] The population of the world is a conditional population; these are not the best, but the best that could

live in the existing state of soils, gases, animals
and morals: the best that could *yet* live; there
shall be a better, please God. This Genius or
Destiny is of the sternest administration, though
rumors exist of its secret tenderness. It may be
styled a cruel kindness, serving the whole even
to the ruin of the member; a terrible communist,
reserving all profits to the community, without
dividend to individuals. Its law is, you shall
have everything as a member, nothing to yourself. For Nature is the noblest engineer, yet
uses a grinding economy, working up all that
is wasted to-day into to-morrow's creation;—.
not a superfluous grain of sand, for all the osten-
tation she makes of expense and public works.
It is because Nature thus saves and uses, laboring for the general, that we poor particulars are
so crushed and straitened, and find it so hard
to live. She flung us out in her plenty, but we
cannot shed a hair or a paring of a nail but instantly she snatches at the shred and appropri-
ates it to the general stock. Our condition is
like that of the poor wolves: if one of the flock
wound himself or so much as limp, the rest eat
him up incontinently.[1]

That serene Power interposes the check upon
the caprices and officiousness of our wills. Its

charity is not our charity. One of its agents is
our will, but that which expresses itself in our
will is stronger than our will. We are very forward to help it, but it will not be accelerated. It
resists our meddling, eleemosynary contrivances.
We devise sumptuary and relief laws, but the
principle of population is always reducing wages
to the lowest pittance on which human life can be
sustained. We legislate against forestalling and
monopoly; we would have a common granary
for the poor; but the selfishness which hoards
the corn for high prices is the preventive of
famine; and the law of self-preservation is surer
policy than any legislation can be. We con-
coct eleemosynary systems, and it turns out
that our charity increases pauperism. We inflate
our paper currency, we repair commerce with
unlimited credit, and are presently visited with
unlimited bankruptcy.

It is easy to see that the existing generation
are conspiring with a beneficence which in its
working for coming generations, sacrifices the
passing one; which infatuates the most selfish
men to act against their private interest for the
public welfare. We build railroads, we know
not for what or for whom; but one thing is
certain, that we who build will receive the very

smallest share of benefit. Benefit will accrue,
they are essential to the country, but that will
be felt not until we are no longer countrymen.
We do the like in all matters : —

> " Man's heart the Almighty to the Future set
>   By secret and inviolable springs."

We plant trees, we build stone houses, we redeem the waste, we make prospective laws, we
found colleges and hospitals, for remote generations. We should be mortified to learn that the
little benefit we chanced in our own persons to
receive was the utmost they would yield.

The history of commerce is the record of this
beneficent tendency. The patriarchal form of
government readily becomes despotic, as each
person may see in his own family. Fathers wish
to be fathers of the minds of their children, and
behold with impatience a new character and way
of thinking presuming to show itself in their
own son or daughter. This feeling, which all
their love and pride in the powers of their children cannot subdue, becomes petulance and
tyranny when the head of the clan, the emperor
of an empire, deals with the same difference
of opinion in his subjects. Difference of opinion is the one crime which kings never forgive.
An empire is an immense egotism. "I am the

State," said the French Louis. When a French ambassador mentioned to Paul of Russia that a man of consequence in St. Petersburg was interesting himself in some matter, the Czar interrupted him, — " There is no man of consequence in this empire but he with whom I am actually speaking; and so long only as I am speaking to him is he of any consequence." And the Emperor Nicholas is reported to have said to his council, " The age is embarrassed with new opinions; rely on me, gentlemen, I shall oppose an iron will to the progress of liberal opinions."

It is easy to see that this patriarchal or family management gets to be rather troublesome to all but the papa; the sceptre comes to be a crow-bar. And this unpleasant egotism, Feudalism opposes and finally destroys. The king is compelled to call in the aid of his brothers and cousins and remote relations, to help him keep his overgrown house in order; and this club of noblemen always come at last to have a will of their own; they combine to brave the sovereign, and call in the aid of the people. Each chief attaches as many followers as he can, by kindness, maintenance, and gifts; and as long as war lasts, the nobles, who must be soldiers, rule very well. But when peace comes, the nobles prove very whimsical and uncomfortable masters ; their frolics turn out to be insulting and degrading to the commoner. Feudalism grew to be a bandit and brigand.

Meantime Trade had begun to appear: Trade, a plant which grows wherever there is peace, as soon as there is peace, and as long as there is peace. The luxury and necessity of the noble fostered it. And as quickly as men go to foreign parts in ships or caravans, a new order of things springs up; new command takes place, new servants and new masters. Their information, their wealth, their correspondence, have made them quite other men than left their native shore. *They* are nobles now, and by another patent than the king's. Feudalism had been good, had broken the power of the kings, and had some good traits of its own ; but it had grown mischievous, it was time for it to die, and as they say of dying people, all its faults came out. Trade was the strong man that broke it down and raised a new and unknown power in its place. It is a new agent in the world, and one of great function; it is a very intellectual force. This displaces physical strength, and instals computation, combination, information,

science, in its room. It calls out all force of
a certain kind that slumbered in the former
dynasties. It is now in the midst of its career.
Feudalism is not ended yet. Our governments
still partake largely of that element. Trade goes
to make the governments insignificant, and to
bring every kind of faculty of every individual
that can in any manner serve any person, *on
sale*. Instead of a huge Army and Navy and
Executive Departments, it converts Government into an Intelligence-Office, where every
man may find what he wishes to buy, and expose what he has to sell; not only produce and
manufactures, but art, skill, and intellectual and
moral values. This is the good and this the evil
of trade, that it would put everything into market; talent, beauty, virtue, and man himself.

The philosopher and lover of man have much
harm to say of trade; but the historian will see
that trade was the principle of Liberty; that
trade planted America and destroyed Feudalism; that it makes peace and keeps peace, and
it will abolish slavery. We complain of its oppression of the poor, and of its building up a
new aristocracy on the ruins of the aristocracy
it destroyed. But the aristocracy of trade has
no permanence, is not entailed, was the result

of toil and talent, the result of merit of some
kind, and is continually falling, like the waves
of the sea, before new claims of the same sort.
Trade is an instrument in the hands of that
friendly Power which works for us in our own
despite. We design it thus and thus ; it turns
out otherwise and far better. This beneficent
tendency, omnipotent without violence, exists
and works. Every line of history inspires a
confidence that we shall not go far wrong ; that
things mend. That is the moral of all we learn,
that it warrants Hope, the prolific mother of
reforms. Our part is plainly not to throw ourselves across the track, to block improvement
and sit till we are stone, but to watch the uprise
of successive mornings and to conspire with the
new works of new days.¹ Government has been
a fossil ; it should be a plant. I conceive that
the office of statute law should be to express
and not to impede the mind of mankind. New
thoughts, new things. Trade was one instrument, but Trade is also but for a time, and
must give way to somewhat broader and better,
whose signs are already dawning in the sky.

3. I pass to speak of the signs of that which
is the sequel of trade.

In consequence of the revolution in the state

of society wrought by trade, Government in our times is beginning to wear a clumsy and cumbrous appearance. We have already seen our way to shorter methods. The time is full of good signs. Some of them shall ripen to fruit. All this beneficent socialism is a friendly omen, and the swelling cry of voices for the education of the people indicates that Government has other offices than those of banker and executioner. Witness the new movements in the civilized world, the Communism of France, Germany, and Switzerland; the Trades' Unions, the English League against the Corn Laws; and the whole *Industrial Statistics*, so called. In Paris, the blouse, the badge of the operative, has begun to make its appearance in the *salons*. Witness too the spectacle of three Communities which have within a very short time sprung up within this Commonwealth, besides several others undertaken by citizens of Massachusetts within the territory of other States.[1] These proceeded from a variety of motives, from an impatience of many usages in common life, from a wish for greater freedom than the manners and opinions of society permitted, but in great part from a feeling that the true offices of the State, the State had let fall to the ground; that

in the scramble of parties for the public purse,
the main duties of government were omitted,
— the duty to instruct the ignorant, to supply
the poor with work and with good guidance.
These communists preferred the agricultural
life as the most favorable condition for human
culture ; but they thought that the farm, as we
manage it, did not satisfy the right ambition
of man. The farmer, after sacrificing pleasure,
taste, freedom, thought, love, to his work, turns
out often a bankrupt, like the merchant. This
result might well seem astounding. All this
drudgery, from cock - crowing to starlight, for
all these years, to end in mortgages and the
auctioneer's flag, and removing from bad to
worse. It is time to have the thing looked into,
and with a sifting criticism ascertained who is
the fool. It seemed a great deal worse, because
the farmer is living in the same town with men
who pretend to know exactly what he wants.
On one side is agricultural chemistry, coolly
exposing the nonsense of our spendthrift agriculture and ruinous expense of manùres, and
offering, by means of a teaspoonful of artificial
guano, to turn a sandbank into corn ; and on
the other, the farmer, not only eager for the information, but with bad crops and in debt and

bankruptcy, for want of it. Here are Etzlers
and mechanical projectors, who, with the Fou-
rierists, undoubtingly affirm that the smallest
union would make every man rich ; — and, on
the other side, a multitude of poor men and women seeking work, and who cannot find enough
to pay their board. The science is confident,
and surely the poverty is real. If any means
could be found to bring these two together!

This was one design of the projectors of the
Associations which are now making their first
feeble experiments. They were founded in love
and in labor. They proposed, as you know,
that all men should take a part in the manual
toil, and proposed to amend the condition of
men by substituting harmonious for hostile industry. It was a noble thought of Fourier,
which gives a favorable idea of his system, to
distinguish in his Phalanx a class as the Sacred
Band, by whom whatever duties were disagreeable and likely to be omitted, were to be assumed.[1]

At least an economical success seemed certain for the enterprise, and that agricultural association must, sooner or later, fix the price of
bread, and drive single farmers into association
in self-defence ; as the great commercial and

manufacturing companies had already done. The Community is only the continuation of the same movement which made the joint-stock companies for manufactures, mining, insurance, banking, and so forth. It has turned out cheaper to make calico by companies; and it is proposed to plant corn and to bake bread by companies.

Undoubtedly, abundant mistakes will be made by these first adventurers, which will draw ridicule on their schemes. I think for example that they exaggerate the importance of a favorite project of theirs, that of paying talent and labor at one rate, paying all sorts of service at one rate, say ten cents the hour. They have paid it so ; but not an instant would a dime remain a dime. In one hand it became an eagle as it fell, and in another hand a copper cent. For the whole value of the dime is in knowing what to do with it. One man buys with it a land-title of an Indian, and makes his posterity princes ; or buys corn enough to feed the world ; or pen, ink, and paper, or a painter's brush, by which he can communicate himself to the human race as if he were fire ; and the other buys barley candy. Money is of no value ; it cannot spend itself. All depends on the skill of the spender. Whether too the objection almost universally felt by such women in the community as were mothers, to an associate life, to a common table, and a common nursery, etc., setting a higher value on the private family, with poverty, than on an association with wealth, will not prove insuperable, remains to be determined.

But the Communities aimed at a higher success in securing to all their members an equal and thorough education. And on the whole one may say that aims so generous and so forced on them by the times, will not be relinquished, even if these attempts fail, but will be prosecuted until they succeed.

This is the value of the Communities; not what they have done, but the revolution which they indicate as on the way. Yes, Government must educate the poor man. Look across the country from any hill-side around us and the landscape seems to crave Government. The actual differences of men must be acknowledged, and met with love and wisdom. These rising grounds which command the champaign below, seem to ask for lords, true lords, *land*-lords, who understand the land and its uses and the applicabilities of men, and whose government would be what it should, namely mediation between want and supply. How gladly

would each citizen pay a commission for the support and continuation of good guidance. None
should be a governor who has not a talent for
governing. Now many people have a native
skill for carving out business for many hands;
a genius for the disposition of affairs; and are
never happier than when difficult practical questions, which embarrass other men, are to be
solved. All lies in light before them; they are
in their element. Could any means be contrived
to appoint only these! There really seems a
progress towards such a state of things in which
this work shall be done by these natural workmen; and this, not certainly through any increased discretion shown by the citizens at elections, but by the gradual contempt into which
official government falls, and the increasing disposition of private adventurers to assume its
fallen functions. Thus the national Post Office
is likely to go into disuse before the private
telegraph and the express companies. The currency threatens to fall entirely into private hands.
Justice is continually administered more and
more by private reference, and not by litiga-
tion. We have feudal governments in a commercial age. It would be but an easy extension
of our commercial system, to pay a private em-

peror a fee for services, as we pay an architect, an engineer, or a lawyer. If any man has a talent for righting wrong, for administering difficult affairs, for counselling poor farmers how to turn their estates to good husbandry, for combining a hundred private enterprises to a general benefit, let him in the county-town, or in Court Street, put up his sign-board, Mr. Smith, *Governor*, Mr. Johnson, *Working king*.

How can our young men complain of the poverty of things in New England, and not feel that poverty as a demand on their charity to make New England rich? Where is he who seeing a thousand men useless and unhappy, and making the whole region forlorn by their inaction, and conscious himself of possessing the faculty they want, does not hear his call to go and be their king?

We must have kings, and we must have nobles. Nature provides such in every society, — only let us have the real instead of the titular. Let us have our leading and our inspiration from the best. In every society some men are born to rule and some to advise. Let the powers be well directed, directed by love, and they would everywhere be greeted with joy and honor. The chief is the chief all the world over, only not his cap and his plume. It is only their dislike of the pretender, which makes men sometimes unjust to the accomplished man. If society were transparent, the noble would everywhere be gladly received and accredited, and would not be asked for his day's work, but would be felt as benefit, inasmuch as he was noble. That were his duty and stint, — to keep himself pure and purifying, the leaven of his nation. I think I see place and duties for a nobleman in every society ; but it is not to drink wine and ride in a fine coach, but to guide and adorn life for the multitude by forethought, by elegant studies, by perseverance, self-devotion, and the remembrance of the humble old friend, by making his life secretly beautiful.[1]

I call upon you, young men, to obey your heart and be the nobility of this land. In every age of the world there has been a leading nation, one of a more generous sentiment, whose eminent citizens were willing to stand for the interests of general justice and humanity, at the risk of being called, by the men of the moment, chimerical and fantastic. Which should be that nation but these States ? Which should lead that movement, if not New England ? Who should lead the leaders, but the Young Ameri-

can ? The people, and the world, are now suffering from the want of religion and honor in
its public mind. In America, out-of-doors all
seems a market ; in-doors an air-tight stove of
conventionalism. Every body who comes into
our houses savors of these habits ; the men, of
the market ; the women, of the custom. I find
no expression in our state papers or legislative
debate, in our lyceums or churches, especially
in our newspapers, of a high national feeling,
no lofty counsels that rightfully stir the blood.
I speak of those organs which can be presumed
to speak a popular sense. They recommend
conventional virtues, whatever will earn and preserve property ; always the capitalist ; the college, the church, the hospital, the theatre, the
hotel, the road, the ship of the capitalist, —
whatever goes to secure, adorn, enlarge these
is good ; what jeopardizes any of these is damnable. The ' opposition ' papers, so called, are
on the same side. They attack the great capitalist, but with the aim to make a capitalist of
the poor man. The opposition is against those
who have money, from those who wish to have
money. But who announces to us in journal,
or in pulpit, or in the street, the secret of
heroism ?

" Man alone
Can perform the impossible." [1]

I shall not need to go into an enumeration of
our national defects and vices which require this
Order of Censors in the State. I might not set
down our most proclaimed offences as the worst.
It is not often the worst trait that occasions the
loudest outcry. Men complain of their suffering, and not of the crime. I fear little from the
bad effect of Repudiation; I do not fear that
it will spread. Stealing is a suicidal business;
you cannot repudiate but once. But the bold
face and tardy repentance permitted to this local
mischief reveal a public mind so preoccupied
with the love of gain that the common sentiment of indignation at fraud does not act with
its natural force. The more need of a withdrawal
from the crowd, and a resort to the fountain of
right, by the brave. The timidity of our public
opinion is our disease, or, shall I say, the pub-
licness of opinion, the absence of private opinion.
Good nature is plentiful, but we want justice,
with heart of steel, to fight down the proud.[2]
The private mind has the access to the totality
of goodness and truth that it may be a balance
to a corrupt society; and to stand for the private verdict against popular clamor is the office

of the noble. If a humane measure is pro-
pounded in behalf of the slave, or of the Irishman, or the Catholic, or for the succor of the
poor; that sentiment, that project, will have
the homage of the hero. That is his nobility,
his oath of knighthood, to succor the helpless
and oppressed; always to throw himself on
the side of weakness, of youth, of hope; on the
liberal, on the expansive side, never on the de-
fensive, the conserving, the timorous, the lock-
and-bolt system. More than our good-will we
may not be able to give. We have our own
affairs, our own genius, which chains each to his
proper work. We cannot give our life to the
cause of the debtor, of the slave, or the pauper,
as another is doing; but to one thing we are
bound, not to blaspheme the sentiment and the
work of that man, not to throw stumbling-blocks
in the way of the abolitionist, the philanthropist; as the organs of influence and opinion are
swift to do. It is for us to confide in the beneficent Supreme Power, and not to rely on our
money, and on the state because it is the guard
of money. At this moment, the terror of old
people and of vicious people is lest the Union
of these states be destroyed: as if the Union
had any other real basis than the good pleasure

of a majority of the citizens to be united.¹ But
the wise and just man will always feel that he
stands on his own feet ; that he imparts strength
to the State, not receives security from it ; and
that if all went down, he and such as he would
quite easily combine in a new and better constitution. Every great and memorable community
has consisted of formidable individuals, who, like
the Roman or the Spartan, lent his own spirit
to the State and made it great. Yet only by
the supernatural is a man strong; nothing is so
weak as an egotist. Nothing is mightier than
we, when we are vehicles of a truth before which
the State and the individual are alike ephemeral.

Gentlemen, the development of our American
internal resources, the extension to the utmost
of the commercial system, and the appearance
of new moral causes which are to modify the
State, are giving an aspect of greatness to the
Future, which the imagination fears to open.
One thing is plain for all men of common sense
and common conscience, that here, here in America, is the home of man. After all the deductions
which are to be made for our pitiful politics,
which stake every gravest national question on
the silly die whether James or whether Robert

shall sit in the chair and hold the purse; after all the deduction is made for our frivolities and insanities, there still remains an organic simplicity and liberty, which, when it loses its balance, redresses itself presently, which offers opportunity to the human mind not known in any other region.

It is true, the public mind wants self-respect. We are full of vanity, of which the most signal proof is our sensitiveness to foreign and especially English censure. One cause of this is our immense reading, and that reading chiefly confined to the productions of the English press. It is also true that to imaginative persons in this country there is somewhat bare and bald in our short history and unsettled wilderness. They ask, who would live in a new country that can live in an old? and it is not strange that our youths and maidens should burn to see the picturesque extremes of an antiquated country. But it is one thing to visit the Pyramids, and another to wish to live there. Would they like tithes to the clergy, and sevenths to the government, and Horse-Guards, and licensed press, and grief when a child is born, and threatening, starved weavers, and a pauperism now constituting one thirteenth of the population?[1] Instead

of the open future expanding here before the
eye of every boy to vastness, would they like the
closing in of the future to a narrow slit of sky,
and that fast contracting to be no future? One
thing for instance, the beauties of aristocracy, we
commend to the study of the travelling American. The English, the most conservative people
this side of India, are not sensible of the restraint,
but an American would seriously resent it. The
aristocracy, incorporated by law and education,
degrades life for the unprivileged classes. It is
a questionable compensation to the embittered
feeling of a proud commoner, the reflection that
a fop, who, by the magic of title, paralyzes his
arm and plucks from him half the graces and
rights of a man, is himself also an aspirant excluded with the same ruthlessness from higher
circles, since there is no end to the wheels within
wheels of this spiral heaven. Something may be
pardoned to the spirit of loyalty when it becomes
fantastic; and something to the imagination, for
the baldest life is symbolic. Philip II. of Spain
rated his ambassador for neglecting serious affairs
in Italy, whilst he debated some point of honor
with the French ambassador; "You have left a
business of importance for a ceremony." The
ambassador replied, " Your Majesty's self is but

a ceremony." In the East, where the religious sentiment comes in to the support of the aristocracy, and in the Romish church also, there is a grain of sweetness in the tyranny; but in England, the fact seems to me intolerable, what is commonly affirmed, that such is the transcendent honor accorded to wealth and birth, that no man of letters, be his eminence what it may, is received into the best society, except as a lion and a show. The English have many virtues, many advantages, and the proudest history of the world; but they need all and more than all the resources of the past to indemnify a heroic gentleman in that country for the mortifications prepared for him by the system of society, and which seem to impose the alternative to resist or to avoid it. That there are mitigations and practical alleviations to this rigor, is not an excuse for the rule. Commanding worth and personal power must sit crowned in all companies, nor will extraordinary persons be slighted or affronted in any company of civilized men. But the system is an invasion of the sentiment of justice and the native rights of men, which, however decorated, must lessen the value of English citizenship.[1] It is for Englishmen to consider, not for us; we only say, Let us live in America, too thankful

for our want of feudal institutions. Our houses
and towns are like mosses and lichens, so slight
and new; but youth is a fault of which we shall
daily mend. This land too is as old as the Flood,
and wants no ornament or privilege which nature
could bestow. Here stars, here woods, here hills,
here animals, here men abound, and the vast tendencies concur of a new order. If only the men
are employed in conspiring with the designs of
the Spirit who led us hither and is leading us
still, we shall quickly enough advance out of all
hearing of others' censures, out of all regrets of
our own, into a new and more excellent social
state than history has recorded.

NOTES

NOTES

NATURE

IN his boyish poem "Good-bye," Mr. Emerson told how, among the cedar and barberry thickets of Roxbury, he found that

> Man in the bush with God may meet.

In his boyhood, though city born, the doors of his grandfather's house by Concord River were always open to him. He knew well thóse meadows, the hills of Waltham and Newton, and the Chelmsford woods in his schoolboy and school-teaching days. The attractions of beautiful and living Nature grew with the increasing repulsion which he felt during his ministry from formalism and Hebraism.

As the little book *Nature* was Mr. Emerson's first venture in letters, yet is still held as one of his most notable works, it seems justifiable to recall, even at some length, its history and the reception it met with in America and in England.

In his journals it does not appear how long he had been meditating this book. The first mention of it occurs in his diary on shipboard, returning from his earliest visit to Europe in 1833. Just three years later the book appeared. It will be remembered that these had been sad and unsettled days for him. His home had been broken up by the death of his young wife, and his recoil from certain forms and rites in worship had driven him to part from his church. He had made the journey to Italy, France, and England to recruit his strength and prepare for a changed life. He writes, September 6, "I like my book about nature, and wish I knew when and where I ought to live. God will show me. I am glad to be on my way home, yet not so glad as others, and my way to the bottom I could find, perchance, with less regret, for I think it would not hurt me, that is, the ducking or drowning.''

In November, 1834, Mr. Emerson came to make his home in Concord and lived for a time with his venerable step-grandfather, Dr. Ezra Ripley. There, in the little room in the southern gable, since known as the Prophet's Chamber, where later Hawthorne wrote the *Mosses from an Old Manse*, he worked on his book. Mr. Cabot in his Memoir ¹ says that probably the first five chapters had been for some time in hand, that the seventh and eighth chapters seem to have been written after his removal to Concord, and the sixth (Idealism) last of all, as the connection of the two. In writing to his brother William, he says: —

CONCORD, JUNE 28, 1836.

My little book is nearly done. Its title is *Nature*. . . . My design is to follow it with another essay, *Spirit*, and the two shall make a decent volume.

AUGUST 8.

The book of *Nature* still lies on the table ; there is, as always, one crack in it, not easy to be soldered or welded ; but if this week I should be left alone, I may finish it.

It was published in September, anonymously ; only five hundred copies were printed, and of these many remained long unsold, so that a second edition was not called for until 1849.

In this essay, as in the *Sermon on the Lord's Supper*, it is interesting to note a more ordered presentation of the ideas — such as was usual in sermons — than Mr. Emerson in the later writings cared to attempt.

¹ *A Memoir of Ralph Waldo Emerson.* By James Elliot Cabot.

Mr. Cabot in his Memoir says that "by the *Christian Examiner*, the chief organ of the Unitarians, *Nature* was treated rather indulgently as a poetical rhapsody containing much beautiful writing and not devoid of sound philosophy, but, on the whole, producing the impression of a disordered dream." He adds, "Transcendentalism was attacked (though more often sneered at) as a threat, however impotent, of radical revolution, but not often, I think, in the person of Emerson. In him, it would be felt, revolution was like the revolutions of Nature, who does not cast off her old leaves until she has got ready the new."

The *Examiner's* view of the work as a poetical rhapsody suggests Dr. Holmes's account of it. "*Nature* is a reflective prose poem. It is divided into eight chapters, which might almost as well have been called cantos. Beginning simply enough, it took more and more the character of a rhapsody, until, as if lifted off his feet by the deepened and stronger undercurrent of his thought, the writer dropped his personality, and repeated the words which 'a certain poet sang to him.'" It is, however, very possible that the passage referred to, in the last chapter of *Nature*, was a poetical rendering of the thoughts of his new-found friend, Mr. Alcott.

Immediately on the appearance of *Nature*, Emerson wrote to Carlyle : —

"I send you a little book I have just now published ; an entering wedge, I hope, to something more worthy and significant. This is only a naming of topics on which I would gladly speak and gladlier hear."

Carlyle thus hailed its appearance : —

"Your little azure-coloured *Nature* gave me true satisfaction. I read it and then lent it about to all my acquaintance that had a sense for such things, from whom a similar verdict always came back. You say it is the first chapter of something greater. I call it rather a Foundation and Ground-plan on which you may build whatsoever of great and true has been given you to build. It is the true Apocalypse, this where the ‘ Open Secret ’ becomes revealed to a man. I rejoice much in the glad serenity of soul with which you look out on this wondrous Dwelling-place of yours and mine, — with an ear for the *Ewigen Melodien* which pipe in the winds round us and utter themselves forth in all sounds and sights and things: *not* to be written down by gamut machinery, but which all right writing is a kind of attempt to write down. You will see what the years will bring you.''

In a letter written in April, 1839, he tells that '' people are beginning to quote you here : *tant pis pour eux*. I have found you in two Cambridge books ; a certain Mr. Richard Monckton Milnes, M. P., a beautiful little Tory dilettante poet and politician, whom I love much, applied to me for *Nature*, that he might write upon it.''

And soon after he received this greeting in a letter from Sterling : [1] —

SEPTEMBER 30, 1839.

I have read very, very little modern English writing that has struck and pleased me so much ; among recent productions,

---

[1] John Sterling, a writer of prose and verse (*The Onyx Ring ; The Sexton's Daughter and Other Poems ; Strafford, a Tragedy, etc.*), now, however, best known as the subject of biographies by Carlyle and Archdeacon Hare. With this brilliant and inspiring man Emerson formed a close friendship by letters, though they never met, lasting until Sterling's early death in 1847. See *A Correspondence between Sterling and Emerson*, published by Messrs. Houghton, Mifflin & Co., 1897.

almost only those of our friend Carlyle, whose shaggy-browed and deep-eyed thoughts have often a likeness to yours which is very attractive and impressive, neither evidently being the double of the other. . . . I trust that you will long continue to diffuse, by your example as well as doctrine, the knowledge that the Sun and Earth and Plato and Shakspeare are what they are by working each in his vocation ; and that we can be anything better than mountebanks living, and scarecrows dead, only by doing so likewise. For my better assurance of this truth, as well as for much and cordial kindness, I shall always remain your debtor.

In this essay Emerson announced his doctrine of the Oversoul, the Universal Mind, which runs through all his work. Its keynote is given in the words " The noblest ministry of Nature is to stand as the apparition of God. It is the organ through which the universal spirit speaks to the individual and strives to lead back the individual to it. . . . The world proceeds from the same spirit as the body of man. It is a remoter and inferior incarnation of God, a projection of God in the unconscious. But it differs from the body in one important respect. It is not, like that, now subjected to the human will. Its serene order is inviolable by us. It is, therefore, to us, the present expositor of the divine mind. It is a fixed point whereby we may measure our departure."

Page 1, note 1.   Mr. Emerson loved to place a motto at the head of his chapter. Dr. Holmes suggested that the hereditary use of a text before a discourse survived thus in him. Before *Nature* in the first edition he placed the words of Plotinus : " Nature is but an image or imitation of wisdom, the last thing of the soul ; Nature being a thing which doth only do, but not know.''

Of the verse containing the doctrine of Evolution which he wrote for the second edition, and which still stands before the Essay, something has been said in the biographical sketch.

The present motto was placed at the beginning of *Nature* in its second edition in 1849 instead of the sentence of Plotinus. But in the new one, Mr. William T. Harris [1] finds this thought of Plotinus, whom he thus quotes : `` We might say that all beings, not only rational ones, but even irrational ones, the plants, and even the soil that bears them, aspire to attain conscious knowledge,'' and credits to Plotinus `` the suggestion of those fine poetic dreams of Schelling and Oken, — that reason dreams in the plant, and feels in the animal, and thinks in man.'' As has been said in the biographical sketch, Plato and his followers had prepared Mr. Emerson's mind to welcome the dawning evolution theories of Lamarck and others, which probably came to him through Lyell's work on Geology, and in conversation with scholars of science. Darwin's *Origin of Species* was not published until 1859.

During his short stay in Paris in 1833, Mr. Emerson visited the *Jardin des Plantes,* and in a lecture called *The Uses of Natural History,* read before the Boston Natural History Society in November of that year, told of what he saw. In it he said : `` The eye is satisfied with seeing, and strange thoughts arise. The universe is a more amazing puzzle than ever as you look along this bewildering series of animated forces. . . . While I stand there I am impressed with a singular conviction that not a form so grotesque, so savage, or so beautiful, but is an expression of something in man the ob-

[1] *Memoir of Bronson Alcott,* by F. B. Sanborn and W. T. Harris.

server. We feel that there is an occult relation between the very worm, the crawling scorpions, and man. I am moved by strange sympathies. I say I will listen to this invitation. I will be a naturalist."

Page 4, note 1. Compare the line in "The Sphinx," *Poems:* —

Thou art the unanswered question.

Page 4, note 2. It should be remembered to how large a part of the educated world the first chapter of Genesis stood in 1836 as the sole and final authority on Creation. Geology and paleontology were in their infancy, comparative anatomy little advanced, and biology hardly born. The new philosophic ideas of progressive development and amelioration, fortified by the new science, were welcomed by Mr. Emerson as harmonizing with the laws of spirit.

Page 7, note 1. In the heavenly bodies Emerson early found his teachers : symbols of light and law, in their beauty, their vast excursion and sure return, they guide his thought and illuminate his works. (See especially "The Poet" [*Poems*, Appendix], "Woodnotes," II., "Character," and "Uriel.") His early journals show that the system of Copernicus widened his views as a minister. In 1833, in Florence, he did homage at the tomb of Galileo. He read the lives of Kepler and Newton, and Herschel's Astronomy, and often expressed the hope that old age might bring him leisure to study the stars. It was his counsel "Hitch your wagon to a star." ("Civilization,"*Society and Solitude.*)

Page 9, note 1. Compare the sentence in a note-book of Mr. Emerson's from Plutarch's essay in the *Morals,* "Why the Pythian Priestess ceases her Oracles in Verse : " —

"The Sun is the cause that all men are ignorant of Apollo,

by sense withdrawing the rational intellect from that which is to that which appears.''

Page 9, note 2. This sentence and what follows are distinctly autobiographical, representing the life that Mr. Emerson led in Concord, going almost daily alone to the woods to attune himself to receive through their symbolic life hints of the spiritual life.

Page 9, note 3.

> Sheen will tarnish, honey cloy,
> And merry is only a mask of sad,
> But sober on a fund of joy,
> The woods at heart are glad.
>
> "Waldeinsamkeit," *Poems.*

Page 10, note 1. Here first appears in his published writings Emerson's doctrine of the Universal Mind or the Oversoul, which thereafter ran through all his works.

The little poem "Pan" (see *Poems*, Appendix) is called to mind by this passage.

Page 11, note 1.

> Methought the sky looked scornful down
> On all was base in man,
> And airy tongues did taunt the town,
> 'Achieve our peace who can!'
>
> "Walden," *Poems*, Appendix.

Page 13, note 1. In the journal for 1855 is written this little prose poem : —

THE YEAR.

There is no flower so sweet as the four-petalled flower which science much neglects; one grey petal it has, one green, one red, and one white.

Page 13, note 2. George Herbert's poem "Man," five stanzas of which are given in chapter viii. of this essay.

Page 14, note 1. Mr. Emerson's friend, Henry Thoreau, wrote : "I do not go there [to the woods] to get my dinner, but to get that sustenance which dinners only preserve me to enjoy."

Page 16, note 1. See first page of "Spiritual Laws," *Essays, First Series.*

Page 17, note 1. The poem "Sunrise," written probably at the same time, while Mr. Emerson lived at the Old Manse, describes the morning seen from the hill opposite. (*Poems,* Appendix.)

Page 18, note 1.

> Ah! well I mind the calendar,
> Faithful through a thousand years,
> Of the painted race of flowers, etc.
>
> "May-Day," *Poems.*

Page 20, note 1. Compare quatrain "Northman," in *Poems.*

Page 23, note 1.

> Thee, gliding through the sea of form, etc.
>
> "Ode to Beauty," *Poems.*

Page 24, note 1. "Each and All" and "Xenophanes," *Poems.*

Page 24, note 2. The theme of "The Rhodora," *Poems.*

Page 24, note 3. This Trinity of the different manifestations of Spirit through the universe, symbolized in matter by the Protean aspects, of light, heat, motion, was a basal thought with Emerson. It is expressed again in the chapter "Spirit" in this essay, in "The Transcendentalist" in this volume, and in the end of "Art," *Society and Solitude*, and as the "three children of the Universe" in the first pages of "The Poet," *Essays, Second Series*. Sidney Lanier, in his last lecture before his death, at the Johns Hopkins University,[1] spoke of this Trinity of Emerson's.

In Thomas Taylor's *Substance of Porphyry's Life of Plotinus*, Plato's and Plotinus's Trinity, the Good, Intellect and the Soul, is discussed, and the author adds, "This theory, the progeny of the most consummate science, is in perfect conformity with the theology of the Chaldæans. And hence is it said in one of their oracles, 'In every world a triad shines forth, of which a monad is the ruling principle.'"

Page 27, note 1. Πάντα ῥεῖ, the doctrine of the flowing of all things, taught by Heracleitus of Ephesus (536–470 B. C.), and often quoted by Plato.

> Far seen, the river glides below,
> Tossing one sparkle to the eyes.
> I catch thy meaning, wizard wave ;
> The river of my life replies.
>> "Walden," *Poems*, Appendix.

> The ripples in rhymes the oar forsake.
>> "Woodnotes," II., *Poems*.

Page 30, note 1.

> To clothe the fiery thought
> In simple words succeeds,
> For still the craft of genius is
> To mask a king in weeds.
>> Quatrain "Poet," *Poems*.

[1] "Moral Purpose in Art," published in the *Century Magazine* for May, 1883.

Page 32, note 1.

> The mountain utters the same sense
> Unchanged in its intelligence,
> For ages sheds its walnut leaves,
> One joy it joys, one grief it grieves.
> > "Nature," Fragments, *Poems*, Appendix.

See also the last passage in the poem "Monadnoc."

Page 34, note 1. "Can such things be?" etc. Shakspeare, *Macbeth*, iii. 4.

Page 39, note 1. Ἀεὶ γὰρ εὖ πίπτουσιν οἱ Διὸς κύβοι. *The dice of Zeus ever fall aright.* From a lost play of Sophocles, Fragment 763; used also in "Compensation," *Essays, First Series;* also "Worship," *Conduct of Life.*

Page 41, note 1. This doctrine expanded in "Sovereignty of Ethics," *Lectures and Biographical Sketches;* ten commandments; compare end of "Prudence," *Essays, First Series.*

Page 42, note 1. The oracle of Nature is overheard by the listener in the wood; "Fragments on the Poet," IV., *Poems*, Appendix.

Page 42, note 2.

> Teach me your mood, O patient stars!
> Who climb each night the ancient sky,
> Leaving on space no stain, no scars,
> No trace of age, no fear to die.
> > "Fragments on the Poet," *Poems*, Appendix.

Page 43, note 1. See "Xenophanes," *Poems.*
Xenophanes of Elea, the rhapsodist and philosopher (570–480 B. C.), taught the unity of God and Nature. His doc-

trine, Ἐν καὶ πᾶν, the One and the All, constantly recurs in Emerson's writings. Xenophanes said, "There is one God, the greatest among gods and men, comparable to mortals neither in form nor thought." Mr. Arthur K. Rogers, in his *Student's History of Philosophy*, says that what Xenophanes taught was "that what we name God is the one immutable and comprehensive material universe which holds within it and determines all those minor phenomena to which an enlightened philosophy will reduce the many deities of the popular faith. The conception is not unlike that of Spinoza in later times."

Page 43, note 2. This passage occurs in a lecture given in December, 1832, before the Boston Society of Natural History.

Page 45, note 1. Although the "degradation" was a Platonic doctrine, I think it so contrary to Mr. Emerson's steady belief in amelioration that the expression here implies merely that the animals are lower steps in an ascending series.

Page 46, note 1. This image, slightly varied, is found in "Pan," *Poems*, Appendix.

Page 46, note 2. Mr. Emerson's brilliant brothers, Edward Bliss Emerson and Charles Chauncy Emerson, had died within the two years before the publication of *Nature*. Of Edward's powers and nobility, his brother tells in his poem, "The Dirge." Of Charles he wrote: "Beautiful without any parallel in my experience of young men was his life. . . . I have felt in him the inestimable advantage, when God allows it, of finding a brother and a friend in one."

Page 47, note 1. Mr. Emerson wrote in one of his Journals, "I remember when a child, in the pew on Sundays, amusing myself with saying over common words, as 'black,' 'white,' 'board,' etc., twenty or thirty times, until the words lost all meaning and fixedness, and I began to doubt which was the right name for the thing, when I saw that neither had any natural relation, but were all arbitrary. It was a child's first lesson in Idealism.''

Page 52, note 1. The flowing universe is told of in many of the poems, as in "Woodnotes," II., "The rushing metamorphosis," etc., and later "Onward and on, the eternal Pan," etc.

Page 53, note 1. Shakspeare, Sonnet lxx.

Page 53, note 2. Shakspeare, Sonnet cxxiv.

Page 53, note 3. In a letter written in December, 1838, to Rev. James Freeman Clarke, then editing in Ohio *The Western Messenger,* to which Mr. Emerson contributed '' The Humble-Bee,'' he says: —

'' I remember in your letter you mentioned the remark of some friend of yours that the verses, ' Take, O take those lips away,' were not Shakspeare's ; I think they are. Beaumont, nor Fletcher, nor both together were ever, I think, visited by such a starry gleam as that stanza. I know it is in *Rollo,* but it is in *Measure for Measure* also ; and I remember noticing that the Malones, and Stevens, and critical gentry were about evenly divided, these for Shakspeare, and those for Beaumont and Fletcher. But the internal evidence is all for one, none for the other. If he did not write it, they did not, and we shall have some fourth unknown singer. What care we who sung this or that ? It is we at last who sing.''

Page 55, note 1.

> The solid, solid universe
> Is pervious to love, etc.
>
> '' Cupido,'' *Poems.*

Page 56, note 1. Leonhard Euler (1707–1783), a Swiss mathematician of remarkable gifts ; also a man of character and wide culture. He was called by Catherine of Russia to the Academy of St. Petersburg as professor of physics, and later of mathematics. Frederick the Great induced him to come to Berlin, where he remained many years, returning, however, to Russia. In total blindness during his last years, he did important work.

Page 57, note 1. Proverbs viii. 23, 27, 28, 30.

Page 58, note 1. Plotinus (204–269 A. D.), of Lycopolis in Egypt, a disciple of Ammonius Saccus of Alexandria, sometimes called the founder of Neo-Platonism, went to Rome and taught philosophy there. Plotinus accompanied the Emperor Gordian in his expedition into Persia, and thus came in contact with the teachings of Zoroaster. He said, " The sensuous life is a mere stage play — all misery in it is only imaginary, all grief a mere cheat of the players ; the soul is not in the game ; it looks on." —*Student's History of Philosophy,* by Arthur K. Rogers.

Page 62, note 1. " The Bohemian Hymn," *Poems,* Appendix.

Page 64, note 1. Milton, *Comus,* 13, 14.

Page 67, note 1. This passage refers to Mr. Emerson's visit to the *Jardin des Plantes* in Paris a few months before. See note to the motto of this essay.

Page 70, note 1. It is very possible that Mr. William T. Harris is right where he says, in speaking of Mr. Alcott's philosophy : " I have been obliged to think . . . that Mr. Emerson attempted to preserve in the last chapter of his book on *Nature* . . . a picture of Mr. Alcott as ' Orphic Poet ' by writing out in his own words and with an effort to reproduce the style of thought, words and delivery of Mr. Alcott, the idealistic theory which he had heard with such great interest.'' — *Memoir of Bronson Alcott*, by F. B. Sanborn and W. T. Harris.

Page 72, note 1. "He who desires to signify divine concerns through symbols is orphic, and, in short, accords with those who write myths concerning the Gods.''— Proclus, *Theology of Plato*, I. iv.

Page 73, note 1. Alexander Leopold Franz Emmerich Hohenlohe (1794–1849), a priest, born at Würtemberg, of a princely family, known for the miraculous cures, attributed to his prayers, in Germany and England, and at Washington, of a Mrs. Mattingly, in 1824.

Page 73, note 2. I am indebted to Dr. Ralph Barton Perry, of Harvard University, for the following information with regard to these expressions : "The phrase (*vespertina cognitio*) signifies the twilight knowledge of man that is contrasted with the full-day knowledge of God (*matutina cognitio*). Knowledge of things in their several natures and particularity is twilight knowledge, while the knowledge of the ideas that constitute the plan of creation is day knowledge. This distinction corresponds to the technical distinction between *a posteriori* and *a priori* knowledge. The distinction between morning and evening knowledge refers to the *direction* of the partial knowledge. To glorify God, or to see him from the standpoint of darkness, is *cognitio matutina ;* to fall away to darkness is *cognitio vespertina.* The angels have both in one, the *vespertina* being contained in the *matutina.* The angels have the *vespertina* in so far as they know the lower only through the higher — or see the higher in the lower — and so always glorify God. The use of these phrases is very curiously mingled with the problem of morning and evening as applying to the period preceding the creation of the sun and moon. — See St. Augustine's *City of God*, Book XI., chapters vii and xxix, Dods's translation. Also the *Summa Theologiæ* of St. Thomas Aquinas, Part I., Quæstio lviii, Art. 6; Quæstio lxxiv, Art. 3.''

Page 76, note 1.

> Wiser far than human seer, etc.
> "The Humble-Bee," *Poems.*

Also : —

> Let me go where'er I will,
> I hear a sky-born music still.
> "Fragments on The Poet," *Poems*, Appendix.

THE AMERICAN SCHOLAR

In 1834 Mr. Emerson had been chosen to give the Poem at the annual meeting of the Phi Beta Kappa Society in Cambridge. Three years later he was invited to give the Address. A month before the meeting he wrote in his Journal : —

29 JULY, 1837.

If the All-wise would give me light, I should write for the Cambridge men a theory of the Scholar's office. It is not all books which it behooves him to know, least of all to be a book-worshipper, but he must be able to read in all books that which alone gives value to books — in all to read one, the one incorruptible text of Truth. That alone of their style is intelligible, acceptable to him.

In his *Memoir of Emerson* Mr. Cabot speaks of this address as "a much needed monition to the cultivated class of persons in New England to think for themselves instead of taking their opinions from Europe or from books."

Mr. Lowell, speaking of this epoch of "the Newness," as the spiritual awakening of New England was sometimes called, said, "The Puritan revolt had made us ecclesiastically, and the Revolution politically independent, but we were still socially and intellectually moored to English thought, till Emerson cut the cable and gave us a chance at the dangers and the glories of blue water. . . . His oration before the Phi Beta Kappa Society at Cambridge, some thirty years ago, was an event without any former parallel in our literary annals, a scene to be always treasured in the memory for its picturesqueness and its inspiration. What crowded and breathless aisles, what windows clustering with eager heads, what enthusiasm of approval, what grim silence of foregone dissent !"[1]

Dr. Holmes records in his Life of Emerson that rarely has any one of the annual addresses before the Phi Beta Kappa Society been listened to with such profound attention and interest. He spoke of it as "Our intellectual Declaration of Independence."

"Nothing like it had been heard in the halls of Harvard since Samuel Adams supported the affirmative of the question, 'Whether it be lawful to trust the chief magistrate, if the commonwealth cannot otherwise be preserved.' It was easy to find fault with an expression here and there. The dignity, not to say the formality of an academic assembly, was startled by the realism that looked for the infinite in 'the meal in the firkin; the milk in the pan.' They could understand the deep thoughts suggested by 'the meanest flower that blows,' but these domestic illustrations had a kind of nursery homeli-

[1] Essay on Thoreau, *My Study Windows.*

ness about them which the grave professors and sedate clergymen were unused to expect on so stately an occasion. But
the young men went out from it as if a prophet had been
proclaiming to them, 'Thus saith the Lord.' No listener ever
forgot that address, and among all the noble utterances of the
speaker it may be questioned if one ever contained more truth
in language more like that of immediate inspiration.''

Carlyle wrote to Emerson about the oration: '' My friend !
you know not what you have done for me there. . . . Lo,
out of the West comes a clear utterance, clearly recognizable
as a *man's* voice, and I *have* a kinsman and brother : God
be thanked for it. I could have *wept* to read that speech ; the
clear high melody of it went tingling through my heart. . . .
Miss Martineau tells me, 'Some say it is inspired, some say it
is mad.' Exactly so ; no *say* could be suitabler. But for you,
my dear friend, I say and pray heartily : May God grant you
strength; for you have a *fearful* work to do! Fearful I call it ;
and yet it is great, and the greatest.''

Page 81, note 1. In the opening passages of an editorial
paper in the *Dial* (April, 1843), '' Europe and European
Books,'' Mr. Emerson speaks of these as still dominant here,
but prophesies thus: '' This powerful star, it is thought, will
soon culminate and descend, and the impending reduction of
the Transatlantic excess of influence . . . is already a matter
of easy and frequent computation. Our eyes will be turned
westward and a new and stronger tone of literature will result.
The Kentucky stump-oratory, the exploits of Boone and David
Crockett, the journals of western pioneers, agriculturalists, and
socialists, and the letters of Jack Downing, are genuine growths
which are sought with avidity in Europe, where our European-
like books are of no value.'' He further says that the moving

centre of population and property of the English race will in
time "certainly fall within the American coast, so that the
writers of the English tongue shall write to the American and
not to the island public, and then shall the great Yankee be
born."

In editing this paper for *Natural History of Intellect* Mr.
Cabot omitted the first three pages.

Page 82, note 1. In the "Symposium" of Plato is a version of this fable, but in his Introduction to Professor Good-
win's edition of Plutarch's *Morals*, Mr. Emerson says, —
"What noble words we owe to him! 'God divided man
into men that they might help each other.'" This idea,
differently expressed, is found in the chapter "Of Brotherly
Love" in the *Morals*, vol. iii. p. 37.

Page 84, note 1.

> The horseman serves the horse, etc.
> "Ode inscribed to W. H. Channing," *Poems.*

Page 85, note 1.

> Line in nature is not found;
> Unit and universe are round;
> In vain produced, all rays return, etc.
>
> "Uriel," *Poems.*

Page 86, note 1. In this address, and throughout the
Essays, and equally the Poems, are evidences of Mr. Em-
erson's reading in the works of the Masters of Science,
— Newton, Laplace, Hunter, Linnæus, Lamarck, Herschel,
Owen, Lyell, Faraday, — and his use of their facts on an-
other plane.

Page 86, note 2. In one of the Journals, Mr. Emerson

quotes a French author's *mot :* " Whether or no there be a God, it is certain that there will be."

Page 88, note 1. This recalls the definition of Art as " Nature passed through the alembic of man," in *Nature,* chapter iii.

Page 89, note 1. Emerson, Thoreau, and Lowell, three young men at that epoch, who set an example to American scholars of independence in thought and originality in expression, spent much of their time during their college terms exploring and reading in the Library at the expense of the prescribed curriculum, thereby incurring censure at the time.

Page 91, note 1. All the influence Mr. Emerson hoped to exert on others was to show them the right of the spirit and the intellect to the same freedom as was claimed for the body. In his Journal for 1856 he writes : " I have been writing and speaking what were once called novelties for twenty-five or thirty years, and have not now one disciple." The would-be disciple must go to the fountain of truth open in himself to every man, and might well get a more generous draught than he.

Compare his poem " Étienne de la Boéce."

Page 93, note 1. Mr. Emerson followed his counsel to the scholar to " read a little proudly." He soon found in a book the passages written for him and lightly passed over the others.

Page 95, note 1. In the addresses called " The Man of Letters " and " The Scholar," which are included in *Lectures and Biographical Sketches,* as well as in this speech, Mr. Emerson steadily holds up to the scholar the duty of active and brave manhood especially imposed upon him by his privileged lot.

Page 95, note 2. The "other me" implies a quite different view from the "Non Ego" of the metaphysician.

Page 98, note 1.

> What prizes the town and tower?
> Only what the pine-tree yields, etc.
>
> "Woodnotes," II., *Poems.*

Page 103, note 1.

> Who telleth one of my secrets
> Is master of all I am.
>
> "The Sphinx," *Poems.*

Page 106, note 1. In an address delivered before the Anti-slavery Society in New York, March 7, 1854, Mr. Emerson said that one comes at last to learn "that self-reliance, the height and perfection of man, is reliance on God." This sentence is the reconciliation of the essays on "Self-Reliance" and "The Over-Soul."

Page 108, note 1. Mr. Emerson wrote in his Journal after this oration: "It was the happiest turn to my old thrum which Charles Henry Warren gave as a toast at the Phi Beta Kappa dinner: 'Mr. President,' he said, 'I suppose all know where the orator comes from; and I suppose all know what he has said. I give you — the Spirit of Concord — *it makes us all of one mind.*'"

Page 112, note 1. Mr. Emerson devotes a chapter to Swedenborg, the Mystic, in *Representative Men.*

Page 113, note 1. The writings of Pestalozzi, the earnest Swiss reformer, whose teachings have wrought so much in the improvement in education in Europe and America, had begun to be read in America. Pestalozzi's beneficent course was dogged through life by apparent failures, partly due to lack of administrative ability in himself, largely to the condition of Switzerland during the Napoleonic wars. Mr. Emerson's friend, Mr. Alcott, in 1825, when he knew little of Pestalozzi, independently introduced a very similar system into his village school at Cheshire, and later in Boston.

Page 115, note 1. This sentence might well stand as a prophecy of much of Mr. Emerson's own history.

ADDRESS TO THE SENIOR CLASS OF THE DIVINITY SCHOOL

This address was given by Mr. Emerson to the Seniors in the Divinity School in Cambridge at their request. The professors in charge of the school had no official part in the choice of a speaker, and therefore were not responsible for his opinions, as, after the address, they clearly made known. Mr. Emerson's journals for the year preceding its delivery contain many expressions of disappointment in the preaching which he, then a regular and hopeful attendant, heard. In the rugged and eloquent prayer and preaching of "Father Taylor" at the Sailors' Bethel, however, he delighted,[1] and spoke of him as "the Shakspeare of the sailor and the poor."

The address was given in the middle of July. On March 14th, he wrote in his Journal : —

"There is no better subject for effective writing than the clergy. I ought to sit and think, and then write a discourse

[1] Rev. Edward T. Taylor, once a seaman, later a Methodist preacher. A passage from Mr. Emerson's diary expressing his admiration for this "Wonderful Man" is printed in full in Mr. Cabot's *Memoir*, vol. i. p. 327.

to the American clergy, showing them the ugliness and un-
profitableness of theology and churches at this day, and the
glory and sweetness of the moral nature out of whose pale they
are almost wholly shut.''

The opportunity to free his mind soon came. He was
approached by some youths from the Divinity School — probably a committee to invite him to make the Annual Address.

Journal, 1st April. '' The Divinity School youths wished to
talk with me concerning Theism. I went rather heavy-hearted,
for I always find that my views chill or shock people at the
first opening. But the conversation went well, and I came
away cheered. I told them that the preacher should be a poet
smit with the love of the harmonies of moral nature: and
yet look at the Unitarian Association and see if its aspect is
poetic. They all smiled No. A minister, nowadays, is plain-
est prose, the prose of prose. He is a warming-pan . . . at
sick beds and rheumatic souls, and the fire of the minstrel's
eye, and the vivacity of his word is exchanged for intense
grumbling enunciation of the Cambridge sort, and for Scripture phraseology.''

Although he knew that what he should say must needs
shock many of the elder clergy, because, tried by his stand-
ards, they were found wanting, it seemed a clear duty that
had come to him to open the minds of these young apostles
to the great possibilities of their calling.

The address provoked a great reaction. The authorities
of the school publicly washed their hands of all complicity in
the occasion. Professor Andrews Norton, a man of great
worth and weight among the more liberal clergy of the day,
strongly attacked the views of Emerson in the Boston *Adver-
tiser*, as making light of revealed Christianity and nearly approaching atheism. Mr. Emerson's revered friend with whom

he had been associated in the Second Church, Rev. Henry Ware, then a professor in the Divinity School, felt that such a doctrine as that "the soul knows no persons" must be resisted, and soon after preached a sermon to the school on this and other points. He sent the sermon to his former colleague with a kind letter, wishing that he be not understood as attacking the new views as Emerson's, not being perfectly aware of the precise nature of his opinions, or the arguments by which they might be justified to his mind. Mr. Cabot in his Memoir says : —

"Emerson replied in a letter which has often been quoted,[1] as it deserves to be, for the entire serenity of temper it displays, but also as a confession that he was incapable of reasoning. There is no one, he says, less willing or less able to be polemic. 'I could not possibly give you one of the "arguments" you cruelly hint at on which any doctrine of mine stands ; for I do not know what arguments mean in reference to any expression of a thought.' He was trying to rouse his contemporaries to a livelier sense of the facts of religion, and this could never be done by argument."

In an early poem, printed after his death, in the Appendix to the *Poems*, "The Bohemian Hymn," which is referred to elsewhere in these notes, Emerson's thought of the inadequacy of man to express Deity is embodied. He said : "I deny personality to God because it is too little, not too much. Life, personal life, is faint and cold to the energy of God. For Reason and Love and Beauty, or that which is all these, — it is life of life, the reason of reason, the love of love." Mr.

[1] The correspondence between these friends, which does honor to both, is printed in full in an Appendix to Mr. Cabot's *Memoir of Emerson*.

Cabot explains that "what he means by personality seems to be nothing more than limitation to an individual. . . . He did not deny self-consciousness to the Supreme Being." He did not want the informing Soul of the universe shut up in Jehovah.

Though much abhorrence or disavowal of the views of this address was publicly expressed, not all the hearers were troubled. Miss Elizabeth Peabody, in a letter to Mr. Alexander Ireland, of Manchester, England, relates that "Dr. Channing regarded the address at Divinity Hall as an entirely justifiable and needed criticism on the perfunctory character of service creeping over the Unitarian churches at the time. He hailed the commotion of thought it stirred up as a sign that 'something did live in the embers' of that spirit which had developed Unitarianism out of the decaying Puritan churches." Mr. Moncure D. Conway tells how the young Theodore Parker went home and wrote in his Journal: "I shall give no abstract, so beautiful, so just and terribly sublime was his picture of the church in its present condition. My soul is roused, and this week I shall write the long-meditated sermons on the state of the church and the duties of these times."

In the circle of Boston and Cambridge there was much disturbance for a time, and, indeed, nearly thirty years passed by before it was felt at the University that Mr. Emerson was a safe or desirable person to be called upon to take any active part in its functions.

In the controversy at the time, as Dr. Holmes wittily says: "Emerson had little more than the part of Patroclus when the Greeks fought over his body." The apparent result of his address must have been somewhat disappointing, and the temporary notoriety was disagreeable to him. He had faithfully delivered his message ; let it work according to its truth. He withdrew himself to Concord to work at his other tasks.

The poem "Uriel," if carefully read, will be seen to be an account, sublimed and impersonal, but accurate in detail, of this experience when a soul, looking from a commanding central point, like the Archangel of the Sun, sees and announces a truth, new and astounding to those whose view, from their position, is more limited and eccentric, so that they cannot see all things moving and returning in their vast orbits in accordance with the beautiful law of the Universe.

On one account only had Mr. Emerson to take immediate action, involving disappointment because of the reception of his address. He had at this time great hopes that Carlyle would come to America, perhaps even to stay, and now had to urge his friend by no means to come until this "foolish clamor be overblown" about his own "infidelity," "pantheism," or "atheism ;" mentioning, however, that if he (Emerson) lived, his "neighbors must look for a great many more shocks, and perhaps harder to bear."

Page 121, note 1. The omnipotence and omnipresence of the perfect law, moral, intellectual, and physical, an inseparable trinity, is everywhere insisted on by Mr. Emerson. "The universe is moral." In the end of "The Poet" (*Poems*, Appendix), the sweetness of the Law is celebrated. See also the motto "Worship," *Poems :* —

> More near than aught thou callest thine own,
> Yet, greeted in another's eyes,
> Disconcerts with glad surprise, etc.

Page 122, note 1. This passage, probably a very startling one to the clergymen present, has in it the doctrine to be found in "The Over-Soul," *Essays, First Series.*

Page 122, note 2. Compare the lines on humility from Keats's "Hyperion," quoted in "The Sovereignty of Ethics," *Lectures and Biographical Sketches :* —

> One avenue was shaded from thine eyes
> Through which I wandered to eternal truth.

Page 123, note 1. Emerson's favorite doctrine of Compensation. See also "Worship" in *Poems :* —

> This is he men miscall Fate, etc.

Page 124, note 1. Hence he did not attack others' belief, sure that the good when rightly shown, without irritating argument or ridicule, would displace the evil.

> Whispered the Muse in Saadi's cot, etc.
> > "Saadi," *Poems.*

Page 124, note 2.

> Around the man who seeks a noble end,
> Not angels but divinities attend.
> > "Fragments on Life," *Poems,* Appendix.

Page 125, note 1. Suggesting the lines in Wordsworth's "Ode to Duty : " —

> Thou dost preserve the stars from wrong ;
> And the most ancient heavens through thee are fresh and
> strong.

Page 125, note 2. To the same purpose as the stanza beginning : —

> Brother, sweeter is the Law
> Than all the grace Love ever saw, etc.
> > "The Poet," *Poems,* Appendix.

Page 126, note 1. In *Representative Men* the debt of Plato to the ancient wisdom of the East is spoken of. Emerson acknowledged the same. His mind prepared for them by Plato and the Neo-Platonists, he early found the Scriptures of the Orient, and, later, delighted in their poets, especially Saadi and Hafiz ; so much in the first, that in several of his poems he adopted *Saadi* or *Seyd* as a generic name for the Poet.

Page 127, note 1. "The divine nature," that is, the over-soul, the divine element shared in measure by every soul. The regeneration of the Calvinist was instantaneous; the regeneration which Emerson found was continuous, if man would only open the gates of his soul to the flood of Spirit.

> Ever the words of the Gods resound,
> But the porches of man's ear
> Seldom in this low life's round
> Are unsealed that he may hear.
> > "My Garden," *Poems.*

Page 129, note 1.

> For what need I of Book or priest, etc.
> > "Fragments on the Poet," *Poems,* Appendix.

Page 130, note 1. Mr. Cabot in his Memoir says that Mr. Emerson "was surprised to find his intention so far mistaken as to leave many of his Unitarian brethren to suppose that he was trying to belittle the character of Jesus. Far from this, he was trying to place the reverence for Jesus upon its true ground, out of reach of the reaction that was sure to set in when the claim of exclusive revelation should lose its force." Mr. Cabot further mentions that Miss Elizabeth Peabody said in her *Reminiscences of Dr. Channing* that a passage to this effect was omitted by Mr. Emerson for want of time in the reading of the address, and she urged him to restore it in the printing, but that he on reflection preferred to let the paper stand as it was read. He would not explain it by what might seem an afterthought.

Miss Peabody urged him at least to put a capital F to the "friend of man," but Mr. Emerson answered, "If I did so, they would all go to sleep."

Page 131, note 1. Wordsworth, *Miscellaneous Sonnets*, "The world is too much with us."

Page 132, note 1. The sublimed doctrine of Self-Reliance.

Page 133, note 1.

> Love's hearts are faithful, but not fond, etc,
> "The Celestial Love," *Poems.*

Page 133, note 2. To call the prophets and saints Bards was to Emerson giving them their due honor, but, perhaps, might seem to some of his clerical hearers making fiddlers of them. In the passage from the Journal, April 1, quoted in the introductory note to this address, he spoke of his wish to make a preacher a true poet.

Page 134, note 1. This is told in verse in "The Problem," *Poems.*

Page 135, note 1. Mr. Emerson once spoke in his Journal of "The corpse-cold Unitarianism of Brattle Street."

Page 137, note 1.

> The Dervish whined to Seyd,
> Thou didst not tarry while I prayed, etc.
>> "The Poet," *Poems,* Appendix.

Journal, 1837. "Among provocations the next best thing to good preaching is bad preaching. I have even more thoughts during or enduring it than at other times."

Page 138, note 1. "Day creeps after day, each full of facts, dull, strange, despised things that we cannot enough despise. . . . And presently the aroused intellect finds gold and gems in one of these scorned facts, — then finds that the day of facts is a rock of diamonds ; that a fact is an Epiphany of God." — "Education," *Lectures and Biographical Sketches.*

Page 142, note 1. The same thoughts in "The Sphinx," *Poems.*

Page 145, note 1. The text "For what is a man profited if he gain the whole world and lose his own soul: or what shall a man give in exchange for his soul," stated freshly.

Page 148, note 1. "Give all to Love," fourth stanza, *Poems.*

Page 150, note 1. Journal, November, 1839. "The Sabbath is my best debt to the Past and binds me to some gratitude still. It brings me that frankincense out of a sacred antiquity."

Page 151, note 1. In parting from his people of the Second Church, Mr. Emerson thus indicated his hope to continue through life to be a preacher of the truth. Of the minister's office he said: "It has many duties for which I am feebly qualified. It has some that it will always be my delight to discharge according to my ability, wherever I exist. And whilst the recollection of its claims oppresses me with a sense of my unworthiness, I am consoled by the hope that no time and no change can deprive me of the satisfaction of pursuing and exercising its highest functions."

Page 151, note 2.

> Line in nature is not found ;
> · Unit and universe are round :
> In vain produced, all rays return ;
> Evil will bless, and ice will burn.
>
> "Uriel," *Poems.*

See also the second paragraph in this address, and the chapter "Circles" in *Essays, First Series.*

LITERARY ETHICS

Mr. Emerson, writing to his friend Carlyle, August 6, 1838, thanking him for his "friendliest seeking of friends for the poor oration" ("The American Scholar") says: "I have written and read a kind of sermon to the Senior Class of our Cambridge Theological School a fortnight ago; and an address to the Literary Societies of Dartmouth College, for though I hate American pleniloquence, I cannot easily say No to young men who bid me speak also. . . . The first, I hear, is very offensive. I will now try to hold my tongue till next winter."

The Dartmouth address followed with but nine days' interval that to the Cambridge Divinity students. Newspapers then had only local circulation, and there was no Northern railroad ; indeed it was a two days' journey by stage which Mr. Emerson made in company with a friend and neighbor, John Keyes, Esq. (a graduate of Dartmouth), and his son, to reach Hanover. "If any rumor of the former discourse," said Dr. Holmes, "had reached Dartmouth, the audience must have been prepared for a much more startling performance than that to which they listened. The bold avowal which fluttered the dovecotes of Cambridge would have sounded like the crash of doom to the cautious old tenants of the Hanover aviary. If there were any drops of false or questionable doctrine in the silver shower of eloquence under which they had been sitting, the plumage of orthodoxy glistened with unctuous repellents, and a shake or two on coming out of church left the sturdy old dogmatists as dry as ever. Those who remember the Dartmouth College of that day cannot help smiling at the thought of the contrast in the way of thinking between the speaker and the larger part, or at least the older part, of his audience. . . . Perhaps, however, the extreme difference between the fundamental conceptions of Mr. Emerson and the endemic orthodoxy of that place and time was too great for any hostile feelings to be awakened by the sweet-voiced and peaceful-mannered speaker."

Page 155, note 1. This opening passage was no formal compliment, but rather a confidential and characteristic utterance by Mr. Emerson to the young scholars of his interest in them, and of his feeling, elsewhere expressed, that "the Scholar has drawn the white lot in life."

Page 155, note 2. Mr. Emerson wrote in his Journal of 1833, speaking of his brother, "Charles's *naif* censure last night provoked me to show him a fact, apparently entirely new to him, that my entire success, such as it is, is composed wholly of particular failures, every public work of mine of the least importance having been, probably without exception, noted at the time as a failure."

Page 158, note 1. In another essay, Mr. Emerson thus asserts his belief: " He did not make his thought : no, the thought made him, and the sun and the stars also."

Page 159, note 1. In the Journal, from which this sentence comes, " The lovely *invention* of the dew " is the expression. The same simile is found in the early poem " Sunrise " in *Poems*, " Fragments on Nature."

Page 160, note 1. Mr. Alexander Ireland of Manchester, England, in the motto to his book on Emerson, calls attention to the following passage in Plutarch's *Life of Cicero*, telling of his consulting the oracle at Delphi, in his youth. " Upon his inquiring by what means he might rise to the greatest glory, the priestess bade him ' follow nature and not take the opinion of the multitude for his guide in life.' "

Page 160, note 2. Mr. Emerson was of the opinion of that admirable American officer, the late General Crook, who told his officers that he thought little of the effect of general orders, saying, " Example is the best general order," and living up to his belief. Mr. Emerson greatly valued biographies, from Plutarch down, and constantly illustrated his lectures by anecdotes.

Page 160, note 3. His interest in Cudworth was not so much in the views of the author, but in Plato, whom he first came upon in Cudworth's pages, when a boy in college. The same is probably true of Tennemann, whose writings on Plato and other philosophers were accessible to him in translations.

Page 160, note 4. The poetical speculations and beliefs of the ancient philosophers were as attractive to him as the systems of the modern metaphysicians were uninteresting. It was the freedom and beauty of the Law, as reported by the prophets and singers, that he cared for. The dogmatic distinctions of the system-makers seemed unprofitable to him.

Page 161, note 1. In a letter, when a Divinity student, to his spiritual confessor, his Aunt Mary Moody Emerson (for his account of whom see *Lectures and Biographical Sketches*), he called himself "Ever the Dupe of Hope." Later in life, he would hardly have said "dupe." He liked to read in Plutarch of Bias's question and answer: "How do the wise differ from the unwise? In a good hope."

Page 162, note 1.

I see it all now; when I wanted a king
'T was the kingship that lacked in myself I was seeking.
　　　　　Lowell, "Two Scenes in the Life of Blondel."

Page 163, note 1.

　　This passing moment is an edifice
　　Which the Omnipotent cannot rebuild.
　　　　"Fragments on Life," *Poems*, Appendix.

Page 166, note 1. At village meetings for good causes, as the old Lyceum, in which debates were sometimes held, or those stirring ones in the days of the Antislavery and Free State movements, Mr. Emerson always attended, and heard with respect and often admired the good and forcible speaking of his neighbors. It was especially so at town meetings.

Journal. "The most hard-fisted, disagreeably restless, thought-paralyzing companion sometimes turns out in the town-meeting to be a fluent, various, and effective orator. Now I find what all that excess of power which chafed and fretted me so much in —— was for." Extempore speech was always very difficult for him.

Page 168, note 1.

　　In dreamy woods what thoughts abound
　　That elsewhere never poet found;

Here voices ring, and pictures burn,
And grace on grace where'er I turn.

Fragments from Notebook.

Page 172, note 1. This passage shows the thought which justified to Mr. Emerson his plan of writing on The Natural Method of Mental Philosophy, which late in his life was partially accomplished in his philosophy courses at Cambridge (see *Natural History of Intellect*). Mr. Cabot says in his *Memoir:* "He had long cherished the thought of a more fruitful method for the study of the mind founded on the parallelism of the mental laws with the laws of external nature."

Page 172, note 2. Heracleitus's Πάντα ῥεῖ, the fluidity of all things, and the reappearance of the one in protean disguises. These doctrines appear everywhere in Emerson's prose and verse.

Page 173, note 1. Mr. Emerson used to say, "My doom and my strength is to be solitary." The gifts of solitude for the scholar are told in "Woodnotes," II., in the *Poems.*

Page 175, note 1. The necessity of the contact with the world and doing one's part there, of action alternating with thought, and the acquiring of facts to translate into thought, is urged alike in the early and later writings.

Page 182, note 1. Mr. Emerson's "lay pulpit," the Lyceum platform, gave such a character as this paragraph suggests to his essays, which were first delivered in country towns and frontier settlements all over the North and West, as well as before cultivated audiences in cities. He would not write down to his audience, but had faith in the perception of humble people. On the other hand, he wrote strong English in short sentences, and in delivery introduced frequent anecdotes which would appeal to them, as they always did to him. Many of these were omitted in the severe pruning of the essays for publication.

Page 186, note 1.

> Ever the words of the Gods resound, etc.
>
> "My Garden," *Poems.*

THE METHOD OF NATURE

In July, 1841, Mr. Emerson betook himself to the single hotel by the beautiful and lonely beach at Nantasket, to write this oration.

He found there delicious airs and sunniest waters, reminding him of the Mediterranean, as he wrote to his brother, saying, "I hoped there to write an oration, but only my outline grew larger and larger, until it seemed to defy all possibility of completion. Desperate of success, I rushed home again." Mr. Cabot hints that in the oration is "a touch of the sea, 'inexact and boundless,' yet distinct in its tone of suggestion."

In his letter to Carlyle, Mr. Emerson, remembering his friend's constant praise of Silence, wrote : " As usual at this season of the year I, incorrigible spouting Yankee, am writing an oration to deliver to the boys in one of our little country colleges nine days hence. You will say I do not deserve the aid of any Muse. O but if you knew how natural it is to me to run to these places! Besides, I am always lured on by the hope of saying something which shall stick by the good boys."

Page 192, note 1. (From the letter quoted above.) " My whole philosophy — which is very real — teaches acquiescence and optimism. Only when I see how much work is to be done, what room for a poet — for any spiritualist — in this great, intelligent, sensual, avaricious America, I lament my fumbling fingers and stammering tongue."

Page 193, note 1. Mr. Emerson would have rejoiced in William Morris's word about a work of industrial art, that it should be "a joy to the maker as well as the user," and that the cotton, or whatever, would be the better, not worse.

Page 195, note 1. To him spiritual matters were out of the possibilities of argument. There was no gainsaying the universal goodness or wisdom or beauty. It was either perceived or not perceived. He said, with Saint Augustine, "Wrangle who will, I will wonder."

Page 196, note 1. The ways were full of "monotones," as Mr. Emerson called them, in those days. Journal. "I so readily imputed symmetry to my fine geniuses in perceiving their excellence in some insight. How could I doubt that . . . [each] was the master mind which in some act he appeared? No ; . . . in new conditions he was inexpert, and in new company he was dumb. The revolving light resembles the man who oscillates from insignificance to glory."

But he received each new guest, even the young student or the visitors of his children, and questioned them as if he thought that the best word might yet come from their mouths.

Page 199, note 1. It was indeed as hazardous a venture as that of Empedocles in his quoted assertion for a speaker to say in the presence of divines and professors, at a New England college festival in those days, that God appeared in man ; that by obedience he became a channel through which deity

was poured out in measure on the earth. Had the oration
been called a sermon and given on Sunday, its heresy would
have been challenged, but, as often happened, Mr. Emerson
found that on a week-day people would listen even with pleasure to words against which on Sunday they would have been
on their guard. Any lapse in the speaker's life due to indulgence of the lower self might have given the satisfaction to
the theologians that the casting forth by Ætna of the sandal
of Empedocles did to the Sicilians.

Page 200, note 1.   The ancient doctrine of "the Flowing" passing into the modern doctrine of Evolution.

Page 201, note 1.

> Line in Nature is not found ;
> Unit and universe are round, etc.
>
>   "Uriel," *Poems.*

Page 202, note 1.   This paragraph and much that follows
is rendered poetically in "Woodnotes," II., in the verses
beginning : —

> Hark, in thy ear I will tell a sign, etc.

Page 206, note 1.   "Here is another of those almost lyri-
cal passages which seem to long for the music of rhythm and
the resonance of rhyme : 'The great Pan of old,' etc."—
Ralph Waldo Emerson, by Dr. O. W. Holmes.

Page 210, note 1.   That men should *listen* in solitude for
the Voice, should obey it, and report its message exactly to
others was Emerson's chief doctrine.

Page 211, note 1.   In this passage he makes what he considered the distinction between genius and talent.

Page 211, note 2.   Compare the passage in the Divinity

School Address where he speaks of the great teachers and prophets as bards. The common preacher argues and proses, the true poet charms and uplifts.

Page 213, note 1.

> Stars taunt us with their mystery.
> "The World-Soul," *Poems.*

Page 213, note 2. Mr. Emerson elsewhere quotes Plato as saying: "The man who is master of himself knocks in vain at the door of poetry."

Page 214, note 1. Probably quoted from Taylor's translation of Proclus, in which the Chaldean oracles are often referred to.

Page 220, note 1. The respect for the high ideals of the men who planted New England, who brought with them the spirit of Cromwell and of Milton, always remained with Mr. Emerson. The fiery faith and noble asceticism of these men and women living in the presence of the other world, outweighed their narrowness and sternness, in his estimation. He often spoke of a wish to write the story of Calvinism in New England, but did not do so. Yet in his "Historical Discourse at Concord" (*Miscellanies*), the "Historic Notes of Life and Letters in New England" (*Lectures and Biographical Sketches*), and the essay "Boston" (*Natural History of Intellect*), he deals with the subject, as also in the Address to the New England Society in New York in 1870, which has been recently printed, with other addresses, by that society.

Page 222, note 1. Ali Ibn Abu Talib, who married the daughter of Mahomet and became caliph.

MAN THE REFORMER

The Mechanics' Apprentices' Library Association, before which this Address was delivered, is mentioned by Mr. Winsor in his *Historic Boston* as doing a modest work with its library of some five thousand volumes as late as the year 1873.

Page 227, note 1. Compare with the passage at the beginning of "The Over-Soul:" "We give up the past to the objector, and yet we hope. . . . We grant that human life is mean, but how did we find out that it was mean?"

Page 229, note 1. A stronger statement of his belief, which appears in so many ways in the prose and poems, that a thought will unsettle the solidest seeming facts; that the scholar's far sight recognizes the true real.

Page 230, note 1. Emerson and many of his friends and contemporaries lived to see their ideas and reforms eagerly claimed by the men of the church, the exchange, or the forum who had rejected, derided, or even persecuted them.

Page 234, note 1. Mr. Alcott and his companions in the short-lived Fruitlands community were confronted by the dilemma that they needed land for their social experiment, yet felt that land could not be rightfully purchased; so they paid money to "redeem from human ownership" their acres of unpromising soil.

Page 236, note 1. Only a few months before the delivery of this lecture, the community at Brook Farm, in West Roxbury, under the leadership of Mr. George Ripley, began an effort to secure for each member the benefits of labor of the body and mind, and for the community the advantages of division of labor. See "Historic Notes of Life and Letters in New England," *Lectures and Biographical Sketches.*

Page 237, note 1. Mr. Emerson had neither the aptitude nor the training for carrying on a farm, or even a large garden, but, especially in his early years as a Concord householder, he took some care of his garden, and preferably of his orchard. But in household matters he disliked to be served by others, especially to call upon servants. He liked the verse from Horace:

> At mihi succurrit pro Ganymede manus
>
> (My own right hand my cup-bearer shall be),

and a proverb, perhaps from the Persian, —

> The king's servant is the king himself.

Page 238, note 1. His respect for labor was great, and is told in Oriental form in the verses, —

> Said Saadi, When I stood before
> Hassan the camel-driver's door, etc.
> "Fragments on the Poet," *Poems*, Appendix.

Page 240, note 1. This passage suggests the lines of George Herbert in his "Church Porch:" —

> Some great estates provide, but not
> A mastering mind ; so both are lost thereby.

Page 248, note 1. A motto for those days in New England might have been the words put in Rob Roy's mouth by Wordsworth : —

> Of old things all are over old,
>   Of good things none are good enough ;
> We 'll show that we can help to frame
>   A world of other stuff.

Page 249, note 1. In Mr. John Albee's excellent *Remembrances of Emerson,* speaking of the many young men whom "his voice reached in the most obscure and unexpected places," he says that Mr. Emerson "received us each and all with his unfailing suavity and deference. His manner towards young men . . . I know no word for but expectancy, as if the world-problem was now finally to be solved, and we were the beardless Œdipuses for whom he had been faithfully waiting. . . . His magnanimous spirit soothed and reassured us, and to the little we brought he added a full store, inserting . . . a silver cup in our coarse sacks of common grain, so that we returned to our brethren with gladness and praise."

Page 251, note 1. Omar the caliph, Mahomet's distant cousin and second successor, who, first warring against him, later became converted. During his reign the Moslems were everywhere victorious. He was rigorously ascetic in his habits. This passage suggests two recent parallels, — the habit of General Gordon of going into the bloody battles of the Chinese war with only a cane in his hand, and the astonishing feat of the religious fanatics, followers of the Mahdi, who, armed with sword and shield and some primitive firearms, broke the square of the English, furnished with the best modern arms, at Tel-el-Kebir, in daylight and open country.

Page 252, note 1. The relation of employer and servants (at that period almost invariably New Englanders from neighboring towns) seemed to Mr. Emerson to put the parties in so false a position that, with his wife's concurrence, the help were invited to sit at the same table at meals. The matter was quickly solved from the kitchen side, for the woman who waited on table explained that the cook was shy and unwilling to eat with Mr. and Mrs. Emerson, and that she herself did not wish to leave the cook alone.

Page 253, note 1. *Treatise of Synesius on Providence,* translated by Thomas Taylor and printed with his *Select Works of Plotinus,* London, 1817. Synesius was later a convert to Christianity and became Bishop of Cyrene; he lived in the early part of the Fifth Century.

Page 256, note 1.

> Times wore he as his clothing-weeds,
> He sowed the sun and moon for seeds.
> > "The Poet," *Poems,* Appendix.

> Sun and moon must fall amain
> Like sower's seeds into his brain,
> There quickened to be born again.
> > "Fragments on the Poet," *Poems,* Appendix.

THE TIMES

This was the Introductory Lecture of a course of eight lectures on "The Times" given by Mr. Emerson at the Masonic Temple in Boston, in the winter of 1841–42. The others were "The Conservative," "The Poet," "The Transcendentalist," "Manners," "Character," "Relation to Nature," "Prospects."

"The Times," "The Conservative" and "The Transcendentalist," also included in this volume, were printed in the *Dial* (July, 1842, October, 1842, January, 1843). "The Poet," in part, is printed in "Poetry and Imagination," in *Letters and Social Aims,* "Manners" and also "Character," in part, in *Essays, Second Series.*

Page 259, note 1. This image of godlike days humbly

disguised appears several times in Mr. Emerson's writings, especially in the poem "Days," and in "May-Day."

Page 260, note 1. As he puts it in his Journal, "Love is the solution of mine and thine."

Page 262, note 1. In this and the next pages appears the ancient doctrine of the Flowing, but applied to the human stream slowly ascending, as spirit more and more informs the clay.

Page 263, note 1. From his boyhood up, Mr. Emerson delighted in oratory. The brilliant, if florid, declamations of some students in college, especially John Everett and certain youths from the South, had a charm which caused their words to remain in his memory from those days, hard to conceive of now, when the whole college flocked to hear the Seniors declaim. As a youth he would walk far to hear Webster's mighty speech, and keenly enjoyed the graceful and studied eloquence of Edward Everett. He admired the elegant bearing, cool mastery of speech, and cutting denunciation of Wendell Phillips, who was never fully himself until challenged or menaced.

Mr. Emerson's own delivery was agreeable, his voice flexible, admirably modulated, especially in reading poetry, and of unexpected power at the right moment. Mr. N. P. Willis, in an amusing article (*Hurrygraphs*, New York, 1851), describes his first hearing of Emerson, and, among other things, says this of the surprise of his voice : "A heavy and vase-like blossom of a magnolia with fragrance enough to perfume a whole wilderness, which should be lifted by a whirlwind and dropped into a branch of an aspen, would not seem more as if it never could have grown there than Emerson's voice seems inspired, and foreign to his visible and natural body."

Page 267, note 1. In Mr. Emerson's copy of Taylor's translation of Plotinus, he marked the definition of time by Archytas the Pythagorean, — *a continued and indivisible flux of hours.*

Page 271, note 1. It should be remembered that this lecture was written in the days when New England bristled with reforms ; and their advocates, striving to outdo one another in the radical quality or the refinements of their schemes, flocked to Mr. Emerson because of his well-known hospitality to thoughts. Therefore his combination of good sense with sympathy, of good temper and of humor with just criticism, and his ability to look on these crowding causes with a due perspective, is remarkable.

Page 274, note 1. Mr. Emerson valued highly the prose as well as the poetry of Milton, especially the *Areopagitica*.

Page 277, note 1. Of this paragraph Dr. Holmes says : " All this and much more like it would hardly have been listened to by the ardent advocates of the various reforms, if anybody but Mr. Emerson had said it. He undervalued no sincere action except to suggest a wiser and better one. . . . The charm of his imagination and the music of his words took away all the sting from the thoughts that penetrated to the very marrow of the entranced listeners."

Page 278, note 1.

> Teach me your mood, O patient stars !
> Who climb each night the ancient sky,
> Leaving on space no shade, no scars,
> No trace of age, no fear to die.
>> " Fragments on the Poet," *Poems*, Appendix.

Page 280, note 1. When the *Dial* was under consideration, Mr. Emerson wrote in his diary, " It ought to contain the best advice on the topics of Government, Temperance, Abolition, Trade and Domestic Life. It might well add such poetry and sentiment as will now constitute its best merit."

When he was urged to edit it, he wrote : "I wish it to live, but I do not wish to be its life. Neither do I like to put it into the hands of the Humanity and Reform men, because they trample on letters and poetry, nor into the hands of the Scholars, for they are dead and dry." Yet he made it always a point of honor to defend or help the reformers at critical times.

Page 282, note 1. An ancestor of Mr. Emerson's, one of the Moodys, a forcible preacher, thus urged his parishioners : " And when ye know not what to do, do not do ye know not what!"

Page 288, note 1. In the poem " Blight " is a very similar passage.

Page 289, note 1. The doctrine of the Oneness of Being, taught by Paul at Athens, and the resulting Immortality. The same in Oriental form appears in " Brahma " (*Poems*).

Page 291, note 1. This passage is almost autobiographical, as is also a very similar one about Osman (an ideal man) towards the end of the chapter, " Manners," *Essays, Second Series.*

THE CONSERVATIVE

This lecture, as has been said elsewhere, was the second in the course on " The Times " given by Mr. Emerson in Boston in the winter of 1841–42. It was first printed in the *Dial* (October, 1842). Dr. Holmes says, in his Memoir of Mr. Emerson, that "it was a time of great excitement among the members of that circle of which he was the spiritual leader. Never did Emerson show the perfect sanity which characterized his practical judgment more beautifully than in this lecture, and in his whole course with reference to the intel-

lectual agitation of the period. He is as fair to the conservative as to the reformer. . . . He has his beliefs and, if you
will, his prejudices, but he loves fair play, and, though he
sides with the party of the future, he will not be unjust to the
present or the past."

Page 296, note 1. Mr. Emerson's eager listening to the
men of science and his use of their facts on a higher plane is
everywhere shown in his prose and verse. In "The American
Scholar" he speaks of "every trifle bristling with *Polarity* that
ranges it instantly on an eternal law;" in "Compensation"
he devotes a paragraph to it, and it appears in the fourth verse
of "The Sphinx" and elsewhere.

Page 297, note 1. Suggesting the lines in the end of
"Threnody:" —

> Silent rushes the swift Lord
> Through ruined systems still restored, etc.

Protagoras's doctrine of "becoming" in Plato's "Theæ-
tetus" is also called to mind.

Page 299, note 1. Mr. Emerson's own strength being
purely individual, and his sympathies and hopes for society
primarily in the advance of the individual, his respectful allowance of the use of organization and the value of the guardians
of what the Past seems to have established, coupled with his
perception of the weaknesses of the reforming class, is the
more interesting.

Page 304, note 1. "The strength of the Egyptians is to
sit still." Isaiah xxx. 7.

Page 312, note 1. Not merely the crack-brained or narrow reformers, "the monotones," as he called them, visited
Mr. Emerson, but high-minded and brave protestants against

the humdrum selfishness or artificiality of life as they found it were his neighbors and friends.

In their first reaction they undervalued the arrangements they found. Thoreau cared little for the roads, and Mr. Alcott, when called on for his tax, said that he used the fields as much, so, since they thought their money was often misapplied, they would not pay. Mr. Emerson's level head was, in the long run, a useful corrective to his friends' extreme views.

E. sits in a mystery calm and intense,
And looks coolly round him with sharp common sense.
                    Lowell, "Fable for Critics."

Page 325, note 1. This paragraph, written in 1841, concerning the hero's resolve, and therefore his own ideal, might with little change have served for Mr. Emerson's epitaph. He respected the laws, written or unwritten, results of the better tendencies of mankind in the past, yet his individual life, not dependent on these, helped to amend them.

THE TRANSCENDENTALIST

This lecture was the fourth in the course on "The Times," but did not, as might seem natural, follow immediately, for contrast's sake, as in this volume, on "The Conservative." "The Poet" came in as a golden mean between the extremes, which he was showing. For Mr. Emerson, when called a philosopher, said, "I am in all my theory, ethics and politics a poet," and, as Sir Leslie Stephen said, "he ridiculed the impression that his transcendentalism was a known and fixed element, like salt or meal, a rigid definite creed. All the argument and all the wisdom, he declares, is not in the

treatise on metaphysics, but in the sonnet or the play." The
intervening lecture "The Poet " was not, however, the essay
by that name in the Second Series, but another, much of
which he printed later, with liberal additions, in "Poetry
and Imagination " in the volume *Letters and Social Aims.*

Dr. Holmes, after speaking of the prejudice naturally existing against "the Transcendentalists" at the time of this
lecture, says : —

"On the other hand we have the evidence of a visitor
who knew a good deal of the world as to the impression they
produced upon him : —

"'There has sprung up in Boston,' says Dickens, in his
American Notes, 'a set of philosophers known as the Transcendentalists. On inquiring what this appellation might be
supposed to signify, I was given to understand that whatever was
unintelligible would be certainly Transcendental. Not deriv-
ing much comfort from this elucidation, I pursued the inquiry
still further, and found that the Transcendentalists are followers of my friend Mr. Carlyle, or, I should rather say, of a
follower of his, Mr. Ralph Waldo Emerson. This gentleman
has written a volume of Essays, in which among much that
is dreamy and fanciful (if he will pardon me for saying so),
there is much more that is true and manly, honest and bold.
Transcendentalism has its occasional vagaries (what school has
not ?), but it has good healthful qualities in spite of them ;
not least among the number a hearty disgust of Cant, and an
aptitude to detect her in all the million varieties of her everlasting wardrobe. And therefore, if I were a Bostonian, I
think I would be a Transcendentalist.' "

Page 330, note 1. Here, as everywhere, appears the sure
faith in evolution and ascension in God's own time. In the

opening passages of the essay "Poetry and Imagination" above referred to, the natural advance of the mind from materialism to idealism is described.

Page 333, note 1. In his Journal for 1838 he says, "The physician tends always to invert man, to look upon the body as the cause of the soul, to look upon man as tyrannized over by his members."

Page 335, note 1. It was charged as heresy to Mr. Emerson that he did not believe in miracles. The happiness of his life lay in his contemplation of the daily miracle wrought by sure and perfect law.

Page 337, note 1. Friedrich Heinrich Jacobi, a contemporary of Goethe, and a writer first of romances, then of treatises, both of a philosophic character. A believer in intuition or divine impulse, he was impatient of the formal systems of the metaphysicians.

Page 338, note 1. Yet in these very years a few of the reformers were led by their enthusiasm and faith to apostolic experiments, to go forth to share with others the light that seemed to them so important, taking no thought for the morrow, — not only bachelors, but men with families. They were bitterly condemned and ridiculed by those who claimed to believe absolutely and *literally* in the words of Jesus : "Consider the lilies of the field ; they toil not, neither do they spin," etc., or "There is no man that hath left house or brethren or sisters or father or mother or wife or children or lands, for my sake and the gospel's, but he shall receive an hundredfold now in this time, . . . and in the world to come eternal life."

Page 342, note 1. In this passage it is Mr. Alcott that his friend alludes to. He wrote of him to Carlyle in 1839: "A man named Bronson Alcott is a majestic soul with whom conversation is possible. He is capable of truth." Later he said of him, " Alcott astonishes by the grandeur of his angle of vision and the heaps of particulars." And again: " He is good as a lens, a mirror, a beautiful susceptibility, every impression on which is to be accounted for, and, until accounted for, registered as an addition to our catalogue of natural facts. It needs one acquainted with the lens by frequent use to make allowance for defects, but 't is the best instrument I ever met with."

Page 342, note 2.

> The civil world will much forgive, etc.
>> " The Poet," IV., *Poems,* Appendix.

Page 347, note 1.

> Well and wisely said the Greek,
> Be thou faithful, but not fond ;
> To the altar's foot thy fellow seek, —
> The Furies wait beyond.
>> " Pericles," Quatrains, *Poems.*

Page 350, note 1. The change to the first person in this paragraph — very likely due to a sheet introduced after the main part of the essay was written — does not mean that Mr. Emerson states here his own views. In this and what follows he only continues to be a mouthpiece for the views of these " children " with whose faith he admits a sympathy, but it is a measured one.

Page 350, note 2. Quoted from Walter Savage Landor's *Pericles and Aspasia.*

Page 354, note 1. This Trinity appears in the first pages of " The Poet," *Essays, Second Series,* and in " Art," *Society and Solitude.*

Page 356, note 1. Sometimes, when "weary of dealing with people each cased in his several insanity," outcries came, in the Journal at least, yet with a touch of humor and always a basis of kindness, as thus : —

Journal, 1842. "Could they not die? or succeed? or help themselves? or draw others? or draw me? or offend me? in any manner, I care not how, could they not be disposed of and cease to hang there in the horizon, an unsettled appearance, too great to be neglected, and not great enough to be of any aid or comfort to this great craving humanity?"

Page 358, note 1. The above passage is a good example of Mr. Emerson's light hand in dealing with a movement that surely had absurd aspects, but more that approached the sublime.

Journal. "Shall it be said of the hero that he opposed all contemporary good because it was not grand? I think it better to get their humble good, and to catch the golden boon of purity and temperance and mercy from these poor" [preachers and reformers].

Page 359, note 1. Mr. Emerson perhaps had here in mind some lines of Juvenal which described the "Sons of the Morning" for whose coming he was ever on the watch : —

> Juvenes queis arte benigna
> Et meliore luto finxit praecordia Titan.

"Blest youths, though few, whose hearts the god of Day
Fashioned with loving hand and from a nobler clay."

THE YOUNG AMERICAN

Concerning the Mercantile Library Association, before which this Address was given, Winsor, in his *Historic Boston*, says that it was founded in 1820, antedating that of New York ; that "it was floated for some years by the most popular system of public lectures in town," and that it succumbed in 1877 before the advancing Public Library, becoming the South End Branch of that institution.

"The Young American" was printed in the April number of the *Dial* for 1844. Two passages in the first pages of the Address as there printed, which Mr. Emerson chose to omit when he printed it among the *Miscellanies*, have now a historic interest which seemed to justify the reprinting of the greater part of them in the notes below. The first of these tells of the reading of the young scholars in the first third of the century. The second describes the additions won from the sea for Boston and the building up of the town into a city, the making of the early railroads, the coming of the Irish laborers and their endurance and cheerfulness under unmerciful taskmasters, and gives a hopeful prophecy for their future.

Page 363, note 1. This passage, printed in the *Dial*, is omitted : —

"Our books are European. We were born within the fame and sphere of Shakspeare and Milton, of Bacon, Dryden, and Pope. Our college text-books are the writings of Butler, Locke, Paley, Blackstone, and Stewart ; and our domestic reading has been Clarendon and Hume, Addison and Johnson, Young and Cowper, Edgeworth and Scott, Southey, Coleridge, and Wordsworth, and the *Edinburgh* and *Quarterly Reviews*. We are sent to a feudal school to learn democracy."

Page 363, note 2. From the *Dial* version : —

"Their alleged effect to augment disproportionately the size of cities is in rapid course of fulfilment in this metropolis of

New England. The growth of Boston, never slow, has been
so accelerated since the railroads have been opened, which join
it to Providence, to Albany, and to Portland, that the extreme
depression of general trade has not concealed it from the most
careless eye. The narrow peninsula, which a few years ago
easily held its thirty or forty thousand people, with many
pastures and waste lands, not to mention the large private
gardens in the midst of the town, has been found too strait
when forty are swelled to a hundred thousand. The waste
lands have been fenced in and builded over, the private gardens,
one after the other, have become streets. Boston proper consisted of seven hundred and twenty acres of land. Acre after
acre has been since won from the sea, and in a short time the
antiquary will find it difficult to trace the peninsular topogra-
phy. Within the last year . . . from twelve to fifteen hundred buildings . . . have been erected, many of them of a
rich and durable character. And because each of the new
avenues of iron road ramifies like the bough of a tree, the
growth of the city proceeds at a geometrical rate. Already a
new road is shooting northwest towards the Connecticut and
Montreal, and every line of road that is completed makes cross-
sections from road to road more practicable, so that the land
will presently be wrapped in a network of iron. This rage
for road-building is beneficent for America, where vast distance is so main a consideration in our domestic politics and
trade, inasmuch as the great political promise of the invention
is to hold the Union staunch, whose days seemed already
numbered by the mere inconvenience of transporting representatives, judges, and officers across such tedious distances of
land and water. Not only is distance annihilated, but when, as
now, the locomotive and the steamboat, like enormous shuttles, shoot every day across the thousand various threads of

national descent and employment, and bind them fast in one
web, an hourly assimilation goes forward and there is no danger that local peculiarities and hostilities should be preserved.

" The new power is hardly less noticeable in its relation
to the immigrant population, chiefly to the people of Ireland,
as having given employment to hundreds of thousands of the
natives of that country, who are continually arriving in every
vessel from Great Britain.

" In an uneven country the railroad is a fine object in the
making. It has introduced a multitude of picturesque traits
into our pastoral scenery. The tunnelling of mountains, the
bridging of streams, the bold mole carried out into the broad,
silent meadow, silent and unvisited by any but its own neighbors since the planting of the region ; the encounter at short
distances along the track of gangs of laborers; the energy with
which they strain at their tasks; the cries of the overseer or
boss ; the character of the work itself which so violates and
revolutionizes the primal and immemorial forms of nature ; the
village of shanties at the edge of the beautiful lakes, until now
the undisturbed haunt of the wild duck, and in the most se-
questered nooks of the forest, around which the wives and
children of the Irish are seen ; the number of foreigners, men
and women, whom now the woodsman encounters singly in
the forest paths ; the blowing of rocks, explosions all day,
with the occasional alarm of frightful accident, and the indefinite promise of what the new channel of trade may do and undo
for the rural towns, keep the senses and imagination active ;
and the varied aspects of the enterprise make it the topic of
all companies, in cars and boats, and by firesides.

" This picture is a little saddened, when too nearly seen,
by the wrongs that are done in the contracts that are made
with the laborers. Our hospitality to the poor Irishman has

not much merit in it. We pay the poor fellow very ill. To work from dark to dark for sixty or even fifty cents a day is but pitiful wages for a married man. It is a pittance when paid in cash, but when, as generally happens, through the extreme wants of the one party, met by the shrewdness of the other, he draws his pay in clothes and food, and in other articles of necessity, his case is still worse; he buys everything at disadvantage, and has no adviser or protector. Besides, the labor done is excessive, and the sight of it reminds one of negro-driving. Good farmers and sturdy laborers say that they have never seen so much work got out of a man in a day. Poor fellows! Hear their stories of their exodus from the old country, and their landing in the new, and their fortunes appear as little under their own control as the leaves of the forest around them. As soon as the ship that brought them is anchored, one is whirled off to Albany, one to Ohio, one digs at the levee at New Orleans, and one beside the water-wheels at Lowell; some fetch and carry on the wharves of New York and Boston, some in the woods of Maine. They have too little money, and too little knowledge, to allow them the exercise of much more election of whither to go, or what to do, than the leaf that is blown into this dike or that brook to perish.

"And yet their plight is not so grievous as it seems. The escape from the squalid despair of their condition at home into the unlimited opportunities of their existence here, must be reckoned a gain. The Irish father and mother are very ill paid, and are victims of fraud and private oppression; but their children are instantly received into the schools of the country; they grow up in perfect communication and equality with the native children, and owe to the parents a vigor of constitution which promises them at least an even chance in the competitions of the new generation. Whether it is this confidence that puts a drop of sweetness in their cup, or whether the buoyant spirits natural to the race, it is certain that they seem to have almost a monopoly of the vivacity and good nature in our towns, and contrast broadly, in that particular, with the native people. In the village where I reside, through which a railroad is being built, the charitable ladies, who, moved by a report of the wrongs and distresses of the newly arrived laborers, explored the shanties with offers of relief, were surprised to find the most civil reception, and the most bounding sportfulness from the oldest to the youngest. Perhaps they may thank these dull shovels as safe vents for peccant humors ; and this grim day's work of fifteen or sixteen hours, though deplored by all the humanity of the neighborhood, is a better police than the sheriff and his deputies.''

Page 364, note 1. Mr. Emerson's own life and his influence on his countrymen was greatly affected by the rapid spreading of the branches of the Railroad tree then recently planted by the Atlantic coast. The seventeen winters following the delivery of this address, excepting that of 1847, spent in England, were passed in arduous and exposing travel, giving lectures in answer to calls from cities, villages, and recent settlements from Maine to the Mississippi, and finally beyond that stream, then dangerous enough in winter.

Page 364, note 2. From the *Medea* of Euripides.

Page 366, note 1. In the Journal of 1838 Mr. Emerson thus acknowledged his own debt : —

'' If my garden had only made me acquainted with the muck-worm, the bugs, the grasses, and the swamp of plenty in August, I should willingly pay a free tuition. But every process is lucrative to me far beyond its economy.''

The next June he admits that when tired with too much talk of the visiting philosophers, he meditates flight beyond the Acton hills. " But my garden is nearer, and my good hoe as it bites the ground revenges my wrongs. . . . I confess I work at first with a little venom, lay to a little unnecessary strength, but by smoothing the rough hillocks, I smooth my temper; by extracting the long roots of the pipe-grass I draw out my own splinters, and in a short time I can hear the bobolink's song, and see the blessed deluge of light and color that rolls around me."

Page 366, note 2. In these very days, George William Curtis and his brother were working as laborers on the farm of Captain Nathan Barrett, and Hawthorne, recently married, was living in the Manse (built by Mr. Emerson's grandfather), all three having served an agricultural and domestic apprenticeship in the community at Brook Farm.

Page 367, note 1. Journal, 1838. " I think Tennyson got his inspiration in gardens, and that in this country, where there are no gardens, his musky verses could not be written. The Villa d' Este is a memorable poem in my life."

Page 368, note 1. The garden at home did not prove always helpful to thought, and a few months after this sentence was written, he bought the beautiful pines, that he had often looked wistfully to while weeding, — his " Sacred Grove" on the shore of Walden. It was there that his young friend, Henry Thoreau, built his cabin the next year, and lived for a time. Two years later, Mr. Emerson wrote to Carlyle of his " new plaything, the best I ever had," which was the high wood-circled Walden Ledge on the farther shore of the pond. Of this he wrote : —

" In these May days, when maples, poplars, oaks, birches, walnut and pine are in their spring glory, I go thither every afternoon, and cut with my hatchet an Indian path through the thicket all along the bold shore, and open the finest pictures." The poem, " My Garden," describes this spot, and what its owner found there. It was close to the new Fitchburg Railroad, and later he wrote how his woods reproached him as he passed by in the train to Boston.

Page 368, note 2. These were the days when the factories, rising along the course of every river in New England, were tempting the boys and girls away from their work beside their fathers in the fields, and their mothers in the farm-house. The first wave of the immigration of the Irish peasantry to build the new railroads made this possible, for most of these, when the railroads were built, sought employment in the country towns.

Page 369, note 1.

> And I affirm my actions smack of the soil.
> > " Hamatreya," *Poems.*

Page 371, note 1. In a letter written shortly before this time to his unseen friend in England, John Sterling, he had said : —

" It seems to me that so great a task is imposed on the young men of this generation that life and health have a new value. The problems of reform are losing their local and sectarian character, and becoming generous, profound, and poetic."

Page 372, note 1. Mr. Emerson's optimism was of a patient kind. He often notices the small balance to the account of good. In his " Historical Discourse at Concord " (*Miscellanies*) he is glad that in the town meetings " if the good counsel prevailed, the sneaking counsel did not fail to be suggested; freedom and virtue, if they triumphed, triumphed in a fair field. And so be it an everlasting testimony for them, and so much ground of assurance of man's capacity for self-government.''

Page 372, note 2. The principle of " effort " recognized by Lamarck, though ridiculed and misrepresented for more than a half century after he announced it, was recognized by Mr. Emerson as consonant with the laws which the great minds of antiquity had announced.

Page 373, note 1. The last part of the " World-Soul " (*Poems*) is a rendering of this passage in verse. The Darwinian doctrine of the Survival of the Fittest appears here.

Page 379, note 1. In the essay " Nature " (*Essays, Second Series*) he speaks of morning sanity, when, " after every foolish day, we sleep off the fumes and furies of its hours,'' as the lesson of the little blue self-heal that grows beneath his study windows.

Page 380, note 1. The three Communities in Massachusetts here alluded to are : —

I. Brook Farm, of which he tells in " Historic Notes of Life and Letters in New England " in *Lectures and Biographical Sketches*. Mr. Charles Lane contributed a paper on the subject to the *Dial*, January, 1844. The magazines contain several articles on Brook Farm, notably those contributed by members of the community, Mr. George P. Bradford,[1] Mrs. Sedgwick,[2] and Mrs. Kirby.[3] Hawthorne was a member, and many amusing comments on the life there are found in his published journals. George William Curtis, also

[1] " Reminiscences of Brook Farm," *Century Magazine*, vol. xxiii. p. 141.

[2] " A Girl of Sixteen at Brook Farm," *Atlantic Monthly*, vol. lxxxv. p. 394.

[3] " A Visit to Brook Farm," *Overland Monthly*, vol. v. p. 9.

a member, told of his experience in his letters to Mr. John S. Dwight.[1]

II. Fruitlands, Mr. Alcott's community at Harvard, Mass., an account of which is given in the very interesting *Memoir of Bronson Alcott*, by F. B. Sanborn and W. T. Harris. An official communication from Fruitlands, by Mr. Alcott and his English coadjutor, Charles Lane, appears in the *Dial*, "Intelligence," in July, 1843, and Mr. Emerson's account of his visit there, and of his forebodings, are given in Mr. Cabot's *Memoir* (vol. ii. page 439), and in *Emerson in Concord*, by E. W. Emerson (p. 203).

III. Hopedale, near Milford, in Worcester County, founded by Rev. Adin Ballou. Its organ was a paper called the *Non-Resistant and Practical Christian*. The Hopedale Home School was established by this community.

All of these Communities were short-lived.

Page 382, note 1. François Marie Charles Fourier (1772–1837), a Frenchman of an artistic temperament and philosophic mind, with a broad humanity. After a short mercantile experience which gave him the opportunity of seeing other countries, yet disgusted him with the selfishness of trade and the social organization, he was swept into the French Revolution, and, after narrowly escaping the guillotine, served as a trooper until disqualified by ill health. In 1808 he published his *Théories des quatres Mouvements, et Destinées générales*, which, after six years' neglect, attracted general notice. His later important work (1822) was the *Traité de l'Association domestique-agricole*, and the *Journal de Phalanstère*. On his gravestone were inscribed his three principles: I. The series distributes the harmonies of the world (*i. e.* all the

---

[1] *Early Letters of George William Curtis to John S. Dwight.* Edited by George Willis Cooke, Harper & Bros., 1898.

harmonies of the universe grow out of a regular and uniform order). II. Attractions are proportioned to destinies (*i. e.* all beings are led and kept in their true sphere, not by a principle of external force, but of internal attraction). III. Analogy is universal. He urged that association of capital, science, and labor would prepare the way for true society; that the living in communities of some eighteen hundred persons each would be economical, secure just and appropriate division of labor, and by variety and sociability rob labor of its irksomeness, and that all the gifts of the members would be used for the common profit and pleasure. Fourier never himself succeeded in carrying out his ideas, but they had much influence in France, England, and America for a time. Mr. Emerson wrote in the *Dial* for July, 1842, "Fourierism and the Socialists," and published the advocacy of these ideas by Albert Brisbane, criticising them good-naturedly himself. Miss Elizabeth P. Peabody wrote the article "Fourierism" in the April number, 1844.

Page 387, note 1. This theme is enlarged on in the essay "Aristocracy," originally called "Natural Aristocracy," *Lectures and Biographical Sketches.*

Page 389, note 1. One of the young men valued by Mr. Emerson, and moved by his teachings, Charles Russell Lowell, in his valedictory oration at Cambridge on the "Reverence due from Old Men to Young," said: "Therefore the old men . . . cannot teach us of the present what should be, for that we know as well as they or better: they should not teach us what can be, *for the world always advances by impossibilities achieved.*" His work in his few years in civil life was remarkable. During the Civil War, as captain in the United States Cavalry, colonel of the Second Massachusetts Cavalry, and finally as commander of the Reserve Brigade of

Cavalry, he showed again and again a power of doing the apparently impossible. He had a share in turning the flood of disaster at Cedar Creek, and died in the moment of victory.

Page 389, note 2.

Tu regere imperio populos, Romane, memento,
(Hae tibi erunt artes) pacisque imponere morem,
Parcere subjectis et debellare superbos.

Virgil, *Æneid*, VI.

Page 391, note 1. At the dark and seemingly hopeless period of the agitation against slavery, it seemed to many abolitionists that, if they failed to do away with it, or check its advance, it might become the duty of the Northern States to repudiate their share in the national crime by secession.

Page 392, note 1. This lecture was delivered during the period of suffering in England, increased next year by the famine, and two years before the triumph of the Anti-corn Law League led by Cobden.

Page 394, note 1. In his second visit to England, although it seemed to Mr. Emerson that the prospects for better social conditions were increasing, and a longer stay there perhaps modified a little the views here expressed, he did not fail to bravely speak his public word, even in the face of some remonstrance, against false, and for real aristocracy.

The Riverside Press

Electrotyped and printed by H. O. Houghton & Co.
Cambridge, Mass., U. S. A.

www.ingramcontent.com/pod-product-compliance
Lightning Source LLC
LaVergne TN
LVHW012208040326
832903LV00003B/188